From Heaven to My Heart

D1003377

Also by Beverly Jane Phillips

Learning a New Language, Speech About Women and God

From Heaven to My Heart

God's Journey with Me

Beverly Jane Phillips

iUniverse, Inc.
Bloomington

From Heaven to My Heart
God's Journey with Me

Prayers by Joyce Rupp are excerpted from *Prayers to Sophia* by Joyce Rupp, ©2000, 2004, 2010. Used by permission of the publisher, Sorin Books®, P.O. Box 428, Notre Dame, Indiana, 46556, www.sorinbooks.com.

Unless otherwise noted, all biblical quotes are from the New Revised Standard Version of the Bible, copyright 1989, Division of Christian Education of the National Council of the Churches of Christ in the United States of America. Used by permission. All rights reserved.

iUniverse books may be ordered through booksellers or by contacting:

iUniverse
1663 Liberty Drive
Bloomington, IN 47403
www.iuniverse.com
1-800-Authors (1-800-288-4677)

Because of the dynamic nature of the Internet, any Web addresses or links contained in this book may have changed since publication and may no longer be valid.

ISBN: 978-1-4502-5993-4 (sc)
ISBN: 978-1-4502-5995-8 (dj)
ISBN: 978-1-4502-5994-1 (ebk)

Printed in the United States of America

iUniverse rev. date: 1/24/2011

To Hattie Kay Williams

Epigraph

"Humankind stands as a bridge between two worlds. Our greatest moments are when we have met, nakedly and face to face, the reality that saves and transforms, and then express this as part of our assimilating the experience. Our records of such experiences give us a further step on the road. They also give others light to find the path they must follow. Everyone's encounter and record brings more light and consciousness into this world and allows the forces of darkness to be beaten back."

--Morton Kelsey, *The Other Side of Silence,*
A Guide to Christian Meditation

Contents

Preface

A campfire is enjoyable for so much more than making s'mores, although they are reason enough. A campfire provides a place for fellowship and warmth with family and friends. Watching the logs burn and collapse, the sparks flare and die may inspire philosophical and theological musings. The sight of a spark flying from the fire and soon dying is a reminder of an idea or an intention that has not been tended. The spark that flies away and lands in some dry tinder creating another fire suggests that some ideas are alive enough to catch fire.

Writing this book about my prayer journals has been like a spark that landed on some tinder and needed fanning. I started writing my prayers to God over three decades ago because it was (and still is) the best way for me to stay focused on God and the conversation at hand. As the spiral notebooks began to pile up, it became obvious that this could become a lifelong practice. I wondered if anyone else would ever read them. Still, never once did I think of throwing them away even as we packed up to move from Illinois to Indiana and from Indiana to Arizona. The boxes of journals were kept in storage and loaded on trucks as matter-of-factly as were boxes of dishes and linens.

The primary value in my journals was writing them. Although the thought did occur to me, from time to time, that there might be ideas and inspiration in them that would be of use to someone else who was on a journey with God. This record of God calling me, meeting me, changing me and of me resisting or responding, rejoicing or lamenting might aid someone else in her efforts to answer God's sure call to friendship. My goal in this book is to highlight how God has worked in my life, an ordinary woman's life. My intent is that God will be the main character.

I want to thank those close to me who have been most involved in the writing of this book. To friends who read the manuscript when it was really a first draft, special thanks to you for trying to make sense out of a very rough draft: Lawn Griffiths, Bonny Henry, JoAnne Dahlmeier, Paige Callahan, Kate Wilmoth. Thanks to my children: Jim Phillips, who did a final edit of the manuscript, and Nancy Baker, who formatted the document the way the publisher required. As always, with everything I have done, I thank Norm, my husband of almost fifty years, for his support and patience in whatever projects I undertake.

Introduction

Writing my prayers came naturally. Most of my life I have been a writer of diaries, lists, articles, sermons, speeches, retreats. However, it never occurred to me that I might write a book until I read the book, *She Who Is, the Mystery of God in Feminist Theological Discourse,* by Dr. Elizabeth A. Johnson, Distinguished Professor of Theology at Fordham University. It took me two starts to read it the first time because it is so profound. I persisted because her theology and her poetic prose moved my spirit onto exciting new pathways of thought and prayer. I knew deep in my heart that I needed to write a book about her book so people who didn't have the time or the background to read hers could be inspired by her life-changing ideas. It took me eight years, with Dr. Johnson's encouragement, to write *Learning a New Language, Speech About Women and God.* Writing it was hard work, but it was one of the most fulfilling things I have done in my life

The idea of writing about my prayer journals crossed my mind many times over the years. Several things held me back. The idea of taking eight years or possibly more of my life discouraged me. Writing what may be classified as a spiritual autobiography was daunting. Would such a book be useful and interesting to anyone else? It seems autobiographies and memoirs are written by people of note, people who have done exceptional things. Brenda Ueland helped me dispense with this worry with these words:

> …writing is this: an impulse to share with other people
> a feeling or truth that I myself had. Not to preach to

them, but to give it to them if they cared to hear it. If they did not—fine. That was all right too.[1]

Even as encouraged as I was by Ueland's wise words, I was still leery of writing this book for several additional reasons. They included reservations that I would be telling too much about myself; that I would not find enough in the journals to make a book; that I would be touched all over again by the sorrows in my life; that no publisher would be interested; that it would make my husband, Norm, and everyone else who has been part of my life nervous not knowing what I was writing but knowing that they would somehow be in it. Another reservation, perhaps the most pressing, is that by making my private practice public, I might lose the Presence I feel in prayer.

Needing encouragement and looking for help, I attended a one day writing class at Chandler Gilbert Community College here in Arizona, which was led by Tom Bird, a writer and teacher from Sedona, Arizona. He has developed a method for writing and for getting published. He claims that you can write your book in thirty days if you write two hours a day six days a week. It seemed like a wild claim, but I bought the large sketch pad he recommended to write on. For two hours each day, six days a week, for five weeks, I wrote about the prayers in my earliest journals. At the end of that time I had 40,000 words which is almost a book. The basics were there but what I wrote was in dire need of rewriting.

The title of this book, *From Heaven to My Heart, God's Journey with Me,* describes the journey I have been on. At the beginning of my prayer life, I believed God to be far off in heaven, wherever that was. My posture was to approach his throne to praise him and to make my supplications. Soon I began to experience God already present in my heart waiting to be discovered there. Of course, God has always been in my heart, but it seems as though he has come from a high and exalted place right into my heart.

The journey has not been a straight line on a super highway. It has been one of ups and downs, of weaving back and forth, mostly on two

---

1 Brenda Ueland, *If You Want to Write, a Book About Art, Independence and Spirit* (St. Paul, Graywolf Press, 1987) 24. The first edition was published in 1938 by G.P. Putnam's Sons

lane roads and on dirt roads. In this book I want to share my intimate moments with God not to show me, but to show God.

The importance of the books I have read cannot be emphasized enough. Many times I copied whole pages of an important book into my prayer journal at the time it was touching my heart. I have cited some of these books and included a bibliography in hopes that, if you are on a search for guides on your own prayer journey, they will be of help to you.

You will soon notice that I alternate the use of masculine and feminine pronouns for God as I speak about God. It seems inconsistent, but it is the way I view God and address God now. Dr. Johnson's book, *She Who Is,* was the high point of my study about God being as much feminine as masculine. After reading it, I could no longer believe that masculine names exclusively are how we should address God. It is very freeing for a woman to know that God meant it when she said that we are created in God's image, male and female. At the same time, and very importantly, it would be less than helpful to always address God as female. That would be as damaging to men as the age old practice of God being "he" has been to women.

These words of Morton Kelsey sum up why I wrote the prayer journals.

> The mystics seemed to feel that it showed lack of respect for the source they sought if they came to an encounter with Love and did not make a record of it.[2]

I encountered Love and made a record of it.

---

2   Morton T. Kelsey, *The Other Side of Silence, A Guide to Christian Mediation,* (NY, Paulist Press, 1976), 197

Chapter One

"If you are not writing enough it is because you are reading too much."
Until I heard Tom Bird, author and teacher, say these words I had never,
ever thought there was such a thing as reading too much! The very idea!
I have always been a book worm to the max. In a conversation with
one of my sisters, I once said, "Remember how when we were kids,
Mom used to get after you for always having your nose in a book?" Her
response was, "That wasn't me! It was you!" Surprised by her comment,
I remembered that it was me who was always reading. To this day I take
a book wherever I go in case I might have a few minutes to wait. Not
only that, I usually take two or three books on vacations. My manner
of reading is to have three, sometimes four books, started at once. Then
I can read what I am in the mood for at any given time and place.

My favorite books will never be of use to anyone else, because as I
read, I mark passages which stand out for my own spiritual growth and
those that I want to use in some future teaching situation that might
present itself. The book shelves in my study are full of books that are
all marked up, ready with ideas that I want to think more about and
to share in writing or teaching. But instead of dwelling on them, I read
another book and mark ideas that strike me as interesting, important
or inspiring. I teach classes, lead workshops and write retreats whenever
I get a chance. But if I live to be one hundred and two I will never use
all the great ideas in those precious books.

Tom Bird's words about reading too much lurk in my mind like
a warning. Many things he said struck deep chords within me. Some
were things I had not thought about before, and some were in harmony

with what I have already thought. He said each one of us has an Author Within, a creative source for whom we may have our own name. "Author Within" suits me fine. In my heart it is a fitting name for God. If God is wanting me to write, then I must write in order to find contentment and the feeling of being in God's flow. If my Author Within is restless because I keep soaking up so many ideas and not using them, then I am reading too much.

It was at the urging of my Author Within that I wrote this book. It may be classified as "memoirs," but I would label it "spiritual autobiography." Memoirs, in my mind, belong to famous people, people who have been involved in the course of world events. If the events of my life are interesting to people who don't know me, it is because they are interested in the experience of living life with God

I've not done things that made me famous. What I have done is write a prayer almost every day of my life for more than thirty years. Not surprisingly, through that practice and over that time I have grown and changed spiritually. If I can describe my journey of faith to you, I will be satisfied. There have been a superabundance of things that have happened to me and to my family and friends that have given God openings to change me, to grow me. There were probably many more times when God, She Who Is, was trying to get through to me, but I was busy doing something else and not listening.

My hope and my plan is that God will be the main character of this book. The wonder of it all is the way God has moved in my life. Unanswered prayers or prayers answered with "no" have been a great disappointment to me and the cause of deep soul searching but they are only a part of the larger picture. The larger picture is the fact that God seeks us out wanting fellowship with us and blessing us in obvious ways but also in many unknown and unnoticed ways.

One of the ways she blesses us is through the communities we live in—our families, our schools, our neighborhoods, our churches, our workplaces, our country. Whoever we are, whether we admit it or not, whether we like it nor not, we are influenced by the people around us. God works with people to grow each one of us—if we are willing—to be the person she wants us to be.

Being more of a solitary, independent person, my recognition of what community has meant to me has been a long time coming. As I look over the prayer journals, I see that the people and their problems that I prayed for were not just objects of my prayer. They were important actors in changing in my life.

7/2/76

Reading my earliest journals, I find that at first I was not faithful to writing every day. There were gaps of days, weeks and even months when, for whatever reasons, I didn't write. The first prayer in the first journal was written on July 2, 1976, and then six months elapsed without another written prayer. During that time I was still praying but only on a catch-as-catch-can basis. It was almost four years later that I worked into the groove of writing a prayer every day. I am a morning person, so it is fitting that morning would be the time I chose for private prayer time. Not only am I at my best then, it has also been a time usually free of interruptions

My first prayers were written out of the anguish of watching a friend die. Soon after that, they resembled grocery lists. In the journal I wrote the name of each person I was praying for and specifically what they needed. What they needed was sometimes determined by what they told me their need was. Sometimes it was determined by what I (in my all my wisdom) "knew" they needed. When I would say to someone, "I will add you to my prayer list" that is literally what I did, added them to a list. I did mean what I said and I did pray for them. There is nothing wrong with writing down the names of those you have promised to pray for. In fact, the very writing of their names can be an act of prayer.

However, in those kinds of prayers, the writing of the prayer was not the act of friendship with God that later came to be the meaning of prayer for me. I was not seeking a direct connection with the Spirit of God in order to experience God's presence. Rather, it was a way of keeping track of whether or not God answered my prayers. One book on prayer I read at the time strongly suggested that prayer requests be written in such a way that there would be space next to them to record, mind you record, when and how God answered each particular prayer.

It was very presumptive and arrogant of me to believe there was some virtue in checking up on God to see whether he had delivered what I asked for. I was operating on the assumption that however I saw the problem or the need was what God willed for that person. I presumed to tell God the answer to every difficult situation.

There are as many ways to pray as there are people doing the praying. A person's theology sets the stage for one's prayer life. Two general theologies are represented in the two ways of praying I have described as mine at different times in my life. One theology assumes that God is somewhere high and lifted up directing the events of each person's life, pulling the strings, so to speak. The other theology says that God is with us in our lives in an intimate way that draws us into relationship with her. My days of keeping prayer lists as such are past. I still do pray for people who ask, but my prayers are much more open-ended. Sadly, there are still plenty of times when I tell God exactly what I think is needed and how she should make it happen.

Finding time for solitude in prayer is the lament I hear most often when I am talking with people about their prayer life. Like most people I was busy every hour of almost every day and still never felt like I had done all the things I needed to do. My solution to the time problem was to have a special place where I could go for precious time with God whenever I was alone during the day. It was my rocking chair, the chair I had used through the infancy of my two children. It was the place they received nourishment for their little bodies when they were babies and it was a place where I could cuddle and comfort them as they grew older. It was then and still is a place where I find nourishment and comfort for myself even though that chair has been moved four times into four different homes since it first became my prayer place.

On the table next to the rocking chair I kept my Bible, the spiral notebook in which I wrote my prayers and any devotional book I was reading. Having this place of prayer was a big step toward writing daily in my prayer journal. It was a sacred space even though it was in my living room. Such a sacred space can be in a more private room, outdoors, in your car, anywhere you can be undisturbed for a period of time. While having the sacred space made it easier to be alone with God, it did not completely solve the problem of praying regularly.

Another problem, besides finding a time when no one was around, was all the waiting household chores. I am a person who likes, I should say, delights in getting things done. So when Norm was off to the church and Jim and Nancy to school, I would think, "now is the time to pray!" But first, I must do the dishes, make the beds, sweep the porch, make a couple of important phone calls and then—you guessed it—then I could sit down and pray. By then, the time I had to be alone was used up. The sacred space was waiting for me and it would continue to wait.

God has always been calling to me to be faithful, and she called to me, in this instance, to find a way to be truly faithful to my prayer time. It occurred to me one day that if Jesus was actually waiting for me in person in my living room, I wouldn't keep him waiting one single second! If he was visible in my living room, I would let those daily chores wait so that I could sit with him. It worked. That was a turning point in my prayer life. From then on, when other things began to use up the time I had to myself, I would picture my loving Lord waiting for me. He was waiting for me because he wanted to spend time with me.

As time went on my sacred space expanded to include any space, and my prayer time expanded to fill any time. Miraculous things happen when you are faithful to God's calling to you. If you truly want to be a person of prayer, you have to really, really want it and go for it.

A haunting fear I have of sharing too openly and too much about my prayer life is the fear that I will lose it. Jesus said we should pray in secret. "…whenever you pray, go into your room and shut the door and pray to your Father who is in secret; and your Father who sees in secret will reward you" (Matt. 6:6). That could mean that we aren't to talk about our prayer practices or it could mean that we shouldn't brag about them. Hopefully, when I am talking and writing, it is safe to share this very private, spiritual practice as long as I am not feeling self-righteous about it.

There were a few years early in God's journey with me, when I believed that sincere prayer, dedicated serious prayer, should be accompanied by fasting. My prayer journal shows that I had a sense of needing to fast. At the same time I was not sure it was what God wanted and whether it was appropriate. At some point during the time I was practicing prayer with fasting, I began to tell others about it. After awhile, I couldn't do it anymore. So now I pray that writing about my prayer life and opening it to others will not diminish it, but rather, will strengthen me on this journey and inspire those who read about it.

The illness of a refugee from Lebanon was the motive for my first prayers with fasting. A Christian agency had an agreement with the government of the United States that Christian refugees could be brought from war-torn Lebanon if there were groups or individuals here who would sponsor them. Sponsoring a family involved helping them find homes and jobs and get settled in their new land. Koshaba was the husband and father of a Christian refugee family from Beirut that our church, Christ Church in Hanover Park, Illinois, sponsored. The family of father, mother and four sons arrived from Beirut in April 1976. By June, Koshaba was critically ill.

The language barrier was a serious and frustrating problem as we dealt with his doctors, nurses and hospitals. He spoke some English but not enough to understand medical terms. His wife spoke five languages, but English was not one of them. The boys soon learned English and, of course, as immigrant children do became very fluent. While helping them get settled into an apartment, gathering furniture and clothes, and getting Social Security numbers, members of our church had worked out a way to converse with them when a translator was not available. It involved much pantomiming and loud voices. I often wondered whether they ever thought, "You don't have to shout! I'm not deaf! I just don't understand English."

It was next to impossible to pantomime the medical details associated with Koshaba's disease and what was being done for him. During this time, things happened that I can only attribute to the work of God. One day not long after he was hospitalized there appeared a doctor who spoke Assyrian! He could talk to him and Virginia to explain the medical terms and diagnoses to them without pantomime and shouting.

During the months of Koshaba's illness, I read many books on prayer and fasting. I didn't just read. I practiced what I read and fasted faithfully not only for him but for other people I knew and for the starving children of our country and of the world. It soon became apparent to me that whether my fasting prayers brought the answers I wanted for my friends, family and the world, they affected me in deep and mysterious ways. Awareness of my hunger when I was fasting seemed to bring clearer awareness of God's presence with me. Wanting

6

to eat something, any little thing, made my promise to God move to the forefront of my mind.

My prayers show that I wasn't always sure that I should fast. This is a prayer of struggle, an argument with God.

> *This is serious and Koshaba and Virginia need help!*
>> *I should fast—should I fast?*
> *Why should I fast? What good would it do?*
>> *If fasting is only of spiritual benefit, why should I <u>fast</u> for <u>them</u>?*
> *Do You want me to fast?*
>> *"If you say you will do it, will you?" --God*
> *Do You want me to fast?*
>> *"If you say you will do it, will you?" --God*
> *Do You want me to fast?*
>> *"If you will say you will do it, will you?" --God*
> *I <u>will</u> do it—liquids only until Koshaba signs the papers.*[1]

I did fast and pray for him to the sign papers he needed to sign to give the doctors permission to do a particular test. Whatever the test was, he was convinced that it would kill him. He just wanted to take his sons and go back to Beirut. The doctors said that without this test, he would die in three months. In great desperation, one of the most desperate I have ever felt in my life, I fasted and prayed.

> *Everyone is away for the 4ᵗʰ of July.*
>> *So is God!*
> *Where are You, God? Where are You? Where are You?*
>> *Do something.*
> *Kneeling, crying. God where are You?*
>> *Obviously not with me, not hearing me, no meaning in fasting.*
> *Bobbi said she would call a priest who is a friend of Koshaba's from Beirut.*
>> *God, send someone who can reach him. God, use the priest.*

God frequently seems to answer prayers more abundantly than we ask or think. Within hours of this prayer a friend of Koshaba's from

---

1   Whenever the prayer I quote involves a conversation in which I knew God was speaking to me, I will identify God's words.

Lebanon was found nearby in Chicago. He was an Eastern Orthodox priest also named Koshaba. Priest Koshaba convinced patient Koshaba to sign the papers!

Praise God! He hears! He cares! Praise God!

Prayer with fasting became a part of my life as his condition grew worse and worse. The results were not what I asked for, not what I wanted. Koshaba died on Labor Day, 1976, six months after the family arrived in the United States. Once he was hospitalized, he never improved enough to go home for even a brief time with his wife and sons.

Burning questions for me were: Does a person fast in order to feel the presence of God? Or must you feel the presence of God in order to fast? Fasting is a time honored practice for hearing the word of God and for sacrificing to God. The question remains for me: what does prayer with fasting accomplish?

Christ Presbyterian Church (USA), Hanover Park, Illinois

6/1/77

Every book I read leaves a trace in my heart and mind, but, every now and then, a book comes along that changes me, that becomes a part of my life and thought permanently. One such book was *With Christ in the School of Prayer* by Andrew Murray, which I read in 1977, shortly after Koshaba's death. Andrew Murray was a man whom you would think least likely to have an effect on the prayer journey of a twentieth century woman. He was born on May 9, 1828, the child of Dutch

Reformed Missionaries from Scotland to South Africa. After studying at the University of Utrecht, he was ordained by the Hague Committee of the Dutch Reformed Church on May 9, 1848, and spent his life serving churches in South Africa. He was a great preacher and wrote more than 240 books. He died January 18, 1917.

Even though his language was exclusively masculine, his words and thoughts spoke directly to me. Exclusively male language didn't start to bother me until almost fifteen years later, but it now drives me to distraction. I can hardly concentrate on any writing that uses only male language for men and women and only male metaphors when referring to God. Recently I defaced a copy of Thomas Merton's *Seeds of Contemplation* by striking out all the male language and substituting feminine. It was an old copy of the book and may have been worth something at a rare book store, but it is no longer valuable to anyone but me. It is only by the love and grace of God that women have loved and served God in spite of being left out of the important formal language of Scripture, theology and worship.

This is a passage from *With Christ in the School of Prayer* which I copied in my prayer journal. I was trying to pray with fasting. That was the topic of the chapter from which this quote was taken.

> Laying aside every weight, as well as the easily besetting sin, afraid of entangling himself with the affairs of this life, he seeks to lead a Nazarite life, as one specially set apart for the Lord and His service.[2]

These words of his brought a soul searching prayer from my heart.

Am I specially set apart?
   No! I felt that once before and took
   pride and soon lost spiritual ground!

If I am "spiritually set apart"
   why should I be? How do I know?
   Because I hunger and thirst after the Word of the Lord.
   because I try to pray constantly, continually.

---

2   Andrew Murray, *With Christ in the School of Prayer* (Fleming H. Revell, Old Tappan, N.J., 1975) 75. The original copyright date was 1933.

> *I AM "specially set apart!*
> *Lord, save me from self-pride and*
> *help me surrender all that I am*
> *to You so that I may be "specially set*
> *apart" for the purpose of serving You in*
> *the lives of others. That You can work through me.*

Some people seem to be specially set apart for noble deeds. They seem to be given special gifts to change troubled situations in the time in which they live. Some people do search for God and want more than anything else to be a consecrated person. Others give it only an occasional thought, and others never think about it at all. So what does "specially set apart" mean? Is it a gift God gives only to special people or can anyone have it?

Summer 1977

During the summer of 1977, I memorized all the Scripture passages I could find, forty of them, which promised that God would give me whatever I asked for. John 14:13, 14 is one example:

> I will do whatever you ask in my name so that the
> Father may be glorified in the Son. If in my name you
> ask me for anything, I will do it.

Learning these passages and living with them embedded in my memory was an attempt to be assured that God would answer the prayers I was offering for all the people on my growing list of prayer needs. But even more pressing than those prayer requests was the deep need to understand why my prayers for healing for our son had not been granted.

My unanswered prayers for healing for Jim were the heart of my wanting God to answer my prayers the way I wanted them to be answered. Jim had severe allergies at a very early age—probably from birth. When they began to manifest themselves as asthma, we took notice. By the time he was eighteen months old, he had attacks during which he had to sit up straight in order to breath. Nothing had ever frightened me so much as waking in the middle of the night to his call

"Mom!" I would get him out of his bed and sit in the rocking chair holding him upright as he struggled to breathe. It seemed to me that each breath might be his last.

When he was two and a half years old, we found Dr. Carlton Lee, an outstanding, innovative allergist in St. Joseph, Missouri. He worked wonders for Jim. Dr. Lee could make the asthma come and go as he tested Jim for different allergies. At times, we would spend every day for a week in Dr. Lee's office with a whole roomful of other people who were suffering various manifestations of their allergic reactions to all kinds of allergens. These were difficult times not only because of Jim's illness but because Nancy, our daughter, was an infant. I had to leave her with friends so much, sometimes whole days for a week. Dr. Lee became so much a part of our lives that when Nancy smashed her thumb in the door at Burger King, she cried, "Take me to Dr. Yee! Take me to Dr. Yee!"

When we moved from Kansas to the Chicago area, we found a highly recommended allergist, but after several months of taking Jim to him, we became so discouraged with his manner, that we started going back to Dr. Lee. Nancy, Jim and I would drive back to Missouri a couple of times a year to have Jim tested and to get more of the antigens that would help him. Thankfully, Norm's parents lived in Topeka, Kansas, so we could stay with them. They took care of Nancy while Jim and I made the daily two hundred mile round trip to St. Joseph, Missouri to Dr. Lee's office.

When we first started with Dr. Lee it was hard to see Jim getting all those shots but after the first day or two, it became evident to me that he didn't seem to mind them. It was as though he knew Dr. Lee was going to make him feel better. The antigen came in the form of shots that I had to give him on a regular basis. I got used to that. My prayers for his healing, and later for healing for Nancy from Type 1 Diabetes, are a constant theme in my journal entries. These were prayers of desperation. I wanted so much for him to be healed! The Apostle Paul wrote to the Romans that the Spirit intercedes with sighs too deep for words (Ro. 8:26). Those were the kinds of prayers, accompanied by tears, that I prayed.

At the time I memorized the prayer verses, we had been taking Jim to Dr. Lee for nine years. Jim would be well for awhile and then the seasons would change causing him to have severe asthma attacks. I believed that all I needed to do was ask and it would be given just as I asked. Those prayers were acts of desperation and of hope.

9/2/77

That summer of filling my mind with promises from the Bible ended with grief on Labor Day. After learning all those verses and using them to claim what I somehow thought God owed me, we discovered that our eight-year-old daughter had Type I (Juvenile) diabetes. We had been on vacation for three weeks, hosting a fiftieth wedding anniversary party for Norm's parents and spending time with mine. During those weeks, she was always thirsty and we couldn't pass a rest area without her needing to use the restroom. A few days after we got home, a friend advised that we take her to the doctor right away. Our family doctor tested a sample of her urine and told us he was sure it was diabetes. We needed to get her to the hospital immediately so he called the hospital and made the arrangements for her to be admitted. While I was bathing her before taking her to the hospital, I could see what I had not seen before: she was very thin, and had a grayish color to her skin.

As we were driving to the hospital, I prayed with great confidence that our family doctor's cursory diagnosis was wrong and that she didn't have diabetes. When we got to the hospital, her blood sugar count was above five hundred which meant she was near falling into a coma. Immediately the doctor ordered insulin and IV's. As I sat by her bed I could see her color changing to the healthy rosy color of a little girl. I knew the diagnosis was right. Our daughter had Type 1 diabetes.

It was apparent that the answer to my prayers was no. It hurt so much to see her in that hospital bed so thin and shaking with fear of the needles. I could hardly stand the thought of those shots. It was unthinkable that she would have to have one or two shots a day for the rest of her life. So my fervent prayer became, "O, God, take it away! Heal her of it!" The answer to these prayers was also no. She still has juvenile diabetes thirty-two years later.

What I had to deal with now was not only two children with serious illnesses, but also a God who, for some reason, was not keeping his promises to me. Why? It wasn't that I was being totally selfish because my prayers were for my children. It wasn't that I was asking for something that God had never done before. Look at all the healings in the New Testament and all the people since who have been healed by prayer. During those first days of dealing with the fact of Nancy's diabetes, my thoughts were that something was wrong with God. He made promises he didn't intend to keep.

Deep in my heart I knew this wasn't true. I knew and had always known that God is good and perfect, all loving and completely caring. Thus, I came to believe there must be something wrong with me. For some reason, God could not answer the prayers of someone like me. I quit praying for my children. My lists of prayers for other people in our congregation continued, but I couldn't pray for my own children or for myself. Even though I thought I was for some reason unworthy of God's attention, I kept struggling with prayer. Oftentimes the struggles came in the form of conversations with God like this one which I wrote on an envelope. It was probably at Nancy's bedside in the hospital some months after the original diagnosis.

> *Why does Nancy have diabetes?*
> *"These things happen. A disease gets started, an accident happens*
> *or a pancreas stops making insulin." --God*
> *Please take it away! Let it be a mistake.*
> *"What will be different if I do? What could she do then that*
> *she is not doing now?" --God*
> *Eat candy and popsicles whenever she wants to.*
> *Not have shots.*
> *"No, I say what could she do that she isn't doing now?"--God*
> *She is doing everything now that she did before and, I'm sure, is in*
> *better condition generally and always will be.*
> *"Then why should I take it away?"--God*
> *Because it's a bother and it's scary and I feel bad for her*
> *sometimes.*
> *"You feel bad. How does she feel?" --God*
> *Great with very few exceptions.*
> *"Then TRUST me. I have a plan for Nancy." --God*
> *In God I trust without a fear. (Ps. 56)*

After more time had passed I wrote this prayer:

O Father, You have worked beautifully in Nancy's life to keep her natural and normal and to accept all of this. I praise Your name. Love, Bev

That prayer was just a little break-through. Maybe in the whole scope of things, that is what prayer is: a series of little break-throughs. It wasn't too long after that when I wrote this companion prayer.

I wish I had been writing things down during the worst years of Jim's asthma attack.
   "What would you have written?" --God
Please take it away.
   "That was about eight years ago. What did it have to do with him as a person?" --God
Made him very sensitive to people who have problems.
   "What else?" --God
It's hard to say.
   "Anything bad?" --God
No, so far as I can tell now.
   "Then why should I take it away?" --God
Because it's been a bother and it's scary and I feel bad for him sometimes.
   "You feel bad. How does he accept it?" --God
Great with a few exceptions.
   "Then TRUST me. I have plans for Jim." --God
"In God I trust without a fear." (Ps.56)

As I reread the prayers above, I realize how much I underestimated the effect their diseases would have on the lives of our beloved children but those positive thoughts helped put things in perspective and were a comfort to me and gave me strength to cope.

9/4/77

The discovery of Nancy's diabetes was an entirely different experience for my pastor-husband. He was shocked and upset about it, too, and wanted it to go away. However, at the very time Nancy was in the hospital this first time, he was ministering to a couple whose oldest daughter had just been killed in a car accident. Barbara was a senior in high school and was riding home with some friends after having decorated the high school gym for the senior prom. Riding in the back seat without a seat belt, she was thrown from the car. No one else in the car was seriously hurt, but she was dead on arrival at the hospital.

It was close to midnight when her mother called Norm to ask him to come to the hospital right away. She was so distraught she only said, "She is dead, and Pete is out of town." Norm had barely arrived at the emergency room when the nurse handed him the phone telling him that it was Barbara's father, Pete, on the line. Her mother wanted Norm to tell her father what had happened. It was Norm's job to tell him his daughter was dead. It was in this context that Norm faced Nancy's diabetes. It gave him a much broader, deeper, more accepting perspective than I. Our friend's daughter was dead. Our daughter had a serious disease, but she was alive.

Words I copied into my prayer journal at this time were from Henri Nouwen's book, *The Wounded Healer.*

> A person comes to the shocking, but, at the same time,
> self-evident insight that prayer is not a pious decoration
> of life but the breath of human existence.[3]

In some sense and in some times prayer had been a "pious decoration" of my life. From this time on, prayer increasingly became for me the "breath of human existence."

12/11/78

Learning to pray was part of growing up in the church. The first time I prayed in public was at a youth banquet in the church in which I grew up. They asked me, in advance, if I would ask the blessing before the meal so I had time to write out my prayer. Even at that, I was so scared! I was a shy person and didn't have much confidence in myself, so this was a big trial. I did it, and I did it well. During my years in youth fellowship, we prayed, and I engaged in prayer in worship. My dear pastor wrote beautiful, long, poetic pastoral prayers. In seminary, I

---

3   Henri J. M. Nouwen, *The Wounded Healer, Ministry in Contemporary Society* (Garden City, Doubleday, 1972), 17.

learned how to write prayers and pray them out loud comfortably. As the wife of a pastor and leader of women's groups, I prayed often and taught others about the importance of prayer. Prayer had been important in my life always. But it was Andrew Murray, combined with my life experiences, who taught me the seriousness of prayer.

> Unless we are willing to pay the price and sacrifice time and attention and what appear legitimate or necessary activities for the sake of the heavenly gifts, we need not look for a large experience of the power of the heavenly world in our work.[4]

There is a price to pay for a rich prayer life. That price is time and attention and setting aside for awhile the duties that press upon us. Moaning about not having time for prayer is not a reason, but an excuse, for not taking time to pray. Paul writes that we should pray constantly. We are missing the richest experience of life when we dismiss his words as impossible because of time limits. In I Thessalonians 5:17, Paul wrote, "Rejoice always, pray without ceasing." That charge seems impossible to carry out, but we are missing something vital to our relationship with God until we try it.

How does one pray constantly? In the early 1970s, my husband was serving a church in a small rural community in northeast Kansas. Every year, the ministerial alliance in the town planned services for Holy Week in which all the churches in town took part. Besides evening services for everyone, the men had daily breakfast together and the women had Bible study later in the morning. Someone of note was always invited to lead the women's Bible study. The year that had the greatest impact on my spiritual life was the year when the topic was prayer. The leader suggested that a way to begin praying constantly was to pray on stimulus. For instance, every time you hear the sirens of emergency vehicles, pray for the people in need and for the responders. When an airplane flies over, pray for the crew and the passengers and for whatever mission they are on. When your phone rings, pray for whoever is calling. Pray when you are moved by some beauty or mystery in nature. Pray when you feel the depth of your love for your spouse or

---

4   Andrew Murray, *The Ministry of Intercession, a Plea for More Prayer*. (Old Tappan, NY, Fleming H. Revell Co., no date) 24.

your children. And so on. Learning to pray in response to stimuli begins to fill life with prayer. It leads to praying without ceasing.

This was an easy habit to get into. It began to foster in me a deep desire for relationship with God which is the main reason for prayer.

5/15/79

One morning when I was feeling depressed and worried about the kids' health, I heard the garbage man singing a cheerful tune in a rich tenor voice! Those were the days before garbage trucks were outfitted with robotics that reach out their long arms and lift the garbage container to empty it into the truck. Those were the days when the guys had to get out of the truck, dump the containers' smelly, gross contents into the back of the truck and then push the lever that would compact it all. This man who was singing so clearly, loudly and joyfully was literally dealing with the garbage of society and he was singing about it! His song comforted me.

How many people I have encountered since who, in desperate circumstances, have been heard singing! One of them was a member of Christ Church who had pancreatic cancer and lived for several years after the onset of the cancer. His faith was so great that he witnessed to all of us throughout the whole long course of his fight with the disease. Many times we thought he was healed, and we believed he was going to be a cancer survivor. I fasted and prayed for him.

Fast until Lloyd is healed. It won't be long. Lord, I get such crazy ideas sometimes. Is this one of them or is it from you? "If we are out of our mind, it is for the sake of God…" (2 Cor. 5:3)

Sometimes when I felt the urge to fast, I wondered whether I was getting to be some kind of religious fanatic. But that was a time of urgency, and I was willing to risk being weird. At that same time, I copied from Catherine Marshall's book, *The Helper:*

> Special filling and special outpouring will be given for tough situations, extremities we alone could never handle. This has been the experience of many individuals across the centuries.[5]

---

5 Catherine Marshall, *The Helper* (Chosen Books, Waco, TX, 1978) 128.

I needed a special filling. I promised to fast until Lloyd was healed. After two days of fasting I reneged on my promise. For fourteen days the cancer was not growing, and he was not having as much pain. The note in the margin of my prayer journal two months later was in red ink

Praise the Lord!!! Lloyd's tumors are gone!

Then he died. A day or two before he died, Norm and I visited him in the hospital. He felt good and was cheerful. He told us he was going home. We believed that by home he meant his house, but he must have known he was going to his heavenly home. It is always interesting how we can express our very own feelings in words that have another meaning for the listener and we think we mean the same thing.

During his illness, when he was able, Lloyd would come to the healing services that Norm conducted at our church. His prayers for others were always beautiful and fervent. He would come back the next Wednesday and tell us his tests were improved after he had been to a healing service. Even if we hadn't prayed for him (he didn't come to pray for himself but to pray for others) he would joke saying that he always benefited from fallout from the other prayers.

7/6/79

Catherine Marshall, spiritual writer and wife of Peter Marshall, the famous preacher and pastor, prayed this prayer.

> Father, this is the promise I make to You: when the Helper prompts me to pray, I will stop what I am doing and pray. When I feel a concern for someone, I will talk with You about it and seek your direction. Keep me alert to the Helper's tug at my sleeve, and give me, Lord as a gift, a high level of willingness to obey and to follow through. [6]

Prayer is not a solitary, sedentary activity. It is movement from your place of quietness and peace out into the world to be God's hands and feet. Everyone has experienced times when they have felt a strong urge to call a friend or write a note to someone long neglected. And lo and behold, it turns out that the call or note was exactly what the person

---

6   Ibid., 144.

needed at that very time. We need to listen to and follow through on those urges because they are quite likely the "Helper's tug at my sleeve."

8/19/79

After a prayer of praise when we thought Lloyd was healed, I wrote this in my prayer journal.

My faith is so strong with regard to your answers to prayers for other people and so weak, almost to the point of nonexistence, for healing for Jim and Nancy. Oh, Lord, forgive me and help my unbelief! Oh, I want Jim and Nancy WHOLE so badly! So much! I can ask You for strength to get them through this day but I can't say with faith "thank You for healing them." My Savior, forgive me. Holy Spirit forgive me. Lord God forgive me.

There are whole books written on the subject of why some prayers are answered and others are not. One reason given for unanswered prayer is that the person praying doesn't have enough faith. This may be the worst and most devastating answer to this question. In a way, that was my feeling about why God didn't answer my prayers for healing for Jim and Nancy. I couldn't believe there was anything wrong with God so it had to be something wrong with me. The loophole in that "logic" was that I was a woman of faith, seeking God's presence and God's will in my life. I was studying the Bible and worshipping regularly. I was helping other people. What more could I do to make myself worthy of having God answer my prayers?

Another reason some people give when confronted with "unanswered" prayer is that God answers our prayers in three ways: yes, no, and wait. He obviously had not said yes to my prayers. There was the possibility that he was saying no, but there was also the always present hope that the time would come when he would say yes, and they both would be healed. It is almost forty years later and Jim still has asthma and Nancy still has diabetes. How long must one wait?

For me, the answer to the question of why some prayers are answered and others are not is that there is no answer. The best I can say is that things happen, and God loves us and suffers with us. The view I had of God during these early days of my prayer life was that he was somewhere removed from us planning everything. My prayers consisted of asking favors from this God who was in heaven determining what was going to happen in everything everywhere. When you see God that way you are seeing God as transcendent. I still believe God is transcendent, above and beyond all things. But now I put more emphasis on the immanence that describes the presence of God in the workings of the world. I believe she dwells with us and in us, that our suffering is her suffering. That still doesn't answer the question about answered and unanswered prayer, but it does strengthen me to know that she abides with me in all that happens in my life and in the lives of my loved ones. That she, too, agonizes when a child can't catch his breath, when a child will not live without insulin shots, when a child is killed in a car accident.

9/21/79

The more I prayed the more I wanted to pray. That is still true today. God lures us toward herself for friendship with her. After six days had passed and I hadn't spent any time in writing prayers, I wrote:

Oh, my Father, why do I let myself get so far away from You? I speak to you often during the day but without the foundation of my morning hour (EVERY DAY!) with you my conversation with You becomes shallow, and I find myself thinking not of the expectations of my prayers, but of the fact that I prayed.

Lord, this close communion with You is hard for me to maintain— what must it be for others who hardly even try except at Sunday worship. How can we help them? How can we teach them?

As I write and share my ideas about prayer, I don't want to dismiss or belittle any other person's ideas or practices of prayer as wrong or unworthy. We are all on a journey, and we are all at different places on the journey. We are all different people, and we reach out to God in many different ways that suit who we are.

What I write, I write out of my own experience. I know that a person can pray while driving the car. I did that a lot when I was traveling through Illinois, Indiana, and Missouri organizing Congressional districts for Bread for the World. Time in a car is perfect for prayer because you are alone with no interruptions. (The advent of cell phones has made that more difficult for some people.) You can pray while you are doing household chores or during intervals at work. Indeed, it makes the work or the drive more pleasant and is a way of reminding us that all we do is done in God's presence.

We can pray and should pray as much as possible during our day, but I believe that God wants time with each of us during which she has our undivided attention. We need times when we can feel her presence over and above everything and everyone else in our lives. And that takes time, determination, and perseverance.

Jesus said that those are blessed who hunger and thirst for righteousness. The practice of daily time alone with God becomes as essential as food and drink to the person who persists in it. In the early years of my growth in prayer, days and even weeks would lapse between prayer times. During those times, I was left weak and thirsty. But for some reason, I persisted. Now hardly one day goes by without the solitude of my prayer time. Sometimes it is short and hurried but without it I am disabled. You have to want it. You have to seriously want it. The more you want it, the more will be given to you. Read again the words of Andrew Murray:

> Unless we are willing to pay the price, and sacrifice time and attention and what appear legitimate or necessary duties, for the sake of the heavenly gifts, we need not look for a large experience of the power of the heavenly world in our work.[7]

9/22/79

Here is an entry from my journal two years after the onset of Nancy's diabetes:

Father, more than anything else I want Jim and Nancy to grow up into deep, continuous fellowship with You. Please help them love you with such depth. Already Nancy says, "I'm not just saying that God loves me. I know he does." When asked how she knows, she said, "Well, I haven't had a sore throat or been in the hospital for a long time."

When she said this, she was showing me a plaque she had made at vacation Bible school by gluing popcorn to a piece of wood. It said,

---

7   Murray, *The Ministry of Intercession*, 24.

"God loves me." For me, there was nothing more important for her to know and to believe than that God loved her and to know it with such certainty. What made her sure of it was not any thought of being healed of her diabetes over the long term. Rather, she was looking at God's love on a day-to-day basis and saw his love in the gift of daily health. Day to day is how we experience God's love. Living in the present moment is the way to know that God loves us.

At about the same time at school Jim was required to answer this question: What two things do you believe in? His answer was "God and myself." I think that this was a teenage boy's way of saying he knows God loves him and that he is able to love himself. That really is what love your neighbor as yourself is all about. When you believe in God and believe that he loves you, you are able to love yourself.

My prayers for my children were being answered, and I was being nurtured. I needed to learn that God is at work in ways I can't even imagine, much less dictate, in the lives of the people for whom I am praying.

By the Way

One of our family albums contains a picture of me in a tree. It was taken when I was in my middle teens. Our family often went to a park in a very small town south of the town in Nebraska where we lived. In that park was a tree with two trunks. One of them grew almost parallel to the ground, and it was wide enough to lie on. In the picture, I am stretched out on that trunk reading a book. The look of contentment on my face is a clue that a tree and a book were my idea of a good time.

My love of trees and books continued. When I was in college, my favorite place to go was the beautiful, tree-filled cemetery a few blocks from the campus. When I had a free hour between classes, I would drive to the remotest corner of that cemetery and study. The life and energy from the trees seemed to give life and energy to my thoughts.

When I was a grown woman, the wife of the minister and mother of two children I still sought places with trees where I could go with a book and my prayer journal. One day when we lived near Chicago, I needed a place to go. I had seen a cemetery not too far from our home. I remembered it as having a lot of trees, just as the cemetery of my college days did, so I went there. It seemed too crowded with very small headstones. It was not as spacious as the one near my college, but I felt like it would do. After all the Chicago area is a crowded place, and you enjoy trees where you find them. I paid homage to the memory of the people who were buried there and went on with my meditation satisfied. Some weeks later I drove past it again on another errand and discovered that it was a pet cemetery!

Now that we live in the desert, I seek places where I can read and meditate without dehydrating. When we first moved here, I discovered the community library is built on the grounds of a marvelous riparian preserve, filled with all kinds of desert plants and birds. The floor-to-ceiling windows in the study area of library provide a perfect place to gaze out into nature and meditate. Recently, I decided to venture out into the "wilderness" of the preserve. It is every bit as inspiring as the woods of my native Midwest. The plants are cacti, sage brush, and mesquite, but I feel the Spirit of God there just as much as in the woods of the Midwest.

Maybe having two sets of grandparents who were farmers put a love of the outdoors in my soul. I have always watched the seasons come and go. In Kansas where Norm served his second pastorate, the best sign of the changing seasons was sugar maples turning colors. There was no need for us to go to New England or anywhere else to "see the colors." The colors lined the streets of Hiawatha, Kansas, a town known for the beauty of the sugar maple trees in autumn. Almost every yard had at least one sugar maple. Most of them had more than one shading their large, country town yards. After the first hard frost, the trees would begin to turn brilliant reds, yellows, gold, and oranges.

They were all beautiful but some were more spectacular than others because of their location or because of the shape of the tree. There were a few trees that had the power to open my heart to God. When I drove around the town of about 4,000 people, I would go out of my way to see trees that were my favorites. They announced to me that God loves beauty. They announced to me that God could and did show herself in the beauty of those trees whose colors were so brilliant they looked as if they were on fire. They announced to me that God loves me.

After we moved to Chicago, I felt the changing of the seasons in the fall when geese would fly overhead in their noisy V formations. The breeze would be warm with a tinge of cold, and the leaves changed colors and began to fall from the trees. In the spring, the feel of the breeze also announced spring time. It would be cold with a tinge of warm and smelled like rich, wet soil. The fall breeze smelled dryer and dusty.

For twenty years, I commuted to the office of the Presbytery of Chicago and to my Bread for the World office in Chicago's Loop. That made me a city person instead of a rural person like my forebears. Being a city person enriched what I appreciated about the outdoors. I began to see some glimpses of God in people hurrying from Union Station to their places of work. I could see God in the magnificent skyscrapers. And, of course, when I got near Lake Michigan, God was there, too, revealing herself. Just as with praying, you have to want to see her. You have to want to have fellowship with her. She meets you more than halfway in her presence in all of creation.

10/2/79

Out of the depth of my disappointment at unanswered prayers for Jim's healing, I memorized Bible passages about God's promises, about God giving me what I wanted. After Nancy became diabetic, my disappointment continued as I prayed for healing for both of my children. As time went on, I began to study Bible passages about healing. I thought I must be missing something. In order to be thorough and remember what I read, I made five columns on a page in my prayer journal: the Bible passage reference; who was healed; whose faith or prayers caused the healing; the method of healing; and the result. It was a good way to analyze the problem, but I didn't come up with answers.

Continuing to search for the meaning of prayer and how to pray aright, I made another list. This time it was a list of Bible passages about prayer. I was on a desperate search for the meaning of prayer, for a way to understand prayer that would enable me to use it for my purposes. What I sought was how to get the results I wanted in situations that burdened me. What I got, I know now, after all these years, was a deep and abiding faith in God. I still ask for specifics, but now the main reason for my praying is to feel God's presence in my heart.

When I read book number three of my prayer journals in preparation for writing this book, I had the dispiriting thought that maybe not much has changed in my prayer life over the years. It is a saddening thought because I have worked so hard to grow and change. "Worked hard" is probably not the best phrase to use. Rather, I have tried hard to become more and more faithful to God in prayer and to have my relationship with her grow ever deeper and richer.

As I read the entries in the journals, it is evident that, in those first years I did not write every day. A recurring prayer was for forgiveness for not praying every day. Usually the cause of the delinquency was that I stayed up too late the night before, so I couldn't wake up before my family did. Along with that came the admission that usually whatever I stayed up doing could have been done better the next day.

When I recall those days, however, there just weren't enough daylight hours to do all I was doing for my husband, my children, my church, my friends and my job. I was doing too much and I was proud of it. My mother was such a hard worker in her home and in her job. It was not unusual for her to have washed several loads of clothes and hung them on the line to dry before my three sisters and I got up at seven o'clock. She might also have baked a batch of cookies or set a pan of dinner rolls to rise. She was the queen of dinner rolls! No one else's could match hers. My love of early morning hours certainly comes from her as does my satisfaction in completing many tasks.

Much of what I wanted to do was to help people out of tough situations. Truth be known I probably wanted to do it for them. This is a characteristic probably inherited from my father. He was always eager to help anyone in any way in any trouble. People used to say, "He is a prince of a guy." And he was. Wherever we would go in my home town he would be greeted by people the rest of the family didn't even know. If any one needed anything they knew they could come to Al.

My wanting to solve people's problems seemed to be more talk than action. I would pray in writing that I was going to do such and such but I didn't always do it. If a problem improved without my help I would think that God had not wanted me to do anything about it anyway. I would have been known as a meddler of the worst kind if I had carried through on all my prayer ideas. Frequently, I was praying for the spiritual well being or growth of another person without their asking me or confiding in me. I was a closet are-you-saved kind of Christian.

My style today is not to pray that I will cleanse people or save them. I am more likely to pray that God will give them wisdom and strength and patience to cope with whatever faces them. Or often I just pray for God to abide with them.

There is, however, a similarity between my first prayers and my prayers today. The likeness is that even then I started each prayer with thanksgiving or with some ascription of praise to God and closed it with a dedication of my life to God. It is a declaration of praise and adoration that unfailingly clears my mind and makes me aware of God in my heart. The formula I use most often and to greatest effect was and still is:

Dear God, my Lord and Savior, You are so great, How great You are and Your greatness is unsearchable. You are so patient! How patient you are and your patience never wears thin. You are so loving. How loving you are and Your love knows no bounds.

Even though the words of praise and thanksgiving are much the same, the words I now use to describe God vary. Thinking about and naming various attributes of God keep me fresh and lively as I pray. They enable me to feel the presence of God in my heart. The attributes of God that can be used in this kind of opening are limited only by a person's imagination about who God is and what God does.

"I never praise God when I pray." Those words were said to me by a colleague in a clinical pastoral education course I took in preparation for my ordination. He went on to say, "It seems like I am buttering up God in order to get what I want." I was floored and have thought about his words often over the years. How can we, beloved creatures of God, inheritors of such love and beauty, not praise God with every breath! The Westminster Confession of Faith's first question is: "What is the chief end of man?" and the answer is "The chief end of man is to glorify God and enjoy him forever." (I would rewrite it to say: "The chief end of every person, man or woman, is to glorify God and enjoy God forever.") We are surrounded by beauty in nature and beauty in other people and in events. Beauty is a creation and a gift of God. As with human gifts, giving thanks and praise is in order. God wants our praise. It helps us in our prayer life to acknowledge how great is the one who hears and answers our prayers.

My written prayers took the form of letters to God. Usually I began, " Dear Lord." When my mother died, my address changed to "Dear Lord our God and Precious Mother." I missed her greatly and was distressed that she died so much sooner than I ever thought she would. The language I was learning about God in my reading of Christian feminist theology opened the way for me to think of God as mother. In one prayer, I wrote that I didn't know what it would be like to be without my mother. She was in the world before I was, and she brought me into it. Those very words apply to a Christian understanding of God. The word "precious" was full of meaning for me as I thought about how precious my mother had been to me and that God was precious to me for many of the same reasons my mother was. Never when I use that phrase do I feel as if I am praying to Mom. I am praying to God who is my mother as well as my father. God far exceeds all of the good, wonderful, loving characteristics of my mother, but she is most certainly like my mother in all her good qualities.

Another similarity in my prayers over the years has been the declaration of my love for God and the plea for God to abide with all whom I love. My closing ascription has become a set one: *Bless all my loved ones this day and always. In Jesus' name and for his sake. Amen and Amen. I love you, Lord! I love you!*

Seldom do I write prayers for my family members by name. Only in times of crisis or great joy do I name them. I pray for them by name in thoughtful prayer during the day and consider that they are covered in the phrase "bless all my loved ones this day and always." This is a "spray the bottles" approach. I heard it described that way once in a seminar on prayer. The story was that you shouldn't just spray over a row of bottles and hope to fill them. Rather you should fill each one individually. I don't have a large family in comparison to some families but if I prayed for each one of them on a daily basis the way I pray for myself and Norm and Jim and Nancy, there would never be time to fill them all. And I don't always know what they need since we don't live close to each other.

I don't know why there are two "amens" and two "I love you, Lords." I do that to this day all these years later. I can't explain why. One would think that one amen is enough. Two "amens" just seem better than one. Musically there are pieces used in corporate worship that consist wholly of repeated "amens." They add a fervency to the prayer just prayed. "So be it!" "So be it!"

The middle section of my prayers has changed over the years. At first the whole prayer was for healing for the kids or for God to help someone with something. Those pleas were followed by an accounting of previous prayers in columns designated for yes or no answers. As my prayer life deepened, the middle section, the body of the prayer, was taken up with lifting up various situations to God and asking that his will be done. In most recent years, it has been reflective of a desire to understand myself and my relationship with God and others.

Writing my prayers helps me stay centered and spend whatever amount of time is needed to express myself and to listen for answers. An affirmation of my spending time to write my prayers came from Lloyd John Ogilvie who wrote:

> On the human level, we will do anything we can to spend time with a person who loves, accepts, and affirms us. A loved one who heightens our self-esteem and gives us fresh courage for life's battles is cherished, and conversation flows naturally.[8]

Just so, our conversations with God should flow freely. Prayer is conversation with God. It is talking with the One who knows us better and loves us more than any of the human beings with whom we come in contact.

By the Way

Reading books about prayer and reading the prayers of other people has been a deep well of inspiration for me. Thomas Merton is one of my favorites. In fact, he inspired me so much that I filled six pages of my prayer journal with quotes from his book, *Seven Storey Mountain*. His words about how the whole universe praises God enriched my praise of God in my daily life:

---

8   Lloyd John Ogilvie, *Autobiography of God* (Regal Books, 1979), 159.

There is not a flower that opens, not a seed that falls into the ground, and not an ear of wheat that nods on the end of its stalk in the wind that does not preach and proclaim the greatness and mercy of God to the whole world. There is not an act of kindness or generosity, not an act of sacrifice done, or a word of peace and gentleness spoken, not a child's prayer uttered, that does not sing hymns to God before His throne, and in the eyes of men, and before their faces.[9]

Writers such as Merton and many, many others have been a community of mentors for me. An example is this prayer by Michael Quoist which was in one of the earliest books on prayer that I used. In my struggles with having enough time to get done everything I wanted to do and needed to do, a prayer of Quoist's expressed my need.

You who are beyond time, Lord, you smile to see us fighting it.
And you know what you are doing.
You make no mistakes in your distribution of time to men [and women, too].
You give each one time to do what you want him [her] to do.
But we must not lose time,
   waste time,
   kill time,
For time is a gift that you give us,
But a perishable gift,
A gift that does not keep.
Lord, I have time,
I have plenty of time,
All the time that you give me,
The years of my life,
The days of my years,
The hours of my days,
They are all mine.
Mine to fill, quietly calmly,

---

9   Thomas Merton, *Seven Storey Mountain* (Orlando, Florida, Harcourt, 1948), 120.

But to fill completely, up to the brim,
To offer them to you, that of their insipid water
>   You may make a rich wine such as you made once in
>   Cana of Galilee.
I am not asking you tonight, Lord, for time to do this and
then
>   that,
But your grace to do conscientiously, in the time that you give
>   me, what you want me to do.[10]

---

10   Michel Quoist, *Prayers,* translated by Agnes M. Forsyth and Anne Marie de
Commaille (NY, Avon, 1975), 98.

Chapter Two

9/22/80

Throughout all the prayer journals, my deepest and most anguished prayers are for the well-being of Jim and Nancy. In 1980 (Jim was fourteen and Nancy was twelve), I was praying in despair. I believed God could do anything he wanted to, so it must be that he didn't want to heal them. That was a primary issue, a grief in my life for all those years and in years to come. If God truly answers prayers then why didn't he heal Jim and Nancy?

The thought that if he had the power to heal them but didn't want to left me bewildered and disappointed. Then the question became, "Why didn't he want to?" It must have been something wrong with me. It couldn't be anything wrong with God because God is perfection in all ways. So I blamed myself that my children were not healed because of my faults and my shortcomings in my faith. My practice was to pray for the kids and hand it over to God and then take it right back again and cry and worry and grieve.

O Father, You know how I've been able to give my job future to You and our retirement future, and our financial matters to You—sometimes I falter. But I know with my whole heart, Lord, that You are taking care of all those things far better than we could care for them ourselves. And I want to know that about Jim's health (and Nancy's too but she is well right now) I really do know it but I keep taking it back from you and am miserable trying to do it myself and failing and denying Your love and Your power. I am so sorry. Please forgive me.

After all these years of struggle with the meaning of prayer, I wish I could say with certainty today, what it is and how it works. The explanation I would give of it is: time spent alone with God. It is time to feel her presence in my heart. It is the feeling that I am in her flow. It is witnessing that when I am in her flow, things go well and I am part of making this world and its people what God intends for them to be. It is commending my loved ones to her flow and seeing that things go more smoothly for them when I do that faithfully.

I can say what, I believe, it is not. For me it is not making a list of wants and seeing if God is going to give them to me. It is not begging that God will heal Jim of asthma and Nancy of diabetes. It is asking that they both will love God and have God's strength and wisdom in their lives. I can't say how it works, but I can say that it does work. The results of my prayers for the kids are that they are fine adults. Nancy is a beautiful, efficient, kind woman who is a wise and loving mother to my very special granddaughter and a loving supportive wife to her husband. Jim is a man of sensitivity to the condition of others and of great generosity to anyone who needs him even to his own sacrifice. They both cope with their diseases with confidence and good spirit. What more could a mother ask. God does answer prayer far more abundantly than we ask or think.

10/26/80

Praying as I read the Bible gives greater depth and richness not only to my study of the Scriptures, but also to my prayer life. I learned this practice from a contemporary Christian woman, but it is an ancient spiritual practice called *lectio divina*. *Lectio divina* involves choosing a passage of scripture, reading it, meditating on it, and praying it. She said, "I stayed in the book of Acts awhile this morning."

Staying in the scripture is a whole different practice than just reading passages with the intent of reading a whole book or even trying to read the whole Bible. Staying in the Scripture means that you want to fill your heart and soul with what God is saying to you through the written word.

If your goal is to read the whole Bible from cover to cover, you won't get it done this way. What will happen is that your heart will be opened to God in ever new and refreshing ways.

11/1/80

Among my prayer concerns for myself are often prayers about my eating too much and weighing too much. It is embarrassing to read that in 1980 I was asking forgiveness for the sin of gluttony and that today, all these years later, eating too much is still a problem. Two weeks ago, I made a promise to lose five pounds, and I have only gained during that time. Our son tried to console me by saying that at my age, I shouldn't worry about it. (He wasn't being unkind about my age just being kind about my weight.) I try on my old clothes or try on new ones and I see my shape and I want to give up and wear sack dresses all the time.

At a women's Bible study circle meeting two decades ago, a friend who was leading the lesson had us read Romans 12. We were to read until God stopped us and then we were to write God a letter about what we were feeling as we read it. I don't have the letter I wrote, but I do have this entry in my journal.

You stopped me at verse 1. ". . . present your bodies as a living sacrifice, holy and acceptable to God, which is your spiritual worship." Forgive me for eating the way I did yesterday! Forgive my gluttony and give me strength to overcome it.

Here is another unanswered prayer, but it is absolutely clear why this one was unanswered and remains so. This is entirely my doing—I really don't want to stop eating so much. I love to eat! For some reason, there is comfort in eating, especially the between-meals stuff I eat, especially any and all chocolate. My father-in-law used to say that he ate to live not lived to eat! Sometimes it is as though I live to eat.

Not only do I eat too much, I don't exercise except when I can be in the pool every day in the five months of hot weather we have in Arizona. I have had physical therapy and steroid shots for backache three different times. The second time especially relieved the pain for quite awhile. But as soon as the therapy was over so was my doing the exercises that so obviously eased the pain. All the while I was in therapy, I would say, "If I only had been doing this all the years since I first was instructed to do them I wouldn't have this pain now." Even that was not enough to make me do what I needed (and still need) to do. In this case, when I pray for relief from the pain or the end of eating more than I need and my prayer isn't answered, I know it is not because God can't or won't but because I can't or won't.

11/11/80

One of the ways I used Scripture in my early days of praying was by reading a passage and substituting my name for the third-person pronouns in the passage. For instance, Jesus' prayer for the disciples and for all the generations to come is one of the passages I read this way in 1980. Referred to as the "Great Priestly Prayer," it is found in chapter 17 of the Gospel of John. Here are just a few verses with my name inserted.

I have made your name known to Bev whom you gave me from the world. She is yours and you gave her to me, and she has kept your word. Now Bev knows that everything you have given me is from you, the words that you gave me I have given to Bev, and she received them and knows in truth that I come from you, and she has believed that you sent me.

Reading these words of Jesus with my name inserted, with him speaking about me directly, not only increases my sense of his presence with me but also affirms my value to God and my worthiness to be spoken of with such divine, loving words.

11/21/80

One of our parishioners asked me to talk with her young son when his father was dying from a brain tumor. This boy was so distraught he was pulling out his eyebrows and eyelashes. I had been giving him organ lessons so it wasn't as though I was being asked to connect only for this desperate situation with someone I didn't know. My prayer the day he and I went out for ice cream was this:

Father, you know Sue wants me to talk to Josh. We made all the arrangements for tonight with much thought and prayer and I pray that You are guiding us! O Father use me to minister to him. Help me answer the questions that he has in his heart—not the ones that his mother is worrying

that he has in his head. I want only You to shine through—not myself.
Forgive me for pride at being asked to do this. Forgive me and take it all
away! Fill me with Your love so that it will encircle and enfold Josh. O Lord
use me to minister to him. I've only remembered John 14:2, 3 to give him.
If there are others that would speak to him help me remember them.

Yeah! Right! Like a ten-year-old wants to be given Scripture passages
to think about. We did go out for ice cream and he talked and talked
and talked. He talked, but not about his father's illness and pending
death; not about what his mother thought was upsetting him so much.
He talked and talked and talked about all the things a boy that age
would talk about when he has the undivided attention of an adult he
knows and admires. I think I did minister to him just by listening. It
may have been the first since the onset of his dad's tumor that anyone
had paid extra attention to him. My prayer was answered even though
God didn't give me any more verses and I didn't even get to use the one
I had. I believe my prayer was answered because God's love did enfold
and encircle this beloved child as God shone through me.

12/7/80

. . .for God did not give us a spirit of timidity, but a
spirit of power and love and self-control. (2 Tim. 1:7.
RSV)

Timidity was the word that caused me to copy this passage in my prayer
journal. The spirit of timidity had been my companion for much of my
life. When I wrote this passage in my prayer journal, I had just been
hired to be the Hunger Action Enabler for Chicago Presbytery. It was
a position which involved speaking, preaching, teaching and writing
about the plight of people who are poor and hungry in the United States
and all over the world. Because poverty is political so is speech dealing
with it. Talking politics in the church is like walking on thin ice. The
adage is true that two things you don't talk about in polite society are
politics and religion.

In the Presbyterian form of government, a presbytery is a geographical
grouping of churches whose representatives, laity and clergy in equal
numbers, debate and vote on issues facing the whole denomination as

well as their own situations. It was my job to be in touch with the one hundred and twenty-seven churches in Chicago Presbytery in as many ways as possible to teach and inspire them to take action for people who were suffering from poverty.

At that time, the federal government was talking of reforming the welfare system in our country. It seems to be an axiom that when it comes to poor and disadvantaged people, legislative bodies talk about reform when what they really mean are budget cuts. There is a parallel to this in churches: when budgets get tight the first funds cut are usually the ones designated for mission.

One way to inform the churches was to give a presentation at the quarterly meetings of the presbytery. Time on the docket of a presbytery meeting is a precious commodity because there is so much business and because so many people have so much to say. The Hunger Committee of the Presbytery of Chicago received permission to do a presentation on the provisions of the welfare legislation and what effects it would have on poor people. It was imperative that we use our time well. The chairwoman of the Hunger Committee spoke boldly about the effect of government actions on marginalized people whenever she got a chance. She and I were to do the presentation, and I was worried that her attention to detail and a style of wordiness would spoil the effect. Not only was I worried about her effect, I was worried about mine. I had strength of heart on the issue, but a timid spirit.

Timothy's words that God has given us a spirit of power, not of timidity, rang in my ears as we prepared for the presentation and as we gave it. She did a good job and so did I. After that event and with that passage as a mantra, I was able to do more bold and persuasive things than I had ever thought I could.

12/25/80

Our Father in heaven, thank You for the gift of Your Son, our Lord and Savior! Thank You for becoming one of us—thank you for your great love, such a love! that would cause you to do that for us. This world can be such a miserable place and Jesus saw and lived through much misery and agony and worry. But, Lord, since you came and showed us the value of it all, it can be truly beautiful.

I don't believe that heaven can be here on earth in its fullness, but I do believe that Your Kingdom can come and has come into our very midst. O Lord, I pray that You will hasten the day when You will dwell in the hearts of all men and women and children. Oh, Lord, use me to change greedy, self-centered hearts to loving and unselfish hearts.

When I prayed this prayer, I believed God was outside human beings and needed to be addressed as one who was separate from his creation. I believed that he directed things from above. Now I am convinced God really dwells in the creation and in the heart of each person who has ever been, is now and ever will be. She doesn't have to be invited in. She already dwells here. But if that is true then questions arise about why some people do such terrible things. I believe God dwells in the hearts of cruel, murderous people, or even people who are mildly evil just as she dwells in yours and in mine. But for some reason, there are people who never know that presence in a way that keeps them from doing bad things. Just so there are many people who do good always who never know that presence in their hearts in a way that gives them a glimpse of the Divine. It is too easy to say that some people are created good and some are created evil. Being greedy or generous, self-centered or caring, doing good or evil must be a choice we make based on whether we know God's presence in our lives. Many influences in our lives either make her presence known or hide her from us.

Somehow knowing and living her presence in my heart has become the chief purpose of my life. It must also be to some degree a deep desire of your heart or you wouldn't be spending time reading this book.

12/30/80

O Lord, change me! You have brought me so far that it would be easy to sit back and be contented with where I am, but I have been at contented places before and have found greater joy beyond them. So, Lord, please keep me moving! Amen and Amen!

12/31/80

One of the surprising things I have been reminded of from reading my journals is that I spent almost five years studying the book of

Revelation! I remember studying it and teaching it, but I had forgotten that it took me that long. My method of Bible study was to use all the commentaries I could get my hands on and go through each verse of a biblical book exploring and looking at each section, phrase by phrase and word by word. I used a study edition of the New International Version of the Bible that had wide margins providing great space for notes and comments. I loved doing it! I remember telling my husband that if I could chose any career in the world it would be to teach the Bible in a college.

After spending that many years studying Revelation, I still doubted my authority to teach it. As I was writing I noted that I didn't know exactly what I would do with what I was learning. No one had asked me to study or to teach that puzzling, beautiful, scary book. My church provided an excellent forum for teaching it though. We were always looking for teachers of adult classes and if they already knew what they wanted to teach that was great! However, sometimes I regarded that as a somewhat iffy proposition . What if they were "out of line" with their theology or Bible scholarship? Using denominational materials in our children's classes kept a check on what was taught there, but the adult classes were pretty much at the discretion of whoever was willing to teach. There were enough people were interested in studying the book of Revelation that it was decided that I should teach a series on it but I was scared. Here is what I prayed:

My Father in heaven, I approach this writing of a Bible study on Revelation with fear and trembling. Who am I to do such a thing? But I also approach it with great excitement and anticipation of teaching it because I want to share the beauty of worship and Your presence that I have found there. I believe you want me to do this so please enable me, Lord, and make it all Your work.

Even with all the time, study and thought that I had invested in the study of the book of Revelation, I still didn't believe I had the authority or the knowledge to write and teach that book on which so much has already been written. It is still hard for me to accept that I have authority to speak or write, even when I feel it is God-given. Sometimes I think that, if I only had some advanced degrees I could more readily accept what I teach and write as authoritative. My only advanced degree is a Bachelor of Divinity degree, which since I earned it, has been changed to a master's degree. It is quite probable that even if I had a PhD, I would feel that I have little authority.

1/30/81

How much I have loved our homes! When I first walk into our living room in the morning, I feel such a sense of peace and the rightness of things. I look around at what we have not only in the things that we have, but the love that we share with each other and with friends and family. I do that at night, too, when I am the last to go to bed or am up sleepless in the night. Someone once told me that my beloved Grandma Harvey used to do that, and I believe that my mom did. Maybe it is something that all women do—all women who have what they need for their families.

The way the light changes throughout the day in any room in our home fascinates me, but most especially it does in the room where I pray and read the Bible. In our other homes, it was the living room while here in our retirement home, it is in the "great room." That sounds so grand, but actually it is kitchen, dining room and living room combined. It has windows and patio doors that let in the light not only of the sun but of the moon at night. It makes me aware of the greatness of God in the changes from darkness to light.

Our living room in Hanover Park had large windows to the west.

I am home alone, and it feels so good. Jim and Nancy and Norm are precious to me, but these moments of silence and of time with You are also precious to me! O Lord, I feel much better than I did when I got up this morning. Your blessings to me are so great! Right now the westering sun is pouring in the living room windows and it is warm and bright in here, and even though it needs cleaning, it is comfortable.

O Lord, I pray that all your children the world over might have the comfort and the joy I have. Lord, give all who care the power to correct injustice and make this the kind of world you want it to be.

2/2/81

This is one of those "Tell me again, Lord, I forget," mornings.

It was early morning prayer time, and I was worrying because Jim had a cold. More often than not, his colds developed into asthma. When Nancy got a cold her blood sugar would rise and upset the balance between her insulin dosage and her food intake. It is apparent from my prayers that I also stewed about them missing school. Over and over again, I would surrender to God their health and well-being. And over and over again, I would take it back and worry about it. Sometimes I would take it back and start the worrying as soon as I said amen to the prayer.

Thanks be to God for her great patience with us.

3/16/81

O Lord, my praise of You and my thanks to You come from deep in my heart, deep in my soul. So much of the time it is even more a feeling than it is words. There is such deep happiness and peace within me and I know, I know it comes from You. O, Lord, I want all of my loved ones to know You this way. Bless them like You've blessed me. Send the right people to them and help them respond in love to You.

The excitement of our deepening relationship is so beautiful and I thank You for it. O, Lord, I know it is a fragile thing on my part because there are so many temptations that, if yielded to, would destroy it. But I also know that You are the rock of my salvation, and <u>nothing</u> can separate me from You and from Your love for me. Praise be to You, O Lord, my God.

There it is: the direction of my prayer life was beginning to change. I didn't realize it happened so early in my desire to be a woman of prayer. Nor did I remember the sheer delight in this new-found understanding of prayer. My prayer practices were leading, drawing me into a closer relationship with God. I was beginning to feel God. I was beginning to know that God was not far away and beyond my reach. He was not sitting on a throne before which I had to kneel and beg for favors. Somehow he was part of my very existence. I rejoiced in the nearness of God to me. I felt it as soon as I sat down in the rocker to write my prayer. My prayers were written as letters to God in which I addressed him by name. At that time, Father and Lord were about the only names I knew or would use. And at the end, I signed the prayer, "Love, Bev."

3/29/81

Oh, dear Lord, I want to know your written word so well that I can say to myself many, many portions of it. I want it to run in my spirit and in my life like the blood runs in my body! It is so frustrating because I learn verses and then forget them. Oh, Lord, supply my need. If Bethel is the answer help me be faithful to it.

Lord, speak to the hearts of our people so that when Norm comes home from Madison and begins to look for people to be trainers that they will know who they are and give themselves to Your work and Your word.

The Bethel Bible Series was the best thing that ever happened to me in terms of my learning the content of the Bible. Even my seminary training had not given me the knowledge of the whole Scripture that Bethel gave me. Bethel is a program for teaching people the scope of God's activity in the Bible starting with Genesis and ending with Revelation. This two-year program which uses the Bible as its text book involves disciplined study and commitment. The study uses a historical approach to the Hebrew-Christian heritage of faith with an overview of the Old and New Testaments.

A congregation enters the Bethel program when the pastor goes to Madison, Wisconsin, for two weeks of training to teach lay leaders in her/his congregation. When Norm came home from that training really excited about the possibilities, he talked with ten members of our church and asked them to be teachers of the classes that would be held for members of the congregation. Ten of us met with Norm once a week for two hours for two years. We memorized concepts from each chapter of each book of the Bible. There were written tests periodically and because of that, flash cards became a part of my daily life. I wrote the chapter and verse of a book on one side of the card and the verse that contained the main concept of the chapter on the other side. As I studied, I memorized them from both directions so that if I were asked what was in a certain passage, I could answer or if I were asked where to find a certain concept I could say where it was.

The printed material of the Bethel series comes with full-color posters and matching pictures in the student's book that are to be used to help students remember the theme of each book of the Bible. Some people complain sarcastically about what poor art the posters are.

However, art is not the point memory is. They are mnemonic devices: a concept is attached to each object in the picture, making it easier to remember. I can still remember the first picture which illustrates that God created everything to be in harmony, and the second where mankind is separated from God, from others, from himself and from nature.

The Bible is becoming less and less important to Christians. Fewer and fewer people attend Sunday Schools and Bible study classes. The loss to the church, to society and to individual lives is grievous. Society at large is losing the foundation of magnificent words and thoughts from which much great literature and music have come. The church and Christians are losing the word that has been sacred for centuries. The Bible is not to be worshipped but it does contain the word of God spoken to and through people for generations. It can be words of support, guidance and affirmation for contemporary people.

By the Way

Without fail when I stay up too late in order to get a whole list of things done I sleep later in the morning and miss my prayer time which always makes things harder for the rest of the day. Friends used to make fun of me and my lists. They would say, "You need a list to keep track of your lists." I had a lot to do, and I had discovered that, if I made a list, then I didn't have to keep rehearsing all the things I needed to get done, and I could do each one with a better spirit. Many, many years ago my dad sent me this prayer that he had copied from somewhere.

> I got up early one morning and
> rushed right into the day;
> I had so much to accomplish that I
> didn't take time to pray.
> Problems just tumbling about me,
> and heavier came each task;
> "Why doesn't God help me?"
> I wondered.
> He answered, "You didn't ask."
> I wanted to see joy and beauty

But the day toiled on, gray and bleak.
I wondered why God didn't show me.
He said: "But you didn't seek."
I tried to come into God's presence.
I used all my keys at the lock.
God gently and lovingly chided:
"My child you didn't knock."
I woke up early this morning and
paused before entering the day;
I had so much to accomplish
that I had to take time to pray.[1]

5/17/81

O Lord, it is truly a miracle how you extend this time to allow me to do so much—when I first give that time to You! Please forgive me for not always turning it over to You. You could accomplish so much more if I did—please help me and guide and strengthen me.

Women are especially good at multi-tasking. Getting many things done has been important to me as long as I can remember. My prayer journals illustrate that fact as I repeat over and over again, almost to the point of embarrassment, that I have too much to do. As near as I can tell there are two maybe three reasons for my wanting to accomplish so many things. First, my Mom always got a lot done. Second, I had a lot to do. Third, I am gifted with many interests and abilities. There was a time when I would not have accepted as true the third one. But that whole scene is for another essay.

My mom was so industrious and so efficient! She was always employed outside our home, but I never thought of her as a "working mom" until my adult years. She worked at a creamery when I was a toddler. Sometimes she would take me with her to work. I can still smell the butter and the cream. Later, she worked cleaning houses for other people and cooking special meals at the Masonic Temple. And she did various jobs over the years at the Hastings Daily Tribune where my dad worked. The reason I didn't realize she worked away from home was that she did all the things a "stay-at-home" mom did and more.

---

1   Grace L. Naessens, Used by permission.

She did the usual housekeeping, cooking, cleaning. She also kept her parents' farm home clean and worked in their garden. She butchered chickens to put in the freezer at the locker plant, and she canned all the produce from the garden that was suitable for canning. She made all of our clothes—there were four of us daughters, and she drove us to and from all kinds of activities. She did the laundry with a wringer washer and it was not uncommon for her to have the laundry done and hanging on the clothesline before we got up at seven o'clock in the morning. Quite often she would also have set dinner rolls to rise by then. She was a whirlwind!

So I could very well have inherited from her the genes for working quickly and efficiently and getting a lot done. Her example prepared me well for the busy life of a minister's wife. All the things Mom did so well I wanted to do well. But I also wanted to be involved in the life of the church Norm was serving and in any Christian Education events Presbytery-wide for which I was needed. Having graduated from seminary but not being ordained, I also wanted to preach in vacant pulpits whenever I was asked.

One of the things Mom did so well was sew. And I did too. I sewed not only my own clothes and clothes for Nancy, but miles and miles of curtains and drapes for the various houses in which we lived. There was no special place for my sewing machine in our first house, but in our second one, I set up a sewing room in one corner of the basement. The kids' playroom, complete with sand table, was also there. So while I was sewing, I could enjoy their play as well as keep my eye on them.

Efficiency genes from my Mom gave me the ability to engage in keeping house, sewing, canning and cooking, engaging in professional activities and giving piano lessons. I had started giving piano lessons in 1966 in order to pay for a piano that I wanted so desperately but couldn't afford. The same month I got the piano the adoption agency called and told us they had son for us. We had been waiting for that call for so many months! We and our families were overjoyed at the news! The piano lessons continued. Two years later when we adopted our daughter there were two babies in the playpen during the lessons.

I had also started playing the organ in 1961 when we moved to our first parish after seminary. They were in need of someone to play the little electronic organ they had just purchased. Since I had taken piano lessons for twelve years, accordion lessons for seven years and had played the organ a little bit I said I would do it. Free lessons came with the little organ, so I got to take the lessons in return for playing for Sunday worship, funerals and weddings. Our second church had a permanent, gifted organist who had been their organist forever so I wasn't called upon to play. When we moved to Hanover Park near Chicago, our third parish, they had an organist, but she quit as soon as she heard that I could play. That began my twenty-year career on the organ bench.

By then, I was even busier with growing children who had health problems, with church activities, with a job and eventually with ordination. All of this points to the fact that I have the ability to do many things. Even as I write this, I can't write words that give me too much credit. It was almost a virtue in my family to downplay your own achievements and abilities. My dad is my model for that, although Mom never did take enough credit for her amazing abilities either. Daddy belonged to Kiwanis Clubs—I use the plural because in the last years of his life he belonged to and attended two and was the official photographer for both. When he died we found in his garage four "Kiwanian of the Year" award plaques. He never displayed them because that would be "tooting his own horn." He also became a Grand Master in the Masonic lodge.

Paul teaches us in Romans 12:3 that we ought not to think of ourselves more highly than we ought to think. However, there is a point at which we should accept our talents as gifts from God and rejoice in them.

Wrapping up the "too many things to do," I can say that today I seldom need lists but what still pertains is that when I start off the day by giving it and my gifts to God I get done what I need to do. As an added bonus, I frequently find myself in a flow of God's activities that surprises and delights me.

6/7/81

O Lord, help me so live that You will have to interrupt my praying to tell me to do things.

I love that sentence. I wrote it, but I love it anyway. It was written in 1981, and it is still my goal today. I love the solitude of my personal prayer time. Sometimes, most of the time, I would rather be alone praying and meditating than doing all the things that I also love to do. Thomas Merton is one of the people whose writings have inspired me over the years. Merton has been described as the most influential American Catholic author of the twentieth century. His autobiography, *The Seven Storey Mountain*, has sold more than a million copies and has been translated into fifteen plus languages. He wrote more than sixty books and hundreds of poems and articles on topics ranging from monastic spirituality to civil rights, nonviolence, and the nuclear arms race.

While he was at Columbia University, he converted to Roman Catholicism and entered the Abbey of Gethsemani, a community of monks belonging to the Order of Cistercians of the Strict Observance (Trappists), the most ascetic Roman Catholic monastic order. An outspoken supporter of the civil rights movement, he referred to race and peace as the two most urgent issues of his time. He was greatly criticized for his activities outside the monastery as he put his beliefs into practice on these two issues. He was referred to as the "conscience of the peace movement." In 1948 in his book, *Seeds of Contemplation,* Merton wrote this about the contemplative life:

> Therefore we have to remember that we look for solitude in order to grow there in love for God and in love for other men [and women]. We do not go into the desert to escape people but to learn how to find them: we do not leave them in order to have nothing more to do with them, but to find out the way to do them the most good. But this is always only a secondary end. The one end that includes all others is the love of God.[2]

Many of the great mystics of the ages have discovered that same connection between the life of prayer and solitude and a life of social action. Catherine of Siena, a fourteenth century mystic in Italy, became one of my favorite mystics after we visited her cathedral in Siena. She had wanted

---

2   Thomas Merton, *Seeds of Contemplation* (New Directions Book, Norfolk, Connecticut, 1948) p. 43

... with all her heart to be a hermit, gave up the solitude
that could have seduced her into a false piety to follow
God into the tabernacle of the world, into the pain and
problems of the people around her, where the one who
said, "Behold, I am with you all days," would surely
be.[3]

Thomas Merton and Catherine of Siena are people who loved
solitude and were drawn into very active lives because Spirit of God
moved them to love and work for others.

By the Way

When I took the Myers Briggs personality test for the first time, my
answers to the questions revealed that I am an introvert. According to
the definition on the Report Form for Myers-Briggs Type Indicator, an
"I" for introversion probably means you relate more easily to the inner
world of ideas than to the outer world of people and things. Several years
later, I took the test again as a requirement of the Presbytery of Chicago
for ordination. The results of taking it the second time were that I
am an extrovert. According to the definition on the Report From for
Myers-Briggs Type Indicator, an "E" for extroversion probably means
you relate more easily to the outer world of people and things than to
the inner world of ideas.

How does being an introvert or an extrovert play into how Thomas
Merton and Catherine of Siena lived their lives? Each of them wanted
more than anything to lose themselves in solitude with God, introversion.
They were both sent out by God to work aggressively among people for
justice and for charity, extroversion.

In the early 1990s, many church people had not yet discovered
that there is a connection between Christian faith and citizenship.
When, as Hunger Action Enabler, I went to churches to lead classes
or seminars, people were often surprised that I was a spiritual woman.
They expected me to be a social activist, which I was. It surprised them
that my activism was spurred by my spiritual life and vice versa. Just

---

3   Joan Chittister, *A Passion for Life, Fragments of the Face of God* (NY, Orbis Books,
2001) 122.

like salt and pepper, bread and butter, meditation and activism go together. Our meditation should send us out. Our activism sends us back to meditation. Anger or distrust or disillusion can be the fuel for activism, but taking action for these reasons eats at our souls and makes us unkind, even ugly, to people who don't agree with what we are doing or who are not as dedicated to the cause as we are.

Sometimes introvert. Sometimes extrovert. God created me both. Mostly, I love the introverted times when I am strengthened and renewed by prayer and meditation. When I am out with people at meetings or worship or Bible study or parties, I am filled with wonder at the diversity of other people and with the enjoyment of their company.

By the Way

Prayers of intercession are risky. They are risky not in the sense that you might get what you pray for. Rather, the risk is in the conceit in thinking that you know exactly what someone else needs. In asking for prayer a person tells you, "This is what I want you to pray for." That is one thing. Another thing is when you look at someone and say, "This is what she needs" and then proceed to tell God what to do.

When my youngest sister and her husband of one year were thinking about adopting two nephews who had been orphaned by a tragedy, I prayed that God would not let the court give the boys to them. They were both still in medical school which, I thought was enough of a strain for newlyweds. Up to that time in my prayer life I would have prayed fervently: "Don't let them have the boys." However, by this time, I had learned a little bit that God is wiser than I am. So my prayers ended with "but do what is right for the boys."

When the court awarded the boys to my sister and her husband it became evident that the answer to the first part of my prayer was a resounding "no." However, as my sister and her husband made a good, safe home for the boys and they grew into fine young men, it became evident that God did know what was best for all of them and for our whole extended family.

7/6/81

The small group ministry that Norm started in Christ Church contributed greatly to my spiritual growth. Christ Church had a small membership and we knew each other well and shared each other's joys and sorrows. In a large congregation getting to know each other through small groups would be important. For us, the primary purpose was to strengthen each other through the study of a Bible passage, discussion of the meaning of that passage for our lives, to pray together and to enjoy each other's company. We met weekly taking turns having the group in our homes.

One night we were asked to meditate for five minutes on an area of our lives we felt was unredeemed, meaning that it was a problem for us. That was a dead end for me. I couldn't think of a single area of my life that was unredeemed. So I prayed fervently to be shown what I couldn't see. I suspect now I wasn't even sure what redeemed meant in the context of my life. I am a good, kind, law-abiding, moral person, and to think of part of me being unredeemed was out of my reach. But I tried.

The next part of the exercise was to meditate for five minutes on the phrase, "Jesus died for me."

I kept saying it over and over. Jesus died for me. Finally the emphasis changed from the words, "Jesus died" to "for me." And my response (Lord, forgive me) was, "He didn't need to do that for me." And that was the first time in my life that I realized that what I had always believed for the corporate body and for terrible sinners was also true for me, Beverly Jane Phillips. That he died for me!

I know the full realization of what this means is yet to come, but the glory and the relief of knowing this "for me" fills my whole spirit with the Spirit and makes me cry.

This meditation was a pivotal point in my spiritual growth. The theory of atonement that says Jesus had to die to save sinners is not my understanding of the atonement now. The awakening was in the "for me" part. However I understood the meaning, the why and wherefore of Jesus' death, the seed was planted in my heart that Jesus did something for me. I held myself in very low esteem. This experience was a crack in a wall of inferiority that let in a ray of light to shine on my sense of self-worth.

7/30/81

Praising God began to appear frequently in my prayers. The opening sentence of my prayer journal entries were always words of praise of God. I felt and do feel God's greatness and want to tell her that I do. Those words are like a key that opens the door of my heart and lets me see that God is waiting in my heart for me to spend time with her. One of these early prayers said,

Dear Father in heaven, I praise Your holy name not only for all of the good and perfect gifts that you have given me, but also and mainly for who You are. For Your perfect love, and patience and justice.

You have most likely noticed that I address the prayers to Father in heaven, but frequently use feminine pronouns for her. In the days of these prayers I would never have used the feminine for God. I hadn't even discovered the idea yet. But now that I have discovered it and written the book, *Learning a New Language, Speech About Women and God*, about feminine language for God, I use it as much as I use the masculine. When I am praying thoughtfully and purposefully, I use the feminine even more. So as I write about these prayers from the past the present seeps back into them.

As I have evolved into a Christian feminist theologian, I have become ever more amazed at the mystery of who God is. The possibilities of God being more than father, king, ruler, judge, have opened whole new vistas of understanding God, ways of seeing God. Even as early in my prayer life as this prayer, God was luring me into amazement and worship of the Great Mystery that is the Divine.

By the Way

Many times my prayer journal became a work book for whatever writing or teaching was occupying me at the time. I discovered early on that very good ideas come to me when I think about tasks in the setting of prayer. As I was writing my book, *Learning a New Language,* I always wrote the first draft immediately after my prayer time and treated that writing as part of my devotions. I firmly believe that, by myself, I never, ever could have written that book. But it became a partnership with God. I knew it was God's idea that I write it, and my prayer was constantly that she would give me the thoughts and the words to write.

"Give me the thoughts and the words" has become a common phrase in my preparation for anything, be it a workshop or adult class lesson or a sermon. It is my goal in each and all of these events to be the bearer of messages from God, not an expounder of "brilliant" ideas of my own. Only once in a while does anyone come to a preacher or teacher to tell her what her words have meant to them. When someone does say thanks it is often couched in the phrase, "It was as though you were speaking right to me." God knows what is in the hearts and minds of the people to whom I am speaking. God knows where they are in their journey and what they need to know. I want to be the bearer of that needed word whenever God wants to use me in that way.

8/16/81

Lord, bless our nation and guide us in the direction You would have us go. Help us live out the principles that were laid down for us in the very beginning of our nation.

The words of the Declaration of Independence and of the Constitution, the writings and speeches of our country's founders are so noble. They could bring peace and well-being to all the citizens of our country and of the world if only we truly believed them. If only we truly practiced them. We take great pride in these documents, but seem to pick out for practice only the ones that affect and/or protect our own special interests.

We treat the Bible the same way. I suspect that people who hold other writings as sacred also pick and choose what they want to believe and practice. Again, emphasizing what is best for themselves and validating what they have already decided to do.

8/31/81

Norm and I have had many great and special times in our marriage, but the two best ones were when we adopted our children. We started the proceedings to adopt Jim in June, 1966. Six months later the agency called to say that they had a two and a half-week-old boy for us. Two years later, we began the process of adopting another baby. With our first, we didn't specify boy or girl, but since we had our son, we decided to ask for a girl. In January, 1969 the agency called and said they had a three and a half-week old girl for us.

The longing for a baby is so deep and so strong that when a couple is finally blessed with children the joy is hard to express! I loved having them and holding them and watching them grow. It was my delight to play with them and go on walks, make cookies and costumes, model with Play Doh and read books. When they got to be school age, I heard other mothers lamenting that summer vacation was starting and then at the end of the summer rejoicing that their kids were going back to school. My emotions were just the opposite. I was always glad when they were home for the summer and sad when they went back to school. Most mothers cry when their children start kindergarten, and I did too, but that was not the only time.

Jim's first day of high school and Nancy's first day of junior high! I want to cry. Not that I would have them be little again, but just that those were such good days for closeness and dependence on each other. They on us—especially on me—for physical needs and me on them for a large measure of my identity.

Much of a woman's identity comes from the roles she plays in the family. In my case, I was the minister's wife and Jim's and Nancy's mom. One day in our second parish in Hiawatha, Kansas, I was in the church kitchen with other women preparing for a special dinner. Our pre-school children were playing around our feet and I heard one child ask the other, referring to me, "Who is that?" The answer was "Jim's mom." It was a pleasure and a satisfaction to be the minister's wife and Jim and Nancy's mom. Those were good roles, good identities, but I did come to learn that I was more even than that.

Chapter Three

9/2/81

Almighty God, our Heavenly Father, thank you for using me last night! I am so nothing and You are so everything! Thank you! Thank you! Thank you! O Lord, may I always be available to You, open to You, so that You may accomplish Your work, Your will through me.

"I am so nothing and You are so everything." My feelings about myself carried echoes of the words of the ever popular hymn: amazing grace how sweet the sound that saved a wretch like me!

In comparison not only to God but to other people I felt like I was nothing. My prayer since I was a child had been that God would "take me and use me." That was a time in my life when God was someone apart from me. God was someone far off who could use me and manipulate me. There was also the counterbalancing language of God active in my heart, hearing my prayers but intellectually I was separate from God and called to be his servant.

Studying feminist theology has enriched my relationship to God so greatly that now, while I still want to do what God wants me to do, I can hardly write the phrase "take me and use me." Now I express it differently. The language I want to use and that I am learning to use is that of partnership. I still mean I want to serve God. However, I no longer feel that I am nothing and God is everything. I feel that God is everything and that I am part of that everything. That I am part of

God and she is part of me. She dwells in my heart. I could even say she is my heartbeat. When I am aware of her presence in my heart I am in "her flow," working **with** her as a partner.

At the same time that I was feeling like nothing, like nobody, I was asking God to prevent me from being proud and arrogant. Everything I have done that was good and successful has been done because God has guided me. Better still, because God has dwelt in my heart and moved me in her flow. When I concentrate, center myself, I feel the movement of God that is my heartbeat. I feel the heartbeat that is God giving me life and energy, ideas and strength. I am not nothing. God is Everything, and I am included in that Everything.

9/16/81

Oh, Lord in my weakness is Your strength!
I am so tired—yet You keep me going.
I need to speak but don't know what to say—You give me words,
ideas and You give me thoughts.
I need wisdom and You give me Yourself.
Praise be to Your Holy Name, O Lord most high and lifted up!

Being the wife of the minister in years gone by was not an easy thing to be. Congregations had high expectations of the woman who was married to their minister, whom they adored most of the time. She was expected to raise their children almost as a single mom because the minister was expected to be at the beck and call of anyone for any emergency, any meeting, any work of the church. At the same time she was expected to keep a clean orderly house, be able to cook not only at home but also with the other women for church dinners. She was expected to be active in "women's work" at the church, to teach Sunday school and, if she could, it would be nice if she played the organ. Heaven forbid that she should have a job away from home and the church! Oh, and her children should be models of behavior for all the other children in the church.

I am sure those expectations have changed to some extent. But they probably still apply in some places and in some denominations. It was not so hard for me to live up to these ideals, because to a certain degree, in some aspects that was who I was. Not only could I do all these things, I wanted to do them. Norm and I met at San Francisco Theological Seminary where we were both studying for ordination. I had the same love of the church and church people that he did. The fact that I was planning to be a minister too didn't negate all the traditional women's roles that were bred inside me. So I made the transition from being a minister to being the minister's wife easily and happily. My call to ministry as a vocation was partially fulfilled by the fact that I worked in the Sunday Schools and women's groups in our churches and as a volunteer in Christian education on the Presbytery level and preached whenever I got a chance.

There is a difference between the "minister's wife" and "the wife of the minister." It is an important distinction. In one, the minister comes first. In the second, although the woman is still identified by her relationship to the minister, at least she is noted as a person. It wasn't easy being the wife of the minister, not only because of congregational demands, but also because I always felt our marriage involved three parties, Norm, me and the congregation. Choices and decisions in such an arrangement are hard to make.

10/9/81

On October 6, 1981, Anwar Sadat, the president of Egypt was assassinated.

O dear Father in Heaven, how You must grieve over the wickedness and cruelty of the human beings You created for goodness and kindness and love. I want to cry over the dangers to men of good will in the Middle East and it must hurt You even more. Forgive us, dear Lord, and guide us to leave wickedness and wars behind. Protect all who go to Sadat's funeral. Especially protect Menachem Begin and our past three presidents. Quiet the fever of evil that day and help the celebration honor the great contributions of Sadat.

Jesus cried over Jerusalem saying, "You have killed the prophets." We have been killing prophets ever since. God sends us courageous people to lead us in the ways of peace and justice and love, and we kill the messenger. Gandhi, King …God still cries over Jerusalem.

Our wedding photo, September 9, 1961.

10/22/81

I want to make a difference for those children I saw on TV last night and the millions like them who have shrunken, fly-covered faces and swollen bellies. Oh, Lord God, I am sorry for the deep grief that must cause You. To see these little ones suffer so. You created them to laugh and play and run, and they are just sitting and starving. Oh, Lord, forgive us all and help us change. Help me work harder in the ways You direct me. Help me make a difference for the starving children. Please, dear Lord.

It was exposure to TV news stories on starving children in India and in Africa that set the direction of my professional career. When I went to seminary in 1958, my intention was to be ordained and go into the mission field. It was so outlandish for me, a woman, to be in seminary at that particular time studying to take what was a man's job. It was outlandish because the Presbyterian Church had only voted in 1956 to ordain women. On a personal level, it was outlandish that shy, unsure me would be called to fill such a role. Women had always been accepted in the mission field. From a little girl to this day, books about Africa have been close to the top of my favorite reading. I felt drawn to the people of that continent. As I thought about why God had called me to the ministry, I was still looking for a safe place to serve, and I must have felt it would be safer to be a missionary than to try to be hired by a church to be their pastor.

When I was examined by my Presbytery to see whether I was fit to go to seminary one question I was asked was "Are you going to seminary just to get a minister husband?" I can't remember now how I answered that question, but, during my seminary days, I would have said there must be an easier way to get a husband! However, I did find a minister-husband there. During my first year in seminary Norm and I started dating and were married in September after I graduated in 1961. This delayed my own ordination by twenty-seven years.

Once, when our children were very young, I attended a conference at which a film on poverty in India was shown. There, right before my eyes, were children drinking out of a sewer, playing in the sewage water that ran down the middle of the street on which they lived. They were dirty and malnourished. All I could do was think of my two clean, well-fed children at home and cry.

For many years after that and still today, I cry when I see the suffering of millions of the world's children. If I cry, how much more must God cry over the gross mistreatment of her beloved children. God answered my prayer that I make a difference for starving children by calling me to the position of Hunger Action Enabler for the Presbytery of Chicago. Under the auspices of the Presbyterian Hunger Program of the Presbyterian Church (USA) I worked to alleviate the hunger of children in our country and in the world for eleven years. My next job was that of regional organizer for Bread for the World having the same goals to educate people about hunger and about how citizens of the United States need to use their influence as citizens to change things for hungry people all over the globe. This was my work for nine years.

10/25/81

There is always a dramatic difference when I prepare and deliver a sermon or speech as an intellectual exercise or as the fruit of prayer. As Hunger Action Enabler my job was to educate the people of the churches in Chicago Presbytery about domestic and world hunger and to guide them into ways they could help alleviate the hunger of millions and millions of people the world over. This work involved preaching and teaching. Early on in my work, I wrote this prayer:

Dear Father in Heaven, when I went to Church of the Cross I spoke my words. I am sorry. Help me this morning speak Your words in the Highland Park Church! Lord, set me on fire with Your message and help them hear and catch fire too!

After that service at the Highland Park church, a lady came up to me and said, "Beverly, you were inspired!" It always works that way. Without fail, if I rely on God to speak to me in preparation for a presentation, I am inspired. When I do it myself it is clunky and heavy for me and, I suspect, for my listeners. God is always ready and willing to give me the thoughts and words that her particular people in a particular place need to hear.

11/9/81

"Take My Life and Let It Be" was one of my favorite hymns when I was in junior high school. Even as an adult I wrote these verses in my journal because they express so well what I wanted God to do for me.

> Take my life and let it be consecrated Lord to Thee.
> Take my moments and my days let them flow in ceaseless praise.
> Take my will and make it Thine, It shall be no longer mine.
> Take my heart it is Thine own; It shall be Thy royal throne.
> Take my love my Lord I pray, I pour it at Thy feet a treasure store.
> Take myself and I will be ever only all for Thee.[1]

This hymn was the inspiration for my earliest prayers: "Take me and use me." My theology, although I would not have given myself credit for having a theology or admitting that someone like me was capable of theology, was that God is the king and director of the universe. I believed he causes to happen all that happens and that he uses individuals to help accomplish the ends he intends to accomplish. Thus the first verse was my offer to let him take me, all parts and times of my life and use them in his plan. The surrender of my own will was part of this prayer. If I am to be "taken," I must have no plans or will of my own. The idea of God being a king is expressed in the words about my heart being God's throne and that I pour my love at his feet a treasure store.

For me, God was high and mighty above all his creation and yet involved in it. He was involved by giving orders from a far-off safe place. This was a place from which he could look down and direct all that was going on. The question of how God can be Love and at the same time cause evil or even tolerate it, is one that I didn't seem to think about. To think about God causing evil would have been outside the concept of the love of God that my family and my church taught me. Even though I wouldn't have said so or acknowledged my thoughts, it was logical in

---

1   *The Presbyterian Hymnal, Hymns, Psalms, and Spiritual Songs,* (Louisville, KY, Westminster/John Knox Press, 1990), 391. Lyrics by Frances Ridley Havergal, 1874, Music by H.A. Cesar Malan, 1827.

my thoughts about God being the One who is in charge of all that is that God does cause, for a good purpose, all the evil in the world.

Today the line of the hymn about his accepting my offer of my heart as his throne is a bridge between what was my faith then and what is my faith now. Today instead of seeing my heart as God's throne, I see it as God's dwelling place. Maybe that was what Frances Ridley Havergal meant when he wrote "Take my heart it is Thine own; It shall be Thy royal throne" in 1874. However, there is a different feeling when a person refers to God on a throne or to God dwelling with us and in us.

My "new" theology, my current theology, is that God does indeed dwell in my heart and in the heart of each one of her creatures, maybe even nonhuman ones. I believe this because I feel it. I know it because when I quiet myself for my prayer time and praise God, the response, "here I am," comes right straight from my heart. It comes in the feeling of warmth and swelling and the sure knowledge that it is God abiding in me. God abides not only *with* us. God also abides *in* us.

One of my favorite pictures of all time has been the one of Jesus knocking on the heart's door. The door is almost overgrown with vines and bushes, and Jesus is standing outside knocking on it wanting to be let in. When my theology began to change, that picture lost its meaning for me. It needs to be turned around, turned inside out. It should be me knocking on the door of my heart where Jesus dwells. It has been my experience that when I knock on that door, Jesus opens it immediately. Jesus is already in my heart. All I have to do is join him there. The keys for me to enter my heart where God dwells are the words of praise and adoration that I use to glorify him.

11/10/81

Take my life and my time and my talents and use them this day in all the ways You can. All power and honor and glory be to Your Holy Name. Lord Jesus, be my teacher as I read Your Holy Word.

At the time I wrote the words of "Take My Life and Let It Be" in my prayer journal, I was studying and teaching the Book of Revelation. I was afraid, not of the contents of this scary, greatly misunderstood book. I was afraid of teaching it. In our first church, a man branded Norm and me as unchristian because we didn't believe in a literal interpretation of the book of Revelation. He took his family and left our church. That is why, I am sure, that in the prayer of mine you just read I prayed that Jesus would be my teacher. There is so much teaching and preaching and so many commonly accepted ideas about the book of Revelation that are misunderstood, distorted and false. All the misunderstandings are accepted by so many as part of the Christian faith and are known and feared by people who know little else about the Bible. Preachers have learned that if you want to scare the hell out of someone in order to make them be good (good as defined by the one doing the preaching) then just hold up this book and preach.

From our experience, I knew there would very likely be people in my class who would believe the common wisdom about this strange book. I knew they would question my knowledge and even my faith for understanding the words of John the way I came to understand them. In spending time studying Revelation I found wonderful phrases of praise for God that still serve as keys to open my heart to God. People who believe this book contains only descriptions of a horrible, gruesome end of this world seem never to have read there what I have read.

> You are worthy, our Lord and God, to receive glory and
> honor and power, for you created all things, and by your
> will they existed and were created. (Revelation 4:11)

This is not the time nor the place to go into a study of the book of Revelation, but it is important to say that John, whoever he was, was a pastor. He did not intend to write a prophecy for generations far in the future. His purpose was to console his readers and give them strength as they faced possible torture and death at the hands of the Romans. The book is written in a coded language whose every word his readers would have understood. They knew it was too dangerous for John, who was already in exile on the Island of Patmos, to write in plain language the message he had for them. In the midst of his mysterious message about what was going to happen in their lives are beautiful words of reassurance that God the Father of their Lord Jesus Christ is in control of all things. Though written so long ago these words still have the power to evoke the knowledge of God's greatness in believers' hearts.

11/21/81

Dear Lord, I love You! You give all the meaning to my life. When I turn away from You I lose strength and my sense of direction. O Lord, thank You for caring so much for us that you are so active in our lives. All power and honor and glory and praise be to You forever and ever.

"All power and honor and glory and praise be to you forever and ever." Phrases like this from the book of Revelation were and are a constant part of my written prayers. Whether anyone who attended the class on Revelation I taught at Christ Church learned anything or was moved in their faith, I was greatly blessed by teaching it. One lady stopped coming to church because I had not presented what she wanted to hear. But for me, the study made a lasting mark on my prayer life. To this day I use words from Revelation and their sequence in my prayers. They are the keys that open my spirit to an awareness of God's powerful presence in my heart. Even the numerical meaning of things in Revelation affect me because I try to write the words of adoration in groups of seven as John often did. Seven was the number of wholeness in that ancient time. Other examples of giving God glory and feeling the mystery and awe of God are Revelation 7:15-17, 15:3-4, 21:1-8.

12/12/81

Dear Lord, thank you for this important day in Daddy's life.[It was the day he received the 33rd degree of Masons] He has really worked hard and made sacrifices for Masons and he has earned this honor. I believe he has done this work as he would have done church work—with dedication and zeal. O Lord, may it be acceptable as work done for You.

Every time I recruited teachers for adult and senior high classes I wished I could find someone who was as dedicated to teaching as my father was. Over the years, he taught individually more than a hundred men who were candidates for joining the Masonic Lodge. The only printed copy of what the men had to learn was in Daddy's possession, but he really didn't need it because he had it all memorized. And the men he taught had to memorize it. He was totally faithful to those men, giving them his time whenever it was convenient for them and oftentimes being out several nights a week working with a candidate

I always wished he would give himself to the church the way he gave himself to the Masons. This lay on my heart as a question: Is other volunteer work as important to God as church work is? His work for the church was coaching a women's soft ball team for many years. His commitment to it began after the first game the girls played with me as coach. It was a disaster. I had taken the job only because no one else would. I was totally inept as a softball coach but I could keep score so he became the coach and I became the scorekeeper. Like the men he mentored for Masons, the women who were on his team always remembered him as their coach.

We often hear of people who have given their lives to a cause and are faithful to their commitment to it to the extent of great self sacrifice. I believe now that anything that is good, that produces light and goodness in the world, is God's work. More than the content of the rules of being a Mason, my father taught all those men what it means to be a man of integrity, a man devoted to helping other people. While walking with Daddy on the streets of Hastings or eating in restaurants there, we would often meet men or members of their family who would greet him. They knew him because he had given himself to them as a mentor. After his death, we had many men tell us how much he meant to them beyond what he taught them about Masons. He was doing God's will for him using the talents God had given him.

1/11/82

Thank You, Father that the bitter cold winds have stopped blowing. I am sure that, for some of Your children in ghetto areas, it is still too cold to be alive.

In January 1982, Chicago had a siege of cold temperatures and bitter winds that lasted without letup for days. During this time our friend Hattie, who lived in the ghetto between the Loop and Hyde Park, was hard pressed to find ways to help her friends and neighbors keep their children and themselves warm. She had so little herself. She did have drapes at the windows of her old, three-story house. She took them down and gave them to people to wrap up in. These were not homeless people. They were people who lived in houses and apartments with no heat. As I remember, the people in public housing had too much heat and had their windows open because many apartments shared only one thermostat that was controlled by the management. Many people who lived in houses were suffering from the bitter cold because they were too poor to pay their gas or electric bill. Sometimes the nights were so bitter cold that the Chicago police would pick up homeless people and shelter them in jail cells for the night.

My daily morning hot shower became a special time to pray for poor and homeless folks. I had just arisen from a warm, clean bed in a warm clean house that had hot water. I was sore and stiff and needed the heat of the water to limber me up. As I washed, I would think about folks who were out in the open all night, maybe sleeping on a bench or in a doorway or under a bridge. How cold they must have been and sore and tired. They spent night after night outdoors without even a warm place to be during the day. And the only relief daylight would bring would be somewhat warmer temperatures and light to see what danger was hidden by the darkness.

By the Way

The minute she introduced herself to us, I knew we were in the company of an extraordinary woman. Hattie Williams had invited the Hunger Committee of the Presbytery of Chicago to meet in her home in the Kenwood Oakwood neighborhood of Chicago. As educators and activists on hunger issues, we wanted to see hunger and poverty first hand in Chicago. And we did!

That afternoon Hattie took us to the home of one of the many, many families she was helping. The family consisted of a mother and six children under the age of twelve. They were the children of several fathers, but not one of them was her husband. The mother admitted to great naiveté in thinking that each man she dated was speaking the truth when he told her he loved her and her children and that he would take care of them.

They lived in a three story tenement that had two apartments on each floor. There was no elevator and the gas and electricity for the building had been turned off. Only two of the six apartments were occupied. Rats ate their way in around the window frames and no amount of steel wool stuffed in the holes could stop them. The apartment was clean as clean could be and all the children who sat in a circle with us visitors were well-groomed and polite. The mother explained that she didn't work because if she did she would have to leave home before the children left for school. Then they wouldn't go to school and she didn't want them to end up like she did.

At the end of our visit Hattie asked us all to stand and hold hands—the children included—while she prayed. My feeling of her specialness was confirmed when she prayed. Hattie Williams prayed with a power that I had never experienced anywhere, any time before! Of all the people in my life who have taught me about prayer, Hattie is unsurpassed.

As a young mother she had seen her neighborhood deteriorating not only in the physical surroundings but in the morals of people on the street. She began to work to get libraries in the schools in her poor neighborhood and for better teachers in those schools. Her home, which was a ramshackle, wooden, three-story building became the place where she held GED classes, classes on sewing, money management, self-esteem, cooking, and even gardening. Where ever she saw a need she tried to meet it or to find people who could meet it. All this she did in the name of God with prayer as her strength and wisdom.

Our church became so involved with Hattie and her work on the south side of Chicago that we garbage-picked mattresses and furniture from the curbside in our suburban neighborhoods. We bought and collected food for her families We also set up a fund for various needs that she might have. At one point there was $256.32 in the fund. A group of Hattie's friends gave a birthday party for her, and we were invited. It had been decided that now was the time to give her that money. It was not doing any good in the bank account. Even at her own birthday party, Hattie was thinking about her neighbors in need. A poster she had made was on a small easel on a table near her cake and the delicious food for the party. She received food to distribute from the Second Harvest Food Bank, and she needed money to pay the minimal price they asked. She needed $256.32! That's the way it was with Hattie and prayer. She got what she asked for. Why God answered her prayers so precisely remains a mystery to me to this day. I have never known anyone else like her. It is a mystery hidden in the grace and mercy of our loving God.

Hattie Kay Williams

1/19/82

Dear Lord God, I love You! I love you more than anything else or anyone else. This time with You is the most important time of each day. Lord, forgive me for all the days when I cut this time short, when I choose to sleep or work instead of giving You my primary attention.

Learning to love God more than I love Norm and Jim and Nancy, more than my parents and my sisters, more than my parents-in-law was a hard lesson to learn. Who I was supposed to love pulled me in two directions—one towards God and one towards my family. What I finally learned was that putting love for God first, putting love for God before my family, helped me love them more and better. Love for God enriched my love for them.

A circle meeting at Christ Church was the occasion for my coming to this conclusion about love. We were studying Matthew 10:37.

> He who loves father or mother more than me is not worthy of me; and he who loves son or daughter more than me is not worthy of me; and he who does not take his cross and follow me is not worthy of me. He who finds his life will lose it, and he who loses his life for my sake will find it.

This is one of the hardest sayings of Jesus. For several women nothing, absolutely nothing, came before their husbands and their children. In these verses we heard God telling us to love him more than these. Our discussion finally led to the discovery that God was not telling us to love our dearest ones less. He was telling us to love him more.

Whatever amount of love we had for God we were being asked to love him more. From my life's experience, I am witness to the fact that the more you love God the more you love your family. Not only do you love them more, you love them better. The quality of love that stems from a deep love of God is a less selfish love. It is a love that sees each person as an individual not as someone whose strings you have to pull to make them be the person you want them to be.

2/18/82

Along with the praise and adoration passages from Revelation, the Psalms took their place in my heart as ways and words with which to praise God.

> I will sing to the Lord as long as I live.
> I will sing praise to my God while I have being.
> May my meditation be pleasing to him, for I rejoice in the Lord.
> (Ps. 104:33,34)

After reading this psalm, I read Psalm 139 and then wrote:

God knows every move we make, every thought we have. There is no place we can go where he doesn't see us and know what we are doing. He created us and knows all about us before we were born. Every one of our days are written in His book even before we are born. How precious to me are Thy thoughts O God!

We are his thoughts. He makes us and moves us. "Search me, O God, and know my heart; try me and know my thoughts!" (Ps. 139:23,24.)

3/31/82

There are so many things that I am capable of doing and so many things that I want to do that until recently I had a really hard time saying "no" when someone asked me to do something for the church. Even though there is so much I enjoy doing there is much that became hard work for me, dreaded, put off. But I would say yes to even jobs such as those.

What finally slowed me down a little in saying "yes" was a practice I believed in and began to use when I was recruiting Sunday School teachers or people to help with Hunger Committee work in Chicago Presbytery. I always made the request, and then said they should pray about it and I would call them back. I really truly did want them to accept the task not because I asked but because God wanted them to. It took a while for me to accept the fact that the same procedure should apply to me as well. After a sour experience with having said "yes" to a job without considering its place in God's flow in my life, I wrote, and I wrote it just like this:

DON'T ACCEPT ANY JOBS AGAIN WITHOUT PRAYER! EVER! EVER!

4/15/82

Maybe one of the reasons I need to pray before I accept a job is because I yearn for the affirmation and praise and the esteem of my friends that accepting it will bring. Everyone needs that kind of support, but maybe I need it to an extraordinary degree. I prayed over and over again, and still do, a prayer that goes like this:

Lord, forgive me for wanting attention; for wanting praise; for wanting people to think highly of me. Forgive me for the means I use to get that praise. Forgive me, Lord.

Once when a group of friends from church were having a party, I decided to make myself a new dress to wear to this special event. It seemed to me that all my other clothes were too well known, too often seen, and that these friends would notice right away that I was wearing something new. I could picture myself saying, "I made it" when they all told me how pretty it was. It was going to be a win/win thing. I would be praised for looking so good and praised for having sewn it myself. The whole evening was a disappointment—not one single person said one single word about my new dress. Not one single person! Not one single word! I was so hurt that I carried that disappointment with me for a day or two afterwards. I love to sew and I had made lots of pretty clothes for myself since high school. Making that lovely dress and feeling good in it should have been enough joy for me, but my enjoyment hinged on the approval of other people.

One way I have of getting attention is by using my extraordinary gift for pouting. A pout, a deep silent pout, is an effective way to get what you want sometimes. But sometimes people just ignore you. It is important that the people you want something from know you are pouting. I'd like to think that I only used the pout on Norm and Jim and Nancy and my family of origin which was bad enough. But, sadly, I seem to remember other occasions, in other groups of friends, when I would pout. Looking back on it, I only hope they didn't notice that I was pouting.

The heart of a pout is that you make yourself so miserable that you are sure others must feel your misery, too, and they will do what you want. On the other hand, it is such a childish, immature way to act that you want to cover it up as best you can. You try to respond briefly to the words of others, or you smile or make feeble jokes. But mostly you say nothing. You respond only when you are drawn into a response. It is a paradox. On the one hand you want the people around you to know how miserable you are, but on the other hand, you don't want to say anything about it or to admit that you are in a pout. You just want the people around you to know what is going on and to care enough to give you the attention you want.

By the Way

Prayers and poems written by other people strengthen me in my resolve to keep time dedicated to daily prayer. This prayer was written by Joan

C. Emden and published in a small newsletter in 1979. I don't know who she was and have never seen anything else written by her, but I know from this prayer she is a woman after my own heart.

> Lord, teach me to watch with thee.
>> Like those in Gethsemane
>> I cannot watch one hour.
> I cannot bend my mind and will
>> Nor keep my restless body still
>> To be with thee this hour.
> Even in my private place
>> On my knees to ask thy grace
>> I do not pray an hour.
> I know thy love for me and yet
>> My perverse self sins and forgets
>> And does not watch that hour.
> I beg thee, Master, wait for me
>> Until I wait for thee
>> And we together live our hour.

7/17/82

The first time I attended a triennial Churchwide Gathering of Presbyterian Women was at Purdue University in West Lafayette, Indiana in 1982. Little did I know as I got ready for that trip that I would attend eight more gatherings. What I have experienced at the gatherings has deepened my spiritual life, broadened my understanding of world events and the relationship of my faith to them, all the while enriching my theology.

One of the things I love most in life is learning, especially book learning. My dad instilled in me this love of books when I was a child. He went to auctions or yard sales and bought boxes of books and brought them home to my sister, Sharon, and me. This was before there was a Peg and Cindy, my other younger sisters. We were free to do with these books whatever we wanted. Usually the first thing we did was make pockets and cards so they could be checked out of our already considerable library. We never really loaned them to any one else. It was all pretend. We also played school with them. I don't remember that we read them because usually they were adult books and we were children. But to this day we love books.

I have also always loved being taught. I enjoyed school all the way through seminary and even now would go back to school if the circumstances allowed. The Churchwide Gathering was a place to learn from all kinds of teachers: Bible scholars, preachers, missionaries, authors, social activists. Every day was full of speakers and workshops and opportunities to view movies and videos on a wide range of topics including international issues and politics as they affect poor and marginalized people. It was a perfect place for me. After that first one, I vowed that nothing short of a broken leg (and I have seen women there with limbs in casts) would keep me from attending all the ones in the future. Here is what I wrote in my prayer journal early in the morning of the second day:

> *I will sing praise to You, Oh Lord,*
> *all this day!*
> *My heart is so filled with joy and excitement*
> *that tears are ready to flow.*
> *Expectation and anticipation are a constant*
> *condition with me.*
> *Each new happening is a wonder.*
> *How amazing, Lord, is Your great love and presence*
> *which binds us, 5,400 of us, together with*
> *one purpose.*
> *How wonderful is Your name, O Lord! How great are*
> *Your works! How beautiful is Your love!*

Going to the Churchwide Gathering of Presbyterian Women was not just an intellectual high for me. It was and always will be a spiritual high as well. The morning session where all are gathered together is more of an information giving session but it is laced with Bible study and music. There are always outstanding musical professionals to lead as we sing old favorites, sing old favorites in new ways, and learn new songs. Thousands of people, mostly women but some men, singing together stirs the soul and creates unity. The evening plenary is worship with more good music, Scripture reading, prayer and good preaching.

The programs always include faith expressions of women from various parts of the world such as dancers from Korea and drummers from Africa.

These activities take place in a carefully planned, colorful setting built to emphasize the theme of the gathering. In 1991 when the Gathering was held at Iowa State University in Ames, Iowa, the theme was "Whose World Is It?" The arena was decorated with cut-paper hangings. The beautiful delicate hangings, which looked like lace, were suspended from the ceiling. They gave the impression of fine white lace or cut work in delicate fabric. Artist Nancy Chinn was the creator of these wonderful works of art which measured four and a half feet by eighteen feet. She created enough of them so that they could be changed eight times during the five days of the Gathering. They presented ten "life zones" which were jungle, polar, desert, ocean, swamp, grasslands, rural life, city life, forest and Australia.

We enjoyed them as the setting for our worship and learning for two days. When we entered the arena on the third day, they had been vandalized! They were torn and hanging in shreds. Some had even been burned. It was a terrible feeling of loss. It was with a feeling of relief that we found out during worship that morning that the destruction was part of the plan to carry out the theme of the gathering. They had not been vandalized but created that way by Nancy Chinn as a vivid parable of what we humans are doing to God's wonderful, intricate creation. We lived with that parable all that day, but when we came to the arena the next day, there were new pristine ones in the place of the ruined ones. The parable made our prayers for the protection of God's creation all the more fervent.

By the Way

As women have become leaders in arenas outside the church and in groups of other kinds, the membership and influence of traditional women's groups has been declining. Over the centuries women's organizations have been the place where women could exercise the leadership they have been denied in a world dominated by men. Sometimes ignored, sometimes ridiculed, sometimes openly and purposely excluded by men in charge, women banded together in groups which have provided a forum for them to develop and to exercise leadership skills. Women's organizations have taken on themselves what are often called "women's issues," but which, in reality, are issues of concern to the whole society. Women through the generations have cared about and worked for children, orphans, widows, the sick and outcast. Women have worked for cleaner, safer neighborhoods and for beauty and the arts. Today much of what women have traditionally done has been taken over by institutions and governments. And, thankfully, women have been increasingly included in the work and decision-making of these public bodies.

Estelle B. Freedman in her book, *Feminism, Sexuality & Politics,* refers to women's groups as a separatist movement. She lauds the fact that women have achieved a greater role in society, but she also emphasizes the need for women to belong to groups which are composed solely of women. A woman working in the world, which is still solidly male-dominated, feels a strong pull to use masculine means to get the job she wants and to get the job done. That woman needs the fellowship and support of other women in order to preserve the attributes of relationship and compassion which characterize women's ways of being.

Every woman needs the fellowship of other women where she can hear and share stories from other women; a group where she can work with other women in women's ways of doing common projects or studying shared topics. For me this need is met by my church circle and by the Churchwide Gathering, as well as by my circle of women friends.

7/25/82

People do like me. This is a pathetic statement but maybe it is one that many women make to themselves. Once when I came home from giving a speech somewhere, Norm asked me how it went. I replied, "They liked me! They really liked me!" Why that came as a surprise to me can only, I think, be explained by a psychiatrist probably after several years of sessions with me on her couch. I have a vague idea about what it is down deep in me that causes me to be surprised when someone does like me. But what causes them to like me is clear: it is God acting in me! When I am preparing a worship service, or sermon, or lesson I pray this prayer or a similar one.

Dear Lord, I am nervous and worried about this sermon. Please let me not lose confidence that it is the message You gave me to speak. I had no ideas in my head Friday a.m. and, Lord, there it was, practically the whole thing.

Thank You, Lord! Please help me deliver it slowly and with force and drama. Take me and use me. Open the hearts and minds of all the people so that they may each one hear what You want them to hear.

Margaret Bourke-White, the legendary photojournalist, was an official Army Air Force photographer. She provided the photographs for the first cover story of *Life* magazine. When she came home from a big trip, she would go on a lecture tour. Of her speaking she wrote:

> Once I made the discovery that my experiences would unfold of themselves on the platform, I never allowed myself to prepare too specifically. I wanted to be surprised, too.[2]

I don't know anything about Margaret Bourke-White's religious orientation, but I feel the same way when I give a sermon or talk that I have not prepared too specifically. God supplies the surprises. God can make something out of even my most feeble efforts. God should not have to go around after me, picking up the pieces when all it takes is for me to tune in to her in my preparation.

7/27/82

Father, please forgive me for being so timid in speaking out about You and the condition of the world. Please make me brave—and fill me with Your message so that what I say will be the truth.

Customarily the two topics not to be discussed in polite company are politics and religion. Unfortunately these are the two topics dearest to my heart so they are what I want to talk about but feel silenced in some conversations. And in others, there is no stopping me.

---

2   Jill Kerr Conway, ed., *Written by Herself, Autobiographies of American Women: An Anthology* (Vintage, NY, 1992)444.

Lord, forgive me for babbling on and on at circle yesterday. I didn't want me to be the center of attention although I look for that sometimes. Forgive me, Lord. Make me want only Your glory and Your praise.

I could talk on and on in a group of women who are dear friends and confidantes about the Bible and theology and my faith experience, and, sometimes, I could even talk with them about politics and world affairs, even though we were not of one mind on these topics. In truth, we were of one mind that it is wrong for children in the United States to go to bed hungry at night, that they have no health insurance, that their parents work full time and still can't rise above the poverty line. Where we disagreed was on the cure and solution to these problems. Anyway, I could talk too much there. But in another setting words about social justice would lodge in my throat.

As I look at it now, still struggling with it, I think it was a matter of authority. Did I have the authority to speak on such issues, and if so, where did I get it? This has been an age-old problem for women. The women mystics in the middle ages who were intelligent and articulate, had a message for the world, but they had little or no authority. They couldn't be priests. They could lead and teach in convents for women but very few of them could beyond these bounds. So they turned to God for their authority. Leaders of all kinds should turn to God and claim God as their authority.

By the Way

I felt confident of my authority when I went to visit members of Congress with fellow members of Bread for the World. Well, I shouldn't use the word "confident" because I was usually scared and nervous going in. Once we were in the presence of the senator or congressman I could speak up.

I recall a time when a group of us went to visit an Illinois Senator in his office in Chicago. We were going to talk against a bill pending in the Senate that would have protected scabs—people who would cross a picket line to do the work of the strikers. It was kind of an Alice in Wonderland setting because here we were, in the city of big shoulders, a bulwark of unionism, and we were on a mission to convince their elected senator to work against a bill that would protect strike breakers and union busters. As we talked with him, he steadfastly maintained his position and resorted to his being part of the leadership as his authority for his position. I had the nerve to ask why since he was a part of the leadership, he could not influence this bill and the changes we were suggesting. I don't remember his response, word for word, but it was something to the effect that being part of the leadership means going along with some things in order to remain part of the leadership.

It was a very unsatisfactory meeting. I think it was colored by a comment made by one of our group as we were walking over to his office. She was a nun who had had many encounters with him over many issues. Her comment to us was, "He is a pig." Our authority to go visit a senator and lobby him on any issue came from our place as citizens of a democracy. But the ultimate authority is God and calling one of her children a pig is not setting a good atmosphere for discussion. We really got nowhere with the senator. Of course, he didn't know what he had been called, but I believe it affected the whole atmosphere of the meeting. When our authority to take bold actions comes from God we should exercise the love of God in our relation to our opponents.

By the Way

For many years when we lived in Hanover Park, there were barn swallows that made nests under the eaves of ours and the neighbors' houses. Their song in the morning was so sweet and cheery. By the time their eggs were hatched, we would have as many as eighteen of them sitting on the phone wire to the house. They were so small and so daring in their flight that they were a joy to watch. An exception to that was the trouble they caused when they built their nests on the front of the neighbor's house right over her mail box. It got so messy that the mailman finally refused to deliver her mail until she took the nest down.

The swallows always reminded me of how the birds sang early in the morning when I was a little girl. I grew up in a small town in Nebraska and there were trees and birds aplenty. Many mornings, I was awakened at sunrise by all the birds' songs. Some mornings I would get on my bike and ride out into the country to enjoy the freshness of the early morning and the beauty of the birds' songs. Meister Eckhart, a fourteenth century Dominican mystic, said that every creature is a word of God and is a book of God. I didn't know about him or this saying until many years later, but the birds of my childhood and of my adulthood are a word of God and a book of God to me.

9/14/82

In my forty-sixth year, I wrote about having an identity crisis. I don't know what precipitated that feeling but my response to it was that it couldn't possibly happen. Little did I know that this one would not be the last one. I wrote with great confidence my statement of faith that it was impossible for me to have an identity crisis.

I can't have an identity crisis! I am a servant of Jesus Christ! That defines who I am as a wife, as a mother, as a Hunger Action Enabler, as a member of Christ Church, as a daughter, as a sister. All these roles are subordinate to the one of servant of Jesus Christ. That servant role defines the others.

Being a servant of Jesus Christ means that all the things I do I do for Him. He gives me my orders, guidance and strength for each day and for each thing He asks me to do. The most basic necessity is to always take time to listen to Him. To have that time alone when He can speak to me and I can hear.

I need to take everything I do to Him in prayer. Then whether I feel success or failure, acceptance or rejection the results are not mine to judge. They are always and completely in His hands, in His plan.

I think maybe an identity crisis now and then is God's will for us. What would life be like if I were today who I was at forty-six? What would life be like if, no matter what happened to me in the intervening years I was unaffected, unchanged?

In different situations, I can change so quickly in my estimation of myself. Am I the woman who wants to be alone or the one who enjoys being with people? Am I the woman who knows many things or am I the one who feels not so smart? Am I the woman who believes in her abilities or the one who needs to be affirmed for almost everything? Identity crises can happen repeatedly. But always, always, always, God is there as a sure foundation to keep me from sinking out of sight.

9/15/82

Dear Lord, this morning I have that nagging feeling that I am worthless.

My mom had a saying that we heard often. It was "I'm not worth shootin' today." She meant that she just didn't have the energy she usually had and wasn't getting all her work done. At least that was the way I took it. It didn't occur to me until years later that feeling like that is really the pits! What could be worse than being of such little value that doing away with you would be a waste of a bullet and of the energy it took to do the shooting. Every time I use the phrase to say what she was saying, I am thinking of my own worthlessness.

This particular case of feeling worthless was triggered by a comment someone made that I was just like a mutual acquaintance. She was a member of the Hunger Committee and when she was asked to give a talk she always talked too much. She could bore the most interested folks into numbness. The comment was justified. He said what he said because I truly had been just like her. I was given the opportunity to speak to a group of people about welfare reform in Illinois. That was a hot topic and meant increased poverty for a lot of people who were already poor. In my preparation, I decided that my audience needed some background. So I gave it to them. My son recently taught me a new phrase: WTMI: Way Too Much Information. That is what I gave them. I am sure that by the time I got to the action I was asking for, I had lost them.

The rest of my prayer was:

Father, I am sorry if that was the case. I can see now, talking with You, that I did prepare too much and should have left it up to You to speak what You wanted them to hear. I didn't have enough confidence in myself to do that and didn't even think about letting You do it. I am sorry, Lord!

I should know better—all the times You've done it for me and made it better than all my planning could ever make it. Take me and use me, Lord. Teach me what I need to know to serve You faithfully and truthfully. Thank You, Lord, for loving me.

10/26/82

Dear Lord, it is so good to take this time to sit quietly with You. I am so tired and everybody expects so much from me and I expect so much from myself. Lord, help me give all of these expectations to You and then You give me back the things You want me to do.

By the Way

"The Cult of True Womanhood" is a phrase used to describe the position of women in the nineteenth century. Elizabeth Schussler-Fiorenza, a gifted Christian feminist theologian, describes the cult this way:

> The modern bourgeois ethos of "femininity" prescribes that "good" wo/men perform unpaid services in and outside the family with selfless love, nurturing care and patient loving-kindness. The ethos of "true womanhood," romantic love, and domesticity defines wo/men's nature as "being for others" in actual or spiritual motherhood. Whereas men are measured by the masculine standards of self-assertion, independence, power, and control, wo/men are called to fulfill their true nature and destiny through self-sacrificing service and loving self-effacement. The cultural socialization of wo/men to selfless femininity and altruistic behavior is reinforced and perpetuated by the Christian preaching of self-sacrificing love and humble service.[3]

Self-sacrificing service and self-effacement described me pretty well. As I write this, I can't help but wonder whether others saw me that way or whether it is just the way I saw myself, but that is beside the point here, I think. I once read that if there is a draft, a woman will sit in it

---

3   Elisabeth Schussler Fiorenza, *Jesus Miriam's Child, Sophia's Prophet, Critical Issues in Feminist Christology*, (New York: Continuum, 1995), 38. Schussler Fiorenza has coined the word wo/men to illustrate that the word "women" is too narrow and confining to describe all women, as is the word "man" to describe all men. She writes on page 24: "…I introduce a particular spelling of 'wo/men' that seeks to indicate that women are not a unitary social group but rather are fragmented and fractured by structures of race, class, religion, heterosexuality, colonialism, age and health."

and if there is chicken, she will eat the back. There is a sense in which women are willing to sacrifice even their own comfort so that someone else doesn't have to sit in the draft or eat the least desirable piece of chicken. That is part of the cult of true womanhood.

I did all the things required of a true woman and was proud of myself—tired, but proud. Maybe if I were to have the chance to do it all over again, I would do the same things. The cult of true womanhood is alive and well in this new century.

Chapter Four

11/3/82

Forgive me, Lord, for being self-centered and for seeking glory and position. Take me and use me, Lord, in whatever ways You want to. Guide me as far as ordination is concerned. I would like to have our three parents present at my ordination, but Lord, I don't want ordination for any of the world's reasons—privilege or economic status. I just want it if I need it to serve You. So take me and use me.

By the way

The story of my being ordained to the office of Minister of Word and Sacrament is a long one. It was thirty-two years from the time I heard God's call to me to be a minister until I was ordained. In 1956, I was serving as a counselor at a junior high church camp which I had done once before in my college years. The director of that camp had become an advisor and guide to me. On the last night of the camp we, counselors and campers, gathered around a big, blazing campfire. We sat on the ground or on logs or leaned against trees in the wooded campsite in western Nebraska. As the fire crackled and burned, we sang camp songs and hymns. Then the director gave a short sermon. The only part of it I remembered later that night and for days and years afterward was the sentence: "You could be a minister." He was speaking to us as a group of fifty to sixty campers and counselors, but for me he could just as well have said, "Bev, you could be a minister."

At first it struck me as funny that I would even hear such a statement as a possibility for me. It had been only two years since women were allowed to be ordained to be ministers in the Presbyterian Church in the United States of America. So I knew it would not be easy to follow that course. And besides that, I was shy and insecure when I was with strangers. For instance, I never wanted to go to a friend's house for a meal because I was afraid I wouldn't know what to say and I might do something stupid. When I was in junior high school I had made a conscious decision (I can even remember where I was standing when I made that choice) not to talk much because people would like me better if I didn't. They wanted to do all the talking, I believed.

As I walked back to my cabin after hearing those words, "You could be a minister," I was laughing to myself over the audacity of my thinking that God wanted me to be a minister! My plan was to be a children's librarian. That seemed to fit more comfortably with who I was than being a minister would. Only a couple of hours later, as I lay wide awake on my bunk, surrounded by eight sleeping junior high girls that my silent laughter turned to weeping. I was overcome by the seriousness of my having heard God speak to me and his asking me to do something so bold, so out of character for me. By the time morning came I knew it was what I had to do.

After breakfast I went to Rev. Roy, the director, and told him what had happened to me. He was not surprised. He knew how active I had been in the youth group and other activities at church. His advice was that I think about it for awhile and then have a talk with my pastor to see what steps I needed to take to start the process. On the surface, that seems simple enough, but it wasn't. I held my pastor in the highest esteem because of his fine preaching, scholarliness, dignity and devotion to his pastoral calling. He was a fine man and a friend of my father. I considered him my friend too, even though my closest minister friends were the associate pastors who worked with us youth.

What made it difficult and scary was that he had, for years, spoken out and voted against the ordination of women. A few days after I got home from camp I made an appointment to see him. I was very nervous as I knocked on his study door. I was sure he was going to react negatively to my announcement and that brought fear into my heart. He offered me a chair in his cool and comfortable book-lined study. We made a little small talk and then I told him about my call to the ministry. He listened intently and then, much to my surprise and great relief, he said, "If God is calling you into the ministry, far be it from me to stand in your way." He became one of my strongest supporters through the whole process and through my seminary years.

My dad's reaction to my announcement was another matter. At first, when he was very upset about it, we had heated discussions. He said I would never make any money and I would be sleeping on park benches and eating crackers. I think the park benches and crackers were his way of adding emphasis to the idea of the poverty he thought I would experience as a minister. In spite of those objections, it wasn't long before he began to be proud of me and would introduce me as his preacher daughter. My whole family and community were proud of me for being a ground breaker for women in the ministry. One of my dad's friends told me what I was doing was very commendable. He meant it as a compliment, but it was, to me, more like an insult. I was not doing this in order to be commended. I was doing it because I had to. It was so clearly what God wanted me to do.

The process to be ordained involved being taken under care by the session of my church and by the Presbytery of which my church was a part. I don't remember the meeting at which the session asked me questions about my faith and my calling, but I do remember the Presbytery meeting. It was in the large sanctuary of a church, and I stood behind the pulpit before a crowd of male ministers and elders and a few female elders. They were allowed to ask questions only about my faith and my calling. The only question I remember was, "Are you going to seminary to find a minister husband?" My answer was that I was going to seminary because I believed God wanted me to be a missionary, but if I did find a minister husband (and I did) that would be God's will for me. They accepted me as a candidate for the ministry.

After two years of the three year seminary course, I was required to appear before the Presbytery again to report on how I was progressing and to answer more questions. A third appearance was required after my graduation in 1961. The questions asked at this appearance were of a factual nature. They needed to know whether I had learned what I was supposed to learn in seminary. They approved me for ordination.

The Book of Order of our denomination mandates that, in order to be ordained a person must have a call to serve a church as pastor or a call from another group which the presbytery recognizes as a suitable organization. By this time Norm and I were engaged to be married. I had no call. Clergy couples are common now, but were unheard of in the Presbyterian church in the 1960s. We were offered one possibility of Norm serving one church and me serving another one with a church-provided house halfway between the two. Having both grown up in the church and knowing what is required of ministers in terms of time and energy, we decided that would not be a healthy option for our new marriage.

Norm was examined by his presbytery and ordained to serve a two church parish in northeast Nebraska. Although I couldn't be ordained without a call, *The Book of Order* did allow for persons in my situation to be examined as fully as for ordination and then be granted a license. The license was good for four years with the option of a one year renewal. At any time during those five years, if I sought and received a call, I could have been ordained without further examination. That was okay with me. During twenty-seven years that were to pass before I was ordained, I served on presbytery committees, preached whenever I was offered the opportunity, led Bible studies and women's retreats. I fit the mold of a good minister's wife and went beyond the call of duty because I was prepared as a clergy person.

During the passage of the four years of my licensure, we adopted our son and our daughter. I was absorbed in their care and in being the minister's wife. Twenty-four years after going through the process the first time I started it again. This time I had a call to be the Hunger Action Enabler for the Presbytery of Chicago.

The rules had changed so that now instead of being examined orally on all the topics, there were written exams as well as appearances before Presbytery. The exams covered the areas of church polity, worship, Bible content, Bible translation and theological capability. It took two days to write the exams. After having been out of seminary for so long, I didn't know whether I had added to my knowledge over the years or whether I had forgotten too much. I needed to decide whether to go back to seminary for some classes in preparation for the exams or just to take them. I decided to take them and then enroll for classes in the subject or subjects which I failed. By the grace and mercy of God, I passed all five exams the first time I took them! It was akin to a miracle. Many people who are fresh out of seminary fail a couple of the tests and have to retake them. The notice I received from the presbytery read: "You passed your ordination exams with flying colors, your ministry as Hunger Action Enabler was validated, and the terms of your call were approved, to take effect July 1, 1988, and the administrative commission to ordain and install you on June 19, 1988 was approved." Thirty-two years after I laughed at being called to the ministry, I was ordained.

2/15/83

Many people have lined my spiritual path. Some of them have been the people I have known in person. Many of them have been writers who shared their personal journey through their writing. In 1983, one of those writer people was John Killinger, who was a pastor of Presbyterian and Congregational churches. He taught at Vanderbilt University for fifteen years and is the author of more than fifty books.

In one of my prayer journals, I filled a whole page with quotes from John Killinger. They addressed my worry about being prideful. Here are two of them.

> . . .Teach me to live in such daily humility before You that I may never offend You while thinking I am performing my duty. For yours is a name above every name, both in heaven and on earth.[1]

---

1   I have carefully looked through four of John Killinger's books and have not found these prayers or the next ones I quote. With his permission I am including them without a specific citation. John Killinger is a prominent lecturer and preacher and has written over fifty books on topics such as Christian history, personal spirituality, world religions, preaching, worship, church politics, a female Christ figure, the Gospels as devotional literature, secular writers and artists, the nature of pastoral ministry, and the relationship between theology and contemporary culture.

> Lord, I want to be a simple person. Remove all my pretensions and unnecessary complexity. Let me meditate on you until all of my life is focused and plain. And then let others see you through me, shining through the apertures of my faith. For your kingdom's sake. Amen.[2]

If you are a book lover as I am, writing a book can make you really proud of yourself. Prayers for humility and for recognizing my place have become more important since the publication of my first book, *Learning a New Language, Speech About Women and God*. Many people who read it have expressed praise and admiration for what I have done. The book is about using feminine language for God. In it I discuss how Christianity came to believe that God is male and what difference it would make if we could see God in her fullness as both male and female and yet as neither. My purpose in writing the book was to share with others what I had learned from Dr. Elizabeth A. Johnson in her book *She Who Is: The Mystery of God in Feminist Theological Discourse*.

Using my book as the starting point for discussion, I have met with many groups of people. And in each group there has been a woman or two who are admiring of me because of what I have taught them about their own worth. It is very freeing for women to see that their being is also part of God's being, that they are indeed a reflection of who God is. There are many women who need this knowledge and assurance so desperately and when they find it in my book, they admire me. A prayer taped to my desk says: "Deliver me from proud thoughts and vain desires."

An example of the importance and the need for this concept of God is in this event. We were at a fiesta for Just Coffee in Tucson. Arizona. Just Coffee is a coffee grower cooperative based in Salvador Urbina, Chiapas, Mexico, with facilities in Agua Prieta, Sonora Mexico, and Douglas, Arizona. The goal of Just Coffee is to develop a Chiapas-owned company providing viable economic incentives for young and old to remain on family lands. The idea behind Just Coffee is to address one of the root causes of labor migration from Mexico to the United States. They market a pure organic Arabic coffee that is grown, harvested and marketed in a spirit of justice. Their members are from a coffee-

---

2   Ibid.

growing community in Salvador Urbina, Chiapas, Mexico, and from the United States.

A number of people from our church were at the fiesta whose purpose, besides celebrating the achievements of Just Coffee, was to raise money for two more coffee roasters. One of my friends introduced me to the "Just Coffee lady" from another church. In my friend's introduction, she said I had written a wonderful book. My new acquaintance asked what it was about. When I told her about it in a couple of sentences, her face lit up, and she grabbed me and hugged me. She said that talking about God using feminine language is just what she had been needing.

I am sure that such happenings are never coincidences. God was answering prayer, carrying out her call to this woman by having us meet each other. The credit for my having written the book belongs only to God as does the meeting with this woman. John Killinger wrote this prayer that applies to each one of us who is tempted to take the glory and credit for something we have done well.

> Lord, as the moon possesses no glory of its own, but reflects the brilliance of the burning sun, help me in my darkness to receive the joy of your presence and reflect it to those who dwell in a land of shadows; for yours is the kingdom and the power and the glory forever. Amen.[3]

2/24/83

Lord, God, accept me into Your Presence this morning. Prepare my heart and mind to bow before You, to worship You and adore You. You are so wonderful! Creating this earth with all of its minute detail and intricacy, the universe with all of its space and brilliant stars and planets.

You are so powerful! Maintaining and sustaining Your whole creation!

You are so wise! Knowing how to create all things and knowing all that happens even in the hearts and minds of men and women.

You are so steadfast! Staying right with Your creatures as they sin and err, waiting for them to return to You

---

3   Ibid.

You are so loving! Sending Your only Son into the world to save us from our sin and error, becoming one of us so that all people can be drawn unto You.
O You alone, O God are worthy of praise and honor and glory and blessing!
Let all the earth sing Your praises. Now and forever more!

2/26/83

Frequently, I meditated on the barn swallows who disappeared all at once as the farm land around Hanover Park became houses and shopping centers.

Almighty God, our Heavenly Father, all praise and honor and glory and power and blessing be to You this day and always! Let every creature sing Your praises. The sweet songs of the barn swallows, and seeing them up close as they sit on the line outside our window and as they dart and flash past our window help me see what a creative and living and imaginative God You are. They must be precious in Your sight! As is all of Your creation each minute part of it.

In the quarter of a century since I wrote that prayer, so many species have disappeared. I am sure there are still barn swallows galore in some places but because of the activity and needs of human beings they are no longer part of the lives of people who need the wonder of such creatures in their lives. Saving the creatures is not just for the benefit of the creatures. It is also for the benefit of human souls and spirits. We need them! We need them to marvel at, to laugh about, to have our spirits enriched.

Now I live in Arizona and don't recognize all the birds by their songs. I do know when it is a house finch singing or a dove cooing. But there is a new gift. And that is the mockingbird. If there is only one of them in your neighborhood you will think you have a great variety of birds because a mockingbird knows and sings so many different tunes. What a marvel of God's creative love.

By the way

Somewhere in the early years of my prayer life I began to base my prayers on the acronym ACTS, which stands for adoration, confession, thanksgiving and supplication These are four elements of a well-rounded prayer. Whether I read it in a book or heard someone talk about it, the formula became very helpful not only in my writing prayers but also when I am called on to speak a prayer. Using ACTS as an outline helps bring ideas to mind for spontaneous prayer.

Adoration is certainly the right place to begin when addressing a being such as God. The one who is the creator of all that is, who sustains and maintains all that is and who dwells in our midst, is certainly deserving of adoration. When I was preparing for ordination, one of the things my presbytery required was that I take a course in pastoral clinical education at a hospital. In that program, people from several denominations who wanted to serve as hospital chaplains attended classes, wrote papers and visited patients in the hospital. One of my classmates was the associate pastor of a church. One day, he and I were discussing prayer, and I mentioned that I used these four actions as the foundation for my prayers. His response was that he never starts a prayer with adoration because "it seems like I am buttering God up so he will answer my prayer."

That may be the way it works with human beings, that we praise someone before we ask them for a favor, but, with God, adoration is received as a natural activity of the human heart. So many things in our lives trigger adoration for God. Seeing a plant blooming can cause us to praise God for the mystery of all of life. Hearing a little child laugh can remind us of God's great gift of innocence and childhood. Feeling a cold rain on a hot day reminds us of how God cares for creation in so many ways. God is waiting to be adored and doing so at the beginning of a prayer opens our hearts to her and makes her real.

Confession is a vital part of prayer. It helps us see ourselves more truly and keeps us from feeling that we are perfect. Being a Protestant and a little skeptical of the Roman Catholic practice of the confessional, it took me a while to realize how important confession is to my soul's well-being. I don't have to confess my sins in order for God to know what they are. I need to confess my sins so I will know what they are.

It is very easy to go through my day thinking that since I didn't do any of the BIG ones—adultery, murder, theft—I don't have anything to confess.

It is common for Presbyterians to have a prayer of confession in the order of worship on a Sunday morning so I had been confessing my sins ever since I was old enough to read the order of service. But that is corporate confession. It is the church, the Body of Christ confessing when it falls short of doing what Christ would have it do. The most moving of these prayers of confession troubled my heart where I needed it personally, but it wasn't until I started including confession as part of my daily prayer that I realized how important it is. It is a way of reminding myself that while I mostly do good things, I also do things that are hurtful to other people and to myself and to God. It is a reminder not to get too proud, too self-righteous, not to think more highly of myself than I ought to think.

Thanksgiving is the easy one. Sometimes near Thanksgiving Day someone asks us to list the things we are thankful for. Without fail people are still listing things when time is closed on the exercise.

Supplication, asking for something, is easy as well. We each have so many things we want changed in our lives and in the lives of others. Supplication is modified and enriched by the adoration and confession which came first. Those two actions serve as standards for what we will ask for. The confession keeps us from setting ourselves up as judges over others. I don't know how many times in my early prayers I was praying for the salvation of someone else's soul. I never said it in the words "save her soul" but rather in words that indicated that I, in my great wisdom and spiritual insight, knew where that person was spiritually and what she needed. Confessing my own sins made me aware that I was on the same journey as my "prayee" and that there were times and places where she could equally as well, be praying for my soul. Expressing my adoration for God, searching for more new words with which to praise God kept me reminded that God is the One who knows the hearts and minds of people because she made us and accompanies us every step of the way along our life's journey.

Adoration, confession, thanksgiving and supplication serve me well as a form for my prayers. Doing things decently and in order is a hallmark of Presbyterianism. This form keeps my prayers decent and orderly.

2/27/83

Dear Lord Jesus, forgive me for turning in upon myself. All my work for others becomes such drudgery when I do that. I can't see them or You and I become more and more inward. Lord, forgive me.

This turning inward of which I was repenting, which I was confessing was a turning inward that nursed my tiredness and fed my resentments or the slights that I felt I had received. Sometimes I was so tired and had such long to-do lists that I really fell into a "poor me" syndrome. Added to that, anything that someone said or did that I perceived as a slight against me sent me into in a pout. A pout is a misery which makes my heart feel dull and heavy and blinds my eyes to anything good in anyone else. Somehow there is an attraction in feeling so bad. It is in some ways a dare to anyone to try to make me feel better, to get over it.

There was a pretty young woman in our church choir who loved to sing so much that when she sang her whole body showed her joy. Especially her long, lovely curls bobbed and danced with joy. Usually I loved to watch her, but one Sunday morning, I was in a pout and didn't want to go to church. I wasn't ready to give up my pout, and I knew watching her sing would make me feel too good to feel bad any longer. The minister's wife who is also the organist and the choir accompanist, as I was, doesn't have a whole lot of choice about going or not going to church. So I went. Sure enough, she made me feel better, and the pout was dissipated.

There is a turning inward that is good for me and that is the kind that acknowledges that I need to do things for myself sometimes. Giving and giving and giving to others wears a person out and down. It took me a long time to learn that going off by myself to read or shop or go out with a friend did not constitute abandoning my family or abdicating all my duties.

By the way

When my Bread for the World office was in the Loop in Chicago there were times when I would turn inward and do something for myself. Usually it was to have lunch in a place that was a little more expensive and therefore more special than the Burger King across the street where I usually ate. The year the cows came to Chicago was a really special time for nurturing myself. Hundreds of cows were on display on the streets of Chicago. No, it wasn't the return of the stockyards. These life-size bovine beauties were works of art that were painted, pomaded and all dressed up for the city by Chicago artists, architects, photographers and designers. Chicago's 1999 summer public art display was originally conceived by Beat Seeberger-Quin and presented in Zurich, Switzerland, during the summer of 1998.

A Chicago businessman had been in Geneva, Switzerland, where they had a display of decorated models of cows. He brought the idea back to Chicago and what a great thing it was! Artists from all over were invited to design and paint the cows which were life size and made of Fiberglas. About 300 local businesses purchased the cows, priced between $2,500 and $11,000. The sale of the cows covered the estimated $750,000 in artists' fees, the cost to ship and install the herd and an abundance of promotional maps and brochures. A grant of $100,000 from the Illinois Department of Commerce and Community Affairs also helped finance this exciting summer activity.

Several cows were added each week, and by the end of the exhibition, there were three hundred and twenty of them. It was my delight to take a little longer lunch break or walk to a meeting in another part of the Loop just to see and take pictures of those cows each one decorated with a special theme. They were delightful in themselves, but what was just as delightful was watching the reaction of people to them. The Parade of Cows drew tourists from all over the country. Over and over again, I saw individuals offer to take a picture of a group viewing a cow so that all members of the group could be in the picture.

I was always by myself when I was out with my camera so I didn't expect to have my picture taken with one of the cows. But one day a man came up out of a hole he was digging in the street near one of them and asked if he could take my picture with the cow I was admiring. These are the kinds of things that nurture me when I turn inward on myself not to pout and grumble but to enrich and broaden me for myself. In case my former boss and friend should read this book, I want her to know that I did get some work done that summer.

Me with one of the Chicago Cows, Summer 1999.

Me at the organ in Christ Church

11/2/83

Dear Lord our God, how great and wonderful You are! Your beginning act of creation was colossal! How everything works together is beyond our comprehending. Praise be to You, too, for the memory that You have given Your human creatures. Father, what a gift that I can sit here in my living room and imagine myself in places I have been like the Tetons and the ocean's edge. That I can see a red-winged blackbird perched on a reed. That I can feel the heat and hear the insects from playing in tall weeds and grass on Grandpa Heeren's farm and from running and playing in the wash outs and gullies on Grandpa Harvey's farm.

My list could go on and on for pages and still not be exhausted—my list of gifts from You, Almighty God, all powerful, all knowing and yet so loving! Even with all Your titles of power You want most of all to be addressed as Father.

May the day come soon when all of your children everywhere will call you Father and will turn their faces toward You instead of turning their backs on you!

When I read this prayer today, I am so happy with the first paragraph. I love it. It describes how I can relive the pleasant experiences of my life and rejoice in them. Calling God "Father" in my journals didn't bother me up until now. It didn't bother me in the first paragraph of this prayer. But when I read, "You want most of all to be addressed as Father," I could hardly copy it down for this manuscript, and then to end the prayer with the supplication that all people everywhere will call him father was just about more than I could take. Two thoughts that occur to me at this point are: first, there are most certainly more names than "Father" that are pleasing to God and, second, it is amazing that women over the generations have been nourished in a faith that would say the best and indeed the only name for God is "Father."

God is so much more than father. When we look at all the activities of God in the world, we see and experience not only God the Father but also God the Mother, God the Creator, God the Lover, God the Giver of Life, God the Source of All That is Good, God our Protector, God the Holy Spirit, God the Son. God is Father, but in the words of an ancient formula God is father. God is not father. God is more than father. God is father in all the good traits we experience in human fathers. God is not father in the experience of human fathers who abuse or neglect their children. God is more than father. God is more than we can ever think or say.

We use the name, father, for God because, we say, it is what Jesus called him. What we fail to realize or to accept is that Jesus also called God a hen who gathers her chicks under her wings; a woman who has lost a coin and searches for it with the same diligence that the shepherd searches for the lost sheep. Jesus used many names for God. Any name we give God is a metaphor because we can only name God from our human experience, not from any sure knowledge that would encompass all that God is.

As for women being nourished by a male-controlled faith, it is only by the strong will of God that women have been able to have faith and to serve a God who is described exactly as a man. Genesis 1:27 tells us something different.

> So God created man in his own image, in the image
> of God he created him; male and female he created
> them.

The story about how the feminine face of God was squelched and almost eradicated is long and complicated. But the point is women are as much in the image of God as men are. If that fact were recognized and made a living part of the Christian faith the world would be a better place. All that is feminine would be valued equally with all that is masculine. The whole idea that some are better and more beloved by God would disappear and not only would abuse and oppression of women cease, but children would be valued more as would all of God's nonhuman creatures and the very world itself. Instead of only the male being of value all would be of equal value. These new ideas take some thinking about and getting used to but it is worth it. The freedom I have now to experience God in myriads of ways as female as well as male has opened up great new vistas for my faith.

12/21/83

Dear Lord my God, I want to praise You with my whole heart!

> *Praise (It must feel good to hear praises when most of what you*
> *hear is complaints and demands.*
> *and honor (what a different world this would be if mankind*
> *would only acknowledge Your greatness and Your power*
> *and give You honor.)*
> *and power (You already have all the power—beyond our*
> *knowing or rather conceiving.)*
> *and might (You are the mightiest Being in the universe and yet*
> *we recognize the might of earthly beings more.)*
> *and riches (All things are Yours, O God.)*
> *and blessing (May all people soon bless You.)*
> *forever and ever. Amen and Amen.*

Father, forgive us for our stubbornness and our willful ignorance!
Forgive us and change us!

1/3/84

One of the most thankless jobs in many churches is that of organist and/ or accompanist. I know because I did it for more than twenty-five years. The reward and the blessing of it came from the conviction that I was doing it for God and from the beauty of the music and the power and versatility of the organ. I loved trying different types of music—some that would be so quiet and peaceful and some that was so loud I would rattle the chairs in the choir loft. Usually I only used that kind of volume when I was in the sanctuary practicing alone. It was a thankless job, but I loved it most of the time. It gave me an opportunity to be by myself in the sanctuary, and I often took part of that time to pray. In a sense, I felt I was honoring my mother who had been faithful in paying for my piano lessons for twelve years when I was growing up. The miracle of her faithfulness was that she kept on paying from a small income even though I seldom practiced.

I describe the job of organist as a thankless job because hardly anyone in the congregation listens to the music you have spent hours practicing. When you are playing the prelude, they are visiting with each other and when you are playing the postlude they are leaving the sanctuary, with some standing there to visit more. A plea for silence so that others could meditate was printed in the bulletin, but not many people paid any attention to it. Norm solved the problem of the prelude by beginning the service with the announcements and then the prelude.

Seldom did anyone say anything to me about my music by way of thanks. However, they always had something to say if I played the wrong tune for the Gloria Patri which I did from time to time. This response to the hard work of an organist or an accompanist is a common experience for the people who do this work in the church.

One Sunday I was thanked. A friend who had a small organ at home and loved organ music, came up to me before I had finished the postlude. She stood there listening until I finished and then thanked me! Some people would come to the organ before I was finished and start talking to me about all sorts of things. Gwen came to thank me!

Thank You for the way I played the organ Sunday. I know it was good because I prayed for Your Spirit to replace the old one of mine, of nervousness and fear and self-doubt. Thank You for hearing my prayer and sending Gwen to thank me. Please guide me as to whether or not I should quit playing for worship.

I was so nervous when I played for worship that I could hardly stand it, so once I took a muscle relaxant before I went to church. It was a drug that a doctor had prescribed for me for a severe backache, and I had some left over. It really worked and I thought I had my problem solved. What I had forgotten was that the first muscle it relaxed was my brain. One morning during a prayer, I was sitting on the organ bench swinging my legs like a child sitting on a fence. At that point, I opted for nervousness rather than the impression of drunkenness, and never again did I take those pills for anything but a backache.

1/7/84

Is this a "dark night of the soul?" I saw glimmers of Your brilliance, Lord, on Thursday. Like a full moon on a cloudy night—the wind moves the clouds and now and then the brilliant light of the moon shines through.

I know You are there, Lord, and I know You are calling me. Please hold on to me and may this be short!

Thank You that you won't desert me or let go of me. I love You, Lord! I love you!

Is my seeking ordination the cause of this? Give me wisdom, Lord. I love you!

Two days later, I prayed:

Thank You, Lord, that that "dark night' is not all pervasive in my life now. It seems like it is still there but either the end of the prophets' discussion or the sending of my ordination papers has caused it to subside. It seems like it was one or the other of both of them that was causing the unrest.

It's strange why can't I say that You have removed it from me. Maybe because I haven't let go of it yet. Maybe because I am not sure of anything yet.

I know without a doubt that I am in Your care. Let me rest there, Lord, and leave all the planning and the decisions up to You.

2/1/84

Lord Jesus, it is amazing to me this morning that You should care so much about me that You <u>want</u> me...You <u>want</u> <u>me</u> to talk to You and listen to You! You <u>want</u> <u>me</u> to be obedient to You and serve You! Amazing that there is anything that <u>I</u> can do for <u>You</u>! Who am I anyway! What am I worth! All that I am is from You, Lord, any strength or possibilities in me are gifts from You!

You are so great and so powerful and so wonderful! You can make great and useful people out of creatures like me. Take me and use me and let me never be proud of myself...only of You!

The question of who I am comes up again and again in the prayer books as does the question about my worth. "Let me never be proud of myself." That is not a good idea! Not ever to be proud? To never value what you have accomplished is not a good thing. There are times when we should be proud of ourselves but give God the glory.

2/3/84

Dear Lord, my God the world that You have created, indeed the universe shows forth Your greatness in so many ways- -in every aspect.

> *<u>You are so perfect!</u> You have created everything so that it works together for the best possible life for all things.*

> > *<u>You are so powerful</u>! You hold all this together and keep it all functioning.*

> > > *<u>You are so wise</u>! You knew how to put it together in the first place and then how to keep it all operating.*

> > > > *<u>You are so loving</u>! You have given it all to us and then also to give Your Son.*

> > > > > *<u>You are so forgiving! You</u> continue to love us and care for us even though we are so disobedient.*

> > > > > > *<u>You are so wonderful!</u> You enter into our lives with such love and to give us such joy!*

Thank you, Lord God! All praise and honor and glory and blessing and riches and power and might be to You now and forever more! Let every knee bow and every tongue confess that Jesus Christ is Lord!

4/10/84

If only I knew more words and could phrase them more beautifully in order to praise You! My heart is full to bursting, my lungs feel it and the tears are coming. Accept all of this, O Lord, as praise and adoration and worship of You. You are worthy, O Lamb of God who was slain for the sins of the world to receive honor and glory and blessing.

Words from the book of Revelation became the words of my private worship of God. The glory and beauty, power and strength of the message of the writer of Revelation is lost in all the furor and fear over the rapture and the destruction of the earth in the last days. All the images of beasts, blood, and devastation take over and the glory of God expressed in this book is completely ignored by popular interpretations of this book.

The purpose of John of Patmos, the pastor, who wrote Revelation, was to reassure his people that God was greater than the emperor, that God's power was greater than the power of Rome. His flock was facing cruel social, economic and political persecution at the hands of the Romans. John wanted to give them courage to stand up to what might lie ahead for them. His reiteration of the greatness and power of God on his throne in heaven, mightier than any earthly emperors, is the message of the book that we all need to take to heart. We have so many gods, and we take our faith so lightly. The book of Revelation says to us that we are not playing a game when we profess our faith in God. We are asking for and receiving a lasting relationship with God who is worthy to receive ALL honor and glory and power and blessing!

The people who read John's message in the first century didn't have to figure out who all the actors were or what the symbols meant. They recognized them in their political and economic lives. The words John used were code for Rome and what she was doing to the Christians. What the people who read the book in the first century needed was confidence that the God whom they refused to deny—even at the peril of a tortured death—was worth such a sacrifice.

So John gives them mighty names with which to envision their God: the Alpha and the Omega; Lord God; the Almighty; the Lamb (God had sacrificed himself as a lamb was sacrificed); our Lord and his Christ; King of Kings and Lord of Lords. This God, says John, is worthy to receive all honor, glory, thanksgiving, blessing, riches, power, wealth, wisdom, might.

It is no wonder that these words have the power to open our hearts to God's presence when we pray.

By the way

> Likewise the Spirit helps us in our weakness; for we do not know how to pray as we ought, but that very Spirit intercedes with sighs too deep for words. (Rom 8:26)

Paul, who is described as the greatest apostle of all, admits that we don't know how to pray as we ought. We don't know what words to say. We don't know how to ask. Thus, quite often, prayer is just sitting in silence. Those moments lead to fellowship with God. There are times when I feel God's presence so strongly that there is no need for words. These times always have as a preface words of praise.

In its written tradition, the Christian faith has been spare in its names for God with the names Father, Lord, King, Judge being the most prominent. In his inspirational book, *One River, Many Wells,* Matthew Fox says that among the world religions, there are many names for God. The Hindu tradition says that there is only one Rama, and he has a thousand names. The Muslim tradition provides a practice in which the worshipper recites and meditates on ninety-nine of the most beautiful names for God. Contemporary feminist theology also insists that the names of God are many.

Our faith would be so much richer if we expressed our praise and adoration of God in prayer using many names for God. Having a list of names for God inside my prayer journal or Bible helps me praise God. Choosing a name that is truthful and appropriate opens up whole new areas of the activity of God and therefore connects me with God through what She is doing.

A few names from the Muslim tradition are: The Protector, The Provider, The Forgiver, The Wise One, The Generous One, The Finder, The Source of All Goodness and the Guide. Some feminist names for God, based on Scripture are Wisdom (Sophia), Midwife, Mother, and Bakerwoman.

What we say about God gives rise to thoughts about God. If we continue to say the same old things, our faith will remain in the same old place. We open ourselves to the Spirit praying in us when we take the time to sit still and address God with many names.

4/19/84

Good Friday: Almighty God, Heavenly Father, whose son was arrested and tortured on this night, betrayed and deserted by his friends. How You must have suffered with Him. Even more deeply and agonizingly that a human parent would with his/her child. How You must suffer and agonize over parents and children who are arrested and tortured and killed in South Africa, in Central America, in Latin America, in North America, in Russia.

O Lord, have mercy on us! Have mercy! Help us change, Dear Lord, help us change. Help those of us who know better to work untiringly for peace and justice for all Your children everywhere. And, Lord, help us make it clear that it is because of You that we are doing it, that we care.

When I wrote this, I was probably thinking more in terms of God not liking such terrible things, not that he was really suffering, acutely suffering with his human creatures. Now I believe God is completely and fully involved in all the agonies of the world. The worship services of the church I grew up in, as well as worship services at seminary, were filled with these descriptors for God: Omnipotent, Omniscient, Omnipresent. That prefix "omni" means "all," so I was brought up and nurtured to believe that God is completely powerful, knows everything and is present in all things. Using these words was a way of giving glory to God, but they also have the power to separate God from us. Even the word "present," when coupled with the prefix "omni," signified to me that God was caring in an "umbrella way," covering all things, not in a personal way.

A very logical question accompanies these words: If God is omni-everything and is Love, why do such bad things happen to people? Some people would be quick to answer that tragedies are punishment for bad behavior. Some would say that these bad things are to educate us, to teach us to do this or not to do that. Some would say it is God's way of showing how strong he is and how weak and dependent we are. If a good and loving God is in control then wouldn't only good things happen to good people and only bad things happen to bad people.

As I studied Christian feminist theology, especially in *She Who Is, the Mystery of God in Feminist Theological Discourse*, by Elizabeth A. Johnson, I came to believe that God, while she is transcendent and is all the things the omni words convey, she is also immanent. She is present in the lives of her creatures more than just being around when we call. She is imminent in our lives as being in each one of us. If she dwells in my heart, and I believe she does, then when I worry about Jim's asthma and Nancy's diabetes, she is suffering with me. When I hear of the tragic death of a child I believe she is grieving even more than the parents because she loves the child, even more than they do. She grieves over the thousands killed in Iraq, in Darfur or anywhere else in the world because these are her beloved children. God, our Loving Mother, would protect and save every one of her children. Believing this about her gives me strength and comfort because I know God is my companion in all the situations of my life. That knowledge also gives me hope that the way things are in the world can change, that the world can become a better, safer, happier place for all human and nonhuman creatures.

5/10/84

Situated on tree-covered rolling hills, the Franciscan monastery was a perfect place for a silent retreat. The buildings were in the style of the early twentieth century and were nestled among paths and ponds. Norm went there for a silent retreat and came home so renewed that he wanted me to have that experience, too.

After clearing my calendar of many responsibilities I drove to this beautiful place in a western suburb of Chicago. On arrival at the retreat center, I was shown to my room and given time to settle in. Then I had an appointment with the spiritual director who was assigned to me. While I am a Presbyterian, having a monk for a spiritual director seemed perfectly natural and, at the same time, amazing. This man who had never met me or talked with me before seemed to know all about me, why I was there and what I needed. Before he got to the spiritual discipline that lay ahead of me, he told me the "rules." It was a silent retreat except for my conversations with him, I was to speak to no one and no one would speak to me for the two days I was to be there.

When I arrived at the dining room for a meal, others were in the room but my place was set at a table apart and even the servers did not speak to me. Nor did anyone I met in hallways or on walks outdoors speak to me. It was an honoring of me and of my purpose for being there. During that time, I had special insights that have stayed with me all these years. Here is what I wrote about one of them on the first morning.

It was really a nice walk, Lord. I took my Bible along in case I found a place to sit and read. (The first bridge would have been a nice place but the beauty and the mystery and the pleasure of Your creation can also be an obstruction so I am back in my room. . .here I feel Your Presence, Lord, just like I do in my place at home.

Your reassurance or assurance that this time is just for me! It is Your special gift just for me! O Lord! That You should love me so!

I'm like that crab Dave and Mary Ellen had in their salt water aquarium. It would walk along and pick up rocks and pieces of coral and other debris and plop them it on its back. Each piece would stick there. And it would walk along and find more. Here on this retreat I need to take off all those things that I carry and get down to just me. Not that they aren't good and aren't part of what I am supposed to be doing, but I need to put them down now for awhile so it is just You and me, Lord! Just You and me! And You can work in me whatever wonders You will!

I wonder if Mary Ellen or Dave had to clean off that crab once in awhile. Or did he have to do it himself. Whichever way it is, Lord, let it be. You have already—last night—removed the piece of coral that is my job. It's like I can't even remember what all the pressing duties are. Thank You, Lord, praise be to You.

My thoughts about the crab and its self-imposed burdens continued.

I don't know what that crab looked like without is burdens, without its coverings. Do I know what I look like without my burdens, without my covering? Show me what You want to show me, Lord!

That little crab had a major influence on my prayer life. It was perfectly obvious to me that I was just like that little pink creation of God. I was walking through life sticking one burden after another on my back. I was always saying "yes" to things people asked me to do and taking on things that no one asked me to do. My prayers express how much I was doing, and I was tired.

During my retreat, God lifted me out of the water and removed all those burdens so I could see who I was underneath it all. I believe that all the things I was doing helped me define myself. They were things that gave me worth. It wasn't that I was miserable. I often wrote and still do write about how much I love all the things I am able to do and all that I am doing. I never knew what to cut out because I enjoyed my busyness. Even in retirement, there are times when I get too many things on the calendar and I still say, "I don't know what to cut out because I enjoy it all!" I still need God's wisdom and guidance in choosing my activities. Sometimes I even ask for it before I say "yes" to yet another obligation.

And "yes," you have probably already guessed, when I got home from my retreat, I started putting it all on again. Praise be to God that she has such unlimited love for me and infinite patience with me!

8/22/84

Dear Lord, I feel as if there is something wrong today. Maybe it is because my day will be so chopped up that I am afraid I will lose control of it; maybe because I still feel bad about not letting LaVerne share what she had learned about two organizations she had researched.

Please forgive me for doing that! She is such an asset to the Hunger Task Force and it would have been better to have let her speak than to always have me be the expert. I am sorry. Help her not feel bad about it.

What a fine line a leader walks. A really good leader, one who truly does know a lot, doesn't have to prove herself. Her goal is to help others grow into knowledge, even into more knowledge than she has; to encourage them in every way to think things through on their own and present their own findings and ideas. It is the leader's privilege to aid people in their own growth and to enable them to speak their feelings and ideas.

What a fine line I walk between thinking I am worthless and thinking I am the last word on any subject. If I were in analysis, the psychiatrist would probably determine that when I get the "know-it-all" attitude it is a ploy to cover the worthlessness I feel. It is a way to make myself important. And when I write that I am worthless and no leader, it is a way of seeking safety from taking responsibility. Whatever the psychology of it is, I am thankful that those two extremes are leveling out in these later years. I am thankful that I usually do know what I am talking about and that I don't need to tell it all in order to think well of myself.

The prayer continued.

About today—I know from Your promises and from all my days of past experience that if I let You be in control of today I will have no problem with it. In fact, it will be a great day. So I give it to You, Lord, and thank You for wanting to plan it and work it out for me! Thank You for wanting to be in our lives.

Today I call this "being in God's flow." I used to see him as one who was over all things directing and stage managing all that happened even in my little life. Now that I see her more as the Spirit that pervades all things, I long to be in her flow. I think she has a good and orderly flow to her life and that I am included in that flow. God does not dictate to me nor does she pull my strings like a puppet. Rather there is a Spirit in me that sings, moves, flows with the Spirit in her. As a result, my days can be so good.

8/31/84

Dear Lord, there is no way that I can thank You enough for being in my life! I am sure, beyond a shadow of a doubt that I couldn't live without You! Two days of my quiet time I have missed and I can hardly cope with getting up in the morning.

O Lord, You are my light and my life. You are my <u>everything</u>: the source of my life, my energy, my happiness, my creativity, my love. You are <u>everything</u> to me. Please hold me close to You and never, never let me leave You!

Almighty God, Creator and Sustainer of the universe, You are so great and so strong, so mighty and so powerful. You are sovereign over the whole universe and over all powers that exist!

You are great and wonderful beyond imagining! A whole lifetime of thinking and meditating and reading and study could not comprehend Your greatness and Your power.

And that is matched by Your love! That one such as You should love one such as me so much that You would live among us and die for us is beyond understanding. And that one such as You has a use, a purpose for one such as me, is such Good News!

9/19/84

Almighty God, I wish I had some new words with which to praise You! You are so much more than <u>great</u>! You are so much more than <u>wonderful</u>! You are so much more than <u>powerful</u>! All glory, praise, honor, thanksgiving be to You! You are great and wonderful beyond compare! You are worthy to receive all honor and glory and power and praise from all Your creatures everywhere. Now and forever!

10/24/84

For it was you who formed my inward parts;
You knit me together in my mother's womb. (Ps 139:13)

Dear Lord and Father, these days at the Career Center have shown me You really did do a good job with me! Help me always keep in mind that you did a good job with all of your creatures and creation. Already the process of ordination has borne fruits for me and for Your Kingdom.

Who was that man coming out of the Jewel store? Was he an angel like my counselor suggests? He said to me, "Good things do come in small packages. You are divine! You are really looking good!" Did you give him those words, Lord? You do such wonderful and mysterious things.

One of the requirements for ordination by Chicago Presbytery was that I attend three days of guidance counseling at the Midwest Career Counseling Center. When we were in seminary, we used to joke that only people who are mentally unbalanced would suffer through seminary to become pastors. We thought that the Apostle Paul himself would fail if he had to take the personality inventories that we had to take to prove us capable of ministry. In truth, our denomination does everything it can to help candidates for the ministry be sure that ordained ministry is a calling for which they have the gifts. That was what the required attendance at the career counseling center was about. We took IQ tests, personality assessments and met with a counselor to talk over the results. My counselor reported to me that my self esteem was very low. That discovery, which was no surprise to me, amazed her because my all test scores were very positive. She encouraged me to think deeply and honestly about the causes of my low self-esteem.

I took a brown bag lunch when I went to the center and would go outdoors to eat it. On the day she and I first started discussing my feelings of inferiority, I ate my lunch outdoors in the clean, crisp fall air and then walked over to a nearby Jewel grocery store to get some cookies for dessert. When I was a few feet from the door, I saw a very tall, sturdy man in casual clothes standing there. He looked at me and said, "Good things do come in small packages. You are divine. You are really looking good."

He wasn't being fresh or flirty. He just looked at me and made those comments. I kept walking into the store but looked around only to find that he was nowhere to be seen. I walked back out into the parking lot to see if I could spot him, but he was not there. I thought he must have been an angel but why would God send an angel to me? When I got back to the center for an afternoon session with my counselor I told her about this man. She was sure he was an angel. She was sure that God had sent him to assure me of my value. I believe he was a supernatural being, but even if he was "just" a man of flesh and blood, he was sent by God to me to impress me in a way not otherwise possible. This blessed encounter did not heal my feelings of inferiority, but it gave me a sound platform from which to work on healing them.

As my counselor and I talked, I remembered an incident in grade school that had traumatized me. It haunted me. I was the teacher's pet in my sixth grade reading class and she was my favorite teacher. Without a doubt, in the teacher's mind or in mine, I was the best reader in the class. There were twin boys in the class who had crushes on me. They wrote me notes to tell me how much they loved me. (This was sixth grade!) I always read the notes but never wrote any back because Mrs. Jones had made it abundantly clear that writing notes in class was in the category of unforgivable sin.

One day, she caught them passing the notes to me. She scolded them and then said to me, in front of the class: "Anyone who reads notes is as dumb as the person who wrote them." It was as though she had slapped me in the face. I knew I was smart. She knew I was smart, and yet she said I was dumb. It changed my view of myself. I am sure there were other incidents and natural traits in me that contributed to my notion of inferiority, but if my favorite teacher of whom I had always been a favorite said I was dumb, it must be true.

When I told my counselor about this incident she said I needed a healing of that memory and that she would help me achieve that healing. But I couldn't wait. I went home and began the process of healing that memory on my own. The process is one that spiritual directors use to help people see, with adult eyes, what happened to them in their childhood. In a quiet meditative state, I imagined myself back in my grade school, walked down the hallway to Mrs. Jones' classroom, walked in, sat down at my desk, received the notes from the boys and heard her say again: "Anyone who reads those notes is as dumb as the ones who wrote them."

Only this time the words that sounded the loudest were "dumb as they are." That must have been a blow to those boys, too. I was smart and I knew it. They were poor readers and did poorly in other classes, as well. My healing began when I realized that what she said may have hurt them more than it did me or at least as much. But what really came home to me was that what she said was not true. It was a lie spoken from angry authority.

I would like to write that the healing I received from that re-creation of the scene cured me of my feelings of inferiority, but it didn't. What it did do, coupled with the visit from my angel, was to enable me to do many things I would never ever before have thought I was capable of.

11/13/84

Time with You, my Lord, is more precious than gold!
  More precious than all the treasures of this world!
Time with You, my Lord, is more precious than family!
  More precious than all the friends in the world!
Without You I cannot love Your gifts,
  my family and friends, aright!
I cannot love them enough!

12/4/84

God must have a good laugh every once in awhile as she listens to the prayers of her children. It would be the kind of a chuckle that a parent has when her child tells her "I will never do that again. I promise." A mom knows that never is a long time and that memories are short.

I want to thank You again and again for the knowledge and the fact that Jim and Nancy are in Your loving arms! I would be such a worrier if I didn't know that and I thank You and praise You!

My prayers show that I did worry about them and still do. I have known some really serious worriers and maybe, quite possibly, I would be one of them if I did not believe firmly that God loves my children even more than I do. She knows them better than I do and I am not a mediator between her and them. I am an advocate for them but she deals directly with them and cares for them.

12/16/8

Dear Lord my God, I <u>need</u> You so much! I need You continually! My satisfaction and contentment cannot be in all the things I get done—because there is always more to do! My satisfaction and contentment can't be in the things I learn because there is always more to learn! My satisfaction and contentment can't even be in the people I love because sometimes they act like they don't love me (nor I them). My satisfaction and contentment can only be in You my Creator and Redeemer! You alone are steadfast and true and loving and patient. You alone know who I am and what it is You want for my life.

12/21/84

Does God need us?

O Father before I fell asleep last night I had such a strong feeling of Your Presence that I couldn't continue laying on my side and, as I rolled onto my back, I thought sure I would see an angel! My conclusion was that You were going to send me a great dream and I would remember it.

This morning I felt let down because I did dream, but I can't remember it. O Lord, if I missed a message You sent please send it again. On the other hand, if Your Presence was for fellowship, for company with me, that is certainly enough for me! Do you get lonesome for us and come into willing hearts to receive love from us? Do <u>You</u> need <u>me</u>?

Nothing would give me more pleasure, more delight, more awe than to have You seek my company just for me, for love and fellowship with me.

Anyone who loves needs loving back. If we think of God only as omnipotent, omniscient, and omnipresent, we can say that God needs nothing. He's got it all. If we see God as present in the world and the affairs of people, if we believe that God suffers with us then we also realize that she needs our love in return, that she needs fellowship with us.

1/2/85

Sometimes a cartoon carries a message as powerful as the writings of the wise men of the ages. One such cartoon, drawn by Pat Brady, is called "ROSE IS ROSE." Pasquale, the bristle-headed star of this cartoon, is drawn in four panels, all of them indicating distress. In the last frame, he says: "I hope I'm not catching a **MOPE!**" It is such a fitting description of how I feel from time to time.

This morning, I slept until 8:40 so didn't have any time alone. I am so tired and draggy and it feels like my face won't smile and my eyes won't look into anyone else's eyes. Dear Lord, help this pass. Take it away before it becomes a big explosive thing in our lives!

I didn't write anything about what was going on and why my mope would cause the explosion in our lives. Maybe it was things I didn't want to write about because of what I thought other people might be feeling. I was afraid that from a mope would come words and feelings that would start an argument. My way was to avoid arguments at all costs. I know that communication is essential to good relationships, but when I think my saying something will lead to a hostile response, I just keep quiet.

By God's grace, I avoided the mope and two days later I was giving thanks to God for helping me avoid it. "O, dear Lord, again, I say with my whole heart—I couldn't live my life without you!"

1/8/85

Yesterday I met with a subcommittee of the candidates committee. They only talked with me for fifteen to twenty minutes. They asked me more about my call and why do I want to be ordained now? I was a little nervous, but I spoke all right.

It was a letdown that I didn't get to tell them more about my experience with You. I wanted to tell them what wonderful things You have done and are doing in my life. In the car on the way home You so filled me with Your Presence that I cried. It is so good to be with You in that way! So good! You let me know in such a loving way that our life together is mainly <u>ours</u>. I know there will be appropriate times to tell it, but I wanted it to be now *before this committee and later before the whole presbytery. I also know that it is by my fruits that they will know You.*

"I Love to Tell the Story" was one of my favorite hymns as a teenager. We sang it often in Sunday School, at youth group and around campfires.

> I love to tell the story of unseen things above,
>   of Jesus and his glory, of Jesus and his love.
> I love to tell the story, Because I know 'tis true.
> It satisfies my longings As nothing else could do.
> I love to tell the story,
> Twill be my theme in glory
> To tell the old, old story
> Of Jesus and his love. [4]

I wanted to tell everyone in the presbytery of Jesus' love for me and how his presence fills my heart so much that I shed tears. "He satisfies my longings as nothing else could do." Writing this book is testimony to the fact that I love to tell the story of God in my life.

1/20/85

How is it, dear Lord and Savior, that I can get so busy and actually be praying so much and not getting the full effect of Your Presence?
   "Because I am always with you, you feel my power but you have been rushing by Me." --God
I have been having good prayer times, but they have been short and sometimes filled with Bethel scripture for study instead of for meditation. Oh, Lord, thank You for calling me and for teaching me. Please don't ever lose patience with me.

Sometimes in my speaking to God, I have experiences of God speaking right back to me. This was one of those times. I don't know why she doesn't do that all the time but her words are precious and appropriate when they come. She puts things in perspective. I hesitate to

---

4   *The Hymnbook,* (NY, Presbyterian Church in the United States, The United Presbyterian Church in the U.S.A., Reformed Church in America, 1955) 383. Lyrics by Katherine Hankey, 1869. Refrain by William G. Fischer. Words William G. Fischer 1869.

say that she speaks to me in words I can write down because phoniness is such a possibility in that kind of claim. But she does.

The plea for patience with me comes from awareness that dealing with me requires a lot of patience. It seems like I make progress in my faithfulness to prayer and meditation and time with God and then I rush on without taking time to be faithful. God has spent years growing me and would be justified in saying, "That's it. I've given you more than enough chances." I know God won't say that. Nothing can separate us from the love of God.

1/29/85

God's imagination and creativity can be a source of worship wherever a person is. The sound of the wheels of the passenger train clicking rapidly on the rails was the only sound in the early morning. I was on an AMTRAK train on my way to Washington, D.C. and the other passengers in my car were still asleep or at least quiet. I was traveling to Washington to attend at home week for Bread for the World organizers. The train was passing through mountains in Pennsylvania.

Dear Lord, my God, how great thou art! How different these mountains are from the Rockies and the Sierras and the Smokies and the Black Hills and the Ozarks. How great and imaginative and creative You are! You are worthy to receive all honor and glory and power and praise and riches and blessing now and forever more!

That was one of my first trips to Washington, D.C. as the field organizer for Illinois, Indiana and Missouri. Every year, the Bread for the World organizers, who had offices in their regions, gathered in Washington, D.C., for "at home week." So as a field organizer for Bread for the World, I would travel to Washington three times a year for this time of planning, support, worship and lobbying.

When I was there, I took every opportunity to visit the awesome museums and memorials of our country. The United States Botanical Garden is located west of the Capitol on the Mall. It would be easy to overlook this amazing place because of the prominence and fame of the other historic buildings along the federal mall. The display of plants, flowering and otherwise, is stunning.

You blessed me with such special moments of worship! How strange it was and wonderful the way You brought me to Yourself through that <u>beautiful</u> purple orchid in the Botanical Gardens in D.C.! How great Thou art to create such a great variety of colors and shapes and sizes in just one species! And then to use that extraordinarily beautiful one to recall me to You!

2/28/85

O Lord God, is this what you want me to see: that you are so faithful to me in my prayer time, but I fulfill my promises to you as it is easy for me—and forget them by saying it really doesn't matter.

I always seek MORE from You and am assured that there are even greater things possible in our relationship and then I give You LESS. Or only what is convenient and what feels good.

Father, forgive me! Having You in my heart is the greatest gift You have ever given me and I thank you and praise You and glorify Your Holy Name! O Father, I know there is more in store for me –for us. Please teach me and make me faithful! And obedient. Praise be to You for Your patience with us! All glory, honor, praise and thanksgiving be to You now and forever! Let all Your creatures every where sing Your praises now and forever more!

3/12/85

Searching for ways to speak about God, to describe God so that I know to whom I belong, has been part of my prayer life long before I discovered that God is more than any name we can give God. When we are in the process of becoming a friend of someone we have just met and liked, we are interested in who they are and what they have done and what they like. So it is when we are in the process of becoming friends with God.

Dear Lord, how great Thou art! How great Thou art! You are so Wonderful, so full of grace and mercy, patient and slow to anger. How great Thou art.

You are God almighty. (Gen 17:1)
You are the Everlasting God. (Gen 21:33)

You are merciful and gracious, slow to anger, abounding in steadfast love and faithfulness. (Ex 34:6)
You are the living God. (Josh 3:10)
You are righteous. (Jn 17:25
You are steadfast and encouraging. (Rom 15:5)
You are the God of hope. (Rom 15:13)
You are faithful. (1 Cor 1:15)
You are merciful and comforting. (2 Cor 1:3)
You are love. (I Jn 4:8)

The Bible is not the only place to learn about God. However, it is the place where we learn what the parameters are. It is the sieve for sorting out what are appropriate names and attributes to use to describe her. In other words, we as Christians cannot just ride off in all directions and name God whatever suits us. When we find a new name for God or a word with which to describe God it should fit the litmus test provided by Love. If it describes love and loving care it is appropriate.

3/15/85

O Lord my God, how great Thou art! I look out the window and see this beautiful spring day and Yours is the praise and adoration for such a wonderful creation! The mystery of it all is too great to comprehend. And then my mind wanders to the people I know and that too gives You glory! They are wonderful and a mystery too. Lord God, I can see why Isaiah and Ezekiel and David and John fell on their faces when they saw a vision of You! You are so wonderful to behold in Your creation, but to be given a vision of You on Your throne would be overwhelming.

All praise and honor and glory and power and praise be to You now and forever more! Let all Your people everywhere sing Your praises!

3/27/85

Almighty God, Creator and Sustainer of this whole, wonderful Universe, what will You do against the powerful forces of evil that grip our world today? They seem indestructible, unbeatable, untouchable.
"I have already done it. Christ's death overcame them." --God.

Father God, they don't look defeated. They look like they are going to burn up Your whole creation.

> *"You are my children, heirs of the promise and yet you look and act defeated." -- God*

I see what You mean and I believe You, but—and I don't mean to sound like the little boy when he wanted to know what heaven was like, but didn't want to go there—I don't want this beautiful creation of Yours to be destroyed. I want it to go on being a part of our lives with You. Are Jerry Falwell and his ilk right? Is Your creation so dirty and evil and hopeless that you will wipe it out by nuclear fire?

The night before I wrote this prayer we heard Helen Caldecott, an elegant and gentle woman, speak passionately about the dangers of the nuclear arms race. She was and still is the single most articulate and passionate advocate of citizen action to remedy the nuclear and environmental crises. While living in the United States from 1977 to 1986, she co-founded the Physicians for Social Responsibility, now an organization of 33,000 doctors committed to educating their colleagues and the public about the dangers of nuclear power, nuclear weapons and nuclear war. On trips abroad, she helped start similar medical organizations in many other countries. The international umbrella group, International Physicians for the Prevention of Nuclear War, won the Nobel Peace Prize in 1985. She founded the Women's Action for Nuclear Disarmament in the United States in 1980.

3/28/85

O Lord my God, forgive my insolence of yesterday and my lack of faith or weakness of faith in Your sovereignty. I am sorry, Father, but I am not sure that it is over yet.

> *"I can take it, my child." --God*

Teach me the truth, Dear Lord. Please teach me the truth. "My child". . .that One such as You should call me Your child! Even when I am being insolent and unbelieving. O Father, I don't doubt that you can save us from nuclear war, but rather do You want to?

> *"How much pain Hiroshima and Nagasaki caused Me! How much any suffering causes me and you ask a question like that! Work as*

hard as You can where I call you and be obedient to me. The whole universe is in my hands. It is my creation." --God

4/15/85

What we say to others can be life-giving or life-stealing. If we tell a child she can't sing or she can't draw, she will grow up believing that she can't sing or draw.

Dear Lord, thank you for arranging it for me to drive James Forbes to the airport! His message (your message) at the conference was so wonderful! And then the affirmation that he gave me on the way to O'Hare!

He asked if I am somewhat charismatic. And when I told him about my heart, he said I am in touch with a Living Power. He said You have been preparing me all these years. That I am a vessel.

When he was getting out of the car, he said he was honored to have been with a chosen vessel and that he will expect to hear more of me. He said it is all right to have a timid spirit because then when you are forceful, You know it is the Spirit.

This was not just a chance encounter—You sent him to me. Praise be to You for witnesses like him!

Remember my telling about my sixth grade teacher who, even though she valued me as an excellent student, said I was just as dumb as the boys who wrote notes to me? These words of James A. Forbes, whom I had never met before, had the opposite effect of the words of my grade school teacher. Whatever we say to each other has a deep and lasting impact. The words of this famous social activist and pastor of Riverside Church in New York City built me up as surely as my teacher's words had torn me down

6/18/85

Oh, Lord God, I am so grateful that You want to spend time with me. What more could anyone want! You are Almighty God, Creator, Sustainer and Redeemer of the Universe and You want to spend time with me!

How amazing! Love so amazing, so divine. Demands my heart, my life, my all.

117

6/19/85

At a wedding in a grand Episcopal Church in Chicago, I read these words on a beam near the ceiling, "Sanctus, Sanctus, Sanctus, Dominus Deus Omnipotentus. The phrase sounds so beautiful so I have been saying it to God. This a.m. I wanted to fill myself with thoughts of Him and so turned to Revelation. There it was in 4:8—"Holy, Holy, Holy, Lord God Almighty." What wonderful gifts You give us, O Lord.

7/23/85

Forgive me, Lord, for trying to live more than one day at a time! Always I am anticipating what I can get done, what lies ahead. Teach me to enjoy today for today's sake. Help me get done in it the things that you would have me get done. And help me do them to Your glory!

Planning. Planning. Planning. I am always planning. Even while I am in the midst of an activity for which I have planned for days, I am planning what should happen next. Planning not only keeps me on edge —I am not giving myself completely to the event at hand -- but also keeps those around me on edge because I plan what I think they should do too.

It took me a long time to recognize this in myself, and it is taking a longer time for me to get over it. But what joy and peace come when I let go and let things just happen, when I relax into the joy of the activities that are mine.

Chapter Five

7/25/85

Occasionally God gifts me with a dream that I remember well into the day. These dreams carry a message for me that fits in with some spiritual change I am experiencing. For several years, I wrote down each dream I remembered and tried to figure out what God was saying to me. Many times they were too complicated to understand even though I had read several books on the meaning of dreams. Some dreams are so bizarre and so complicated I can't figure them out. One that I thought I had figured out was this one.

Dear Lord my God, save and protect me. My awful dream was of someone who was trying to change me into something I am not and did not want to be. That person tried to use one person to do it and he wouldn't. Then he/she selected another and as the dream ended the selected one had plans to do it whenever he was told to. They were so sure of doing it that I was free to walk around—it was almost inevitable that they would have their way. Whatever it was, was not blatantly evil, but it had a feeling of evil. I wonder if it was feminism.

I can hardly believe that I was so afraid of becoming a feminist! It was at the beginning of my searching feminist theology to see what it was about and not knowing yet how it would enrich and broaden all my perspective. The problem was that I had bought into the prevailing idea that anyone who was a feminist hated men. I didn't and I don't.

At the time I was writing this prayer, an old friend who did hate men was visiting in our home. She had experienced great discrimination from the men in her profession who had the power, and she was bitter about it. She embodied what I thought at the time was a feminist. She was a woman who had a grudge against men and wanted to get revenge by showing them she could do anything as well or better than, they could. I wrote:

O Lord, save and protect me from forces that would encourage and coerce me into hating any group of Your people. Forgive us, Lord, for all the dividing of Your children that we do.

Little did I know at the time that Christian feminism was taking root in my soul. What the dream and the prayer did for me was to help me avoid the pitfall of hating men as I came to feel strongly the wrong that has been done and is being done to women in a male dominated world. A sure and steady part of my feminism is that God created male and female in God's own image. That means that, though we are different from one another, together we are greater than the dominant male and the submissive female.

7/28/85

Dear Lord my God, here I am at 6:30 on Sunday morning with a sermon that I consider half-baked and I will be preaching at 10:00! O Lord, I love doing it this way—preaching without a manuscript—because I don't have the pain of writing it all down and struggling with getting it just right. Even more than that I love doing it without a manuscript because I do it better because You speak through me. But since I don't write it down, I don't feel like I am prepared; I don't think that I am prepared.

"You are not prepared. I am. You don't have to be. For two weeks, I have been giving you thoughts and ideas for this message. It is mine!" --God

All I have to do is be open so it can flow through me. O my Lord, You are so great and wonderful! I know You can do that! But can I?

"You've done it before." --God

The outline and the message seem so strong and so negative and so depressing.

"That outline isn't the whole thing, and the message needs to be delivered. It is mine." --God

O Lord, what would I do without this close relationship with You! What would I do? I think I would perish.

"Don't change the subject yet. Look at the outline." --God

O Holy Spirit, it is good. It will be Your message and it will be good. Use Norm and all of Your preachers everywhere to sound Your message of love and justice and peace throughout the entire world.

On Monday morning this was my prayer:

O dear Lord, You were so prepared for the worship at Mt. Prospect yesterday! I felt the stimulus of the Holy Spirit as soon as I sat down with the worship leader. You and she wrote a beautiful service—and she even said, "The Holy Spirit has sure been busy this week!" The service You wrote and the sermon You delivered went together perfectly!

The sermon was beautiful! And one of the women is sending me a check to help the children! Her sister said I was an inspiration to her; one man said the worship leader and I were fantastic, but we both know who was fantastic! It was You! It is You! It will always be You!

May that whole service bear many fruits for the children of the world, for all their needs. Thank you for using me that way! Forgive me for my doubts and help me be ever more dependent on You.

8/15/85

Bless Norm on this his fiftieth birthday! Help him not feel old! Help him feel the energy and the vigor that your Holy Spirit can provide for us. What would you have me say to him in a note this day?

How old a half century sounds! How depressing to think that two thirds of our lives are gone. Not to deny those two ways of stating the fact, but how wonderful it is to have been growing together for more than half our lives! How satisfying it is to have friendships that are that old and enduring! How stimulating it is to view the world the way we view it now! How exciting it is to know that even being a half century old, we still have the unknown of career growth and changes ahead of us. . .people to minister to, programs to develop, ideas to be explored, our faith to be deepened.

May God fill our second half-century. May we accept all the abundance that God has for us in our second half century. All honor and glory and praise be to God.

8/23/85

Father, this is a long slow process, isn't it? Turning me from a full time wife, mother and homemaker into a full time worker for justice for Your children everywhere! Several years ago, I didn't want to be something else, now I do, but it is hard to get rid of the old ways and the old burdens. To stop caring whether every corner of the house is cleaned and organized. I still do want to be a full time wife and as much of a mother as Jim and Nancy need, but there are parts of that role that are unneeded any more. Help me be the wife that Norm heeds (help him to be the husband I need) and help me be the mother that Jim and Nancy need.

At this time the Hunger Committee, the Presbytery, the Presbyterian Hunger Program and I were trying to figure out ways to make the part time hours I had been working as Hunger Action Enabler into full time hours. The stickler was finding the funds to do it. There had always been work enough to fill a full time job, but there wasn't enough money or enough will in Chicago Presbytery to pay for it.

Over the years, I had told Norm that when it was time for me to work away from home, he would have to push me out the door, lock it and not let me back in until I had a job. That was how much I enjoyed being a homemaker. God worked in me and grew me to the point that I wanted to spend more time in my hunger ministry and was willing to make it my full time job. I could see that it would change everything and that was unsettling but I was being called. The above prayer continued:

And help me be Your servant in whatever ways You want me to be. I honestly don't know what to do about this clinical pastoral education thing. Now that the regional Hunger Action Enabler is squelched, do I need to take the CPE now or wait until next fall?

And I am back to the question, what will I be ordained to? It seemed like the regional HAE was going to be it. I know this is all in Your hands and I AM SO GLAD! I surely wouldn't want to be figuring it out on my own.

You are my life and my breath and my strength and my reason for being. Thank you for dwelling with me and guiding me.

The passion of my heart was to continue the work of HAE. Ever since I had seen a movie of starving children in India playing in the sewer I wanted to do something about hunger and poverty. Being a resource person for those issues with the one hundred and thirty-five churches of Chicago Presbytery had fulfilled that calling. But being ordained could end it for two reasons. One was that the money to pay me was hard to find and the second was whether the Hunger Action Enabler was an ordainable position. The man who had charge of candidates in Chicago Presbytery wanted me to be ordained to be the pastor of a small inner city church (of which there were several) part time and be HAE part time. That way they could raise the money and the question of the appropriateness of HAE for ordination would be sidestepped. As it turned out those two issues were resolved, and I was ordained to the position of HAE for Chicago Presbytery. God's hand was in it all.

8/29/85

Almighty God, You are so wonderful! You created us out of such great love! And You created everything perfect for our lives. Every detail of the earth's being is created to go with every other detail, so that one thing depends on another. You are worthy to receive all honor and glory and power and praise and thanksgiving—now and forever more! O Lord, God, let every creature every where sing Your praise.

God, our Father, how Your heart must break and Your tears flow as You see children of Yours being beaten and threatened by other children of Yours. You mean for us to live in peace and harmony with each other and instead we hate and fight. Father, forgive us, all of us even those who don't carry the whips and the sticks, but still have a part in the oppression of other people.

9/3/85

Take me and use me in this strange new situation: Clinical Pastoral Education at Alexian Brothers hospital. The sixteen hours a week for six months stretches out like an eternity before me, but I am sure it is something You want me to do so may I do it for your sake and your glory.

The same man who wanted me to be ordained to the pastorate instead of Hunger Action Enabler told me to "keep a low emotional involvement in CPE." I think he was responding to my doubts about the value in doing it. I was afraid they wanted to make a hospital chaplain out of me, and I didn't want to do that at all! Can you imagine keeping a low emotional involvement in a hospital setting where I would be visiting sick and dying people every day!

As it turned out, a large part of CPE was discovering things about myself and sharing them with others in my class. In fact, many times the others were the ones to point out what was "wrong" with me. We confronted ourselves in what was called verbatims. Part of our assignment each day was to visit new patients in their rooms and offer whatever services we could provide to them and their families in their time of illness. For each visit, we were required to write down what we said and what they said word for word. That way our mentors could help us see areas of weakness or strength in ourselves. It was good for me.

9/15/85

Lord Jesus, my Savior and my Friend, I don't know when You have asked me to do something that I didn't want to do as much as I don't want to do this CPE! Especially this first "on call" duty! There have been some things that I was overly nervous about, but I wanted to do them. Lord, I don't want to do this! I don't want to spend the time and the energy on it! I don't want to be away from Norm and Jim and Nancy this much! Lord, I don't want to do it. Can't I be ordained without it! Can't I be a whole person without it!

Help me be obedient, Lord! Help me be obedient! Even as I was writing the above paragraph, I knew that this will be good for me and for whatever You have in mind for my ordination. Already, I am learning some things about myself that I need to know and that I know will make me a better, more useful servant of Yours. And I want that to happen! I want that to happen with my whole heart!

I want my whole life to be in service to You! I love You and You are my life and my strength!

I wrote this prayer in the morning and by 11:00 that very evening I was thanking God for what a wonderful day it had been. When we were on call overnight we had a small room with a bed where we could sleep between calls for help if there were any. I was sitting on the bed in that room when I wrote a prayer of thanks for the leaders of my CPE and for my fellow chaplains. I even began praying for patients by name.

It wasn't that I became devoted to being a hospital chaplain, but I began to see how important that work is and also to feel God's Spirit in the hospital. It also became evident that I was there as much or more for my own good as I was for anyone else's.

God took special care of me and of the patients. All of my calls, when I was on night duty, were as easy as an emergency call can be. In all the nights I was there, I had only three calls and they were for a man brought in who was dead on arrival, an elderly man who had been dying of cancer, and a young man who had a heart attack at work on his night job and died in the ambulance on the way to the hospital.

In this later case a coworker of the deceased had called his wife and told her only that her husband had been taken to the hospital by ambulance. She had a twenty minute drive to get to the hospital. By the time she arrived, she had a feeling that he was dead. It was my job as chaplain on call to be the one who said, "Your husband has died." She had come alone so I sat with her until the doctor came to give her the details. In that situation, I felt like I did a good job.

The members of my class who wanted to be hospital chaplains had numerous calls during their night duty. And they were for tragedies such as car accidents, stabbings, and crib deaths. Since I got the "easy" calls, I began to feel certain that God wasn't calling me to the hospital chaplaincy. I was there in order to know myself better and to experience the needs of people.

The priest who was in charge of the CPE program prayed with me and called me a holy woman. Again, what is said to and about us and what we say to and about other people has a powerful influence on who we become.

O Lord, I want to be a holy woman and by Your power and Your grace and Your presence in me! I want to be a holy woman for Your sake and for the sake of your lonely, hurting, oppressed children everywhere.

10/5/85

Lord, You have given me great strength to do the things I am doing and, I believe, You have made me calm about the ordination exams. I thank You and I praise You. I know that You are also giving me dreams to help me, but I just can't get up in the night to write them down. I already ask so much from You, but one more request is that I not miss writing down a dream that You especially want me to write down.

As I reread my journals in writing this book, I found my dreams written down but with little or no interpretation. When I wrote them, I could remember small details but felt unprepared to say what they meant. Most dreams fly away as soon as I awaken, but some stay vivid in my mind even after I have gotten out of bed, showered, brushed my teeth and gotten dressed. These are the dreams I try to pay attention to. In literature about dreaming, they are called numinous dreams because their content and images create a powerful emotion, linger in the mind, and are not easily dismissed.

Here is one such dream that I recorded because it was so real to me and so clear.

I went into a store to buy tampons and the employees were having a reunion with a former employee who had moved away and come back to visit. No one wanted to wait on me so they took my money and then were going to give me a key to the machine so I could get them myself. I was sitting there waiting and watching them trying to find the key and suddenly there was this <u>very fierce</u> bulldog right beside me and kind of under my arm. He was snarling and so angry that he was shaking—such power. I thought if I let go of him, he will eat those people so I just held on very tightly!

When I woke up I realized right away that he was my anger at being kept waiting. And later I thought he is my anger over a lot of things. When I was at the office I told a couple of friends about it and they both said he would eat me not other people.

Lord, help me with this! I really didn't know or wouldn't accept that anger has this much power within me. Help me use it, Lord, for you and Your work. I really don't know how that is to be done so, please, as I enter situations that produce anger help me:

    1. *express it in an appropriate way—to tell the person who is making me angry that that is what they are doing, or to express*

anger over a given situation to the proper person. Please show me how.

2. *turn that energy to something else. Please show me how.*

10/9/85

Many strong emotions can beset a person whose faith has been challenged: defensiveness, bewilderment, judgment of the challenger, questioning of her faith, uncertainty about her view of God. All these flooded into my life for days after one of the leaders of the CPE class spoke to me in a private conference. He said that my kind of faith scares him and makes him uncomfortable. His explanation of his discomfort was that by claiming God's authority, I might bypass, overlook or deny his authority as a leader. He said his mother has a faith like mine, and he has trouble with her faith.

That afternoon I wrote this in my journal:

Lord, his words actually make me have smidgeons of doubt about our relationship. Forgive me, Lord. And strengthen me. You know sometimes I wonder if it is made up and induced by me. But I know it isn't.

Why doesn't he understand? Does he believe such a relationship is not possible or desirable? You know and I know that I could not be doing what I am doing without the presence of Your Spirit! Even this little incident has deflated me for tonight. I would be flatter than a pancake without You. I am nothing without You—that would probably upset him with all his psychological training.

In this case of my faith being attacked, I went through all these emotions. So where did I come out? I came out with a stronger and surer faith in God's presence with me than I had before. Whatever this man's faith life was like, there was something that made him want to be the highest authority in my life. Since I was not that important in his life, what he had to say had more to do with him than with me. I didn't understand it at the time but he was a perfect example of how some men can be led to feel and act like they are the authority. I didn't respond to him, as timid as I was in those days, I just gulped and held my feelings inside.

The next day I wrote:

I sure let him upset me yesterday. I'm sorry, Lord, to have let his doubts and limitations cause me uncertainty over what You and I have together! The answer to why some people know You so personally and some don't is not mine to give or maybe not even to dwell on. And if You want to use me in his life then help me speak to him Your words.

10/31/85

In 1958, when I appeared before Platte Presbytery in Nebraska as a candidate for ordination, there were no written exams. The candidate met with a committee of ministers from the Presbytery who asked questions about his faith as well as questions of a factual nature. If the candidate was approved by that committee he was presented to the Presbytery and questioned orally before the whole body by any and all who had questions.

In the late 1960s, the use of written exams was instituted. The subjects of the exams are Bible Content, Open Book Bible Exegesis,[1] Theological Competence, Worship and Sacraments and Church Polity. After having been out of seminary for twenty-four years, it was hard for me to decide whether to go back to seminary for some classes in preparation for the exams or to just take them. I decided to take them and then go back to school for the ones I failed. As it turned out I passed them all the first time I took them.

However, I didn't know in advance that I was going to do so well so I agonized over the prospects of taking them. Study guides were provided and I took one class at McCormick Seminary in Chicago. The exegesis exam worried me the most because the only clue I had as to what part of the New Testament I would be asked to exegete was that the passage would be from Colossians or Galatians.

Be with me today and help me study aright for the ordination exams tomorrow and Saturday. I feel confident, but it really does all depend on You! Thank You for all the people who love me and will be and are praying for me. Lord, help me do Your will!

---

1   Exegesis is the study of a part of the Bible in which one looks at the text in the original language, considers the time and place it was written, learns about the author, and then writes a translation and commentary on its relevance to a modern issue.

Speak to me now as I read and study Galatians.

11/2/85

Lord Jesus, You know how much fun the exegesis part of the exams was yesterday! Your word is always fun and profitable for study. I felt the power of the Holy Spirit as I wrote it. But the polity test was something else! Even when I felt on the verge of panic, I didn't even pray!

I am sorry, Lord, I want to do all these things out of obedience to You and with Your help and then I don't even ask for Your help. Please be with me today. Theology and worship are sure to be hard ones! Help me recall Your truths and express them. There is so much that is beautiful in the Directory for Worship and in the Confessions.

11/10/85

My dear Lord Jesus, help me do the CPE without becoming a pain in the neck to everyone around me! And without impairing my job too much and without driving myself crazy!

My schedule was really overloaded when I was taking the Clinical Pastoral Education training. I was required to spend sixteen hours a week at the hospital which was ten miles from our home. My job as Hunger Action Enabler was part time and my office was at home but when I needed to be at the Presbytery office in Chicago, an hour train trip from home and longer when I drove. Part of my job description was to go to Presbyterian churches in the Chicago metro area to preach, teach or meet with committees. Besides preparation for these kinds of events, I wrote a monthly newsletter for the Hunger Committee as well as writing worship services and publicity for them.

At the same time, I was the organist and choir accompanist for our church as well as being active in adult education and in Presbyterian Women. I was doing so many things that sometimes my family wasn't sure where I was. One time Norm had taken me to the hospital for CPE duty. When I was through, I called Jim to come get me. I waited and waited and waited, and he didn't come. I went back inside the hospital to call him again (pre-cell phone days). He was at home. Thinking I was coming home from Chicago, he had gone to the train station to meet me and figured when I didn't get off the train that I had missed it.

Even though I grew very tired I was proud of all I could accomplish. God never failed to accompany me and inspire me in all these activities.

11/25/85

I didn't want to put an amen on my prayer today Jesus, help my prayer continue all day. Let Your power flow into me and out of me the whole day!

12/10/85

In Jesus' name and for His sake. . . no amen yet. . .let my prayer continue as long as my life continues.

1/17/86

I received word that I had passed all five of the ordination exams.

Dear Lord my God, I can't tell You how grateful I am that I passed the ordination exams! You have been so present with me my whole life guiding and directing its events that all things have led to this place. Lord, stay with me always and continue Your guidance and direction in all that I do. Always, only so that my life may glorify You!

2/10/86

Some of my dreams are so vivid that the impression they leave lasts into the day's activities and beyond. One such dream came on a night when I was on call at the hospital. One of the other CPE students had stayed in our classroom late that night writing a theological reflection that was due the next day. He was a young priest for whom CPE had opened up many questions about his call to be celibate. He was searching for answers and was asking my wisdom. I think this dream came to me as a validation of my ability to counsel him.

O Lord my God, when I woke up after the dream about the penis, I thought it must have had sexual connotations, but as I thought about it this morning, I think it was like a seal of approval or a grade perhaps on how far I have come. It was big and strong and clean and flesh color (not red and throbbing) and I held it in my hand. There was only the shadow of memory of another person present.

As I look at that dream and think of what I have done here it might mean that I have what it takes to make it in the world today. There's nothing wrong with being a woman—I love being a woman and wouldn't want to be a man—but it is necessary to know that you are as well equipped as a man to do the work at hand.

I guess—if this dream comes from You and I am interpreting it rightly, that penis was given to me by You as kind of a diploma. It doesn't signify finished or accomplished, but like a school diploma signifies an accomplishment along the way.

Being given a penis as a sign of work well done seems far-fetched at first but it is clearly a mark of strength and power in a world where being the possessor of a penis gives you authority over others. I was at that time seeking meaning and authority outside the womanly realm. I really didn't want a penis. I just wanted to be taken as seriously in what I was working toward as a man would have been.

Decades later, I read the book *The Mad Woman in the Attic.* It is an analysis of women writers of the nineteenth century and why they wrote so often about women who were hidden away, locked in attics, captives in their own homes. A quote from that book confirms my understanding of this dream.

Is a pen a metaphorical penis? Gerard Manley Hopkins seems to have thought so. In a letter written in 1886 he confided a crucial feature of his theory of poetry.

> The artist's most essential quality is masterly execution, which is a kind of male gift, and especially marks off men from women, the begetting of one's thought on paper, on verse, or whatever the matter is. . .the male quality is the creative gift. Male sexuality, in other words is not just analogically but actually the essence

of literary power. The poet's pen is in some sense (even more than figuratively) a penis."[2]

Women writers were either ignored or degraded because they were women. They were without penises.

The Greek philosopher, Aristotle, wrote that a human being is born female because of a lack of certain qualities and that there is a natural defectiveness in females that makes them misbegotten males. In other words, women are the victims of birth defects. If all human beings were born perfect, they would each have a penis.

Sigmund Freud wrote that women's problem is that they envy men having a penis. This is the way Freud describes penis envy in *Some Psychical Consequences of the Anatomical Distinction between the Sexes* (1925). He writes that the little girl notices the strikingly visible and well-proportioned penis of a brother or playmate, immediately recognizing it as the superior counterpart of her own small and hidden little organ and from then on she is subject to penis envy. She has seen it, knows that she does not have it, and wants it.

My dream was a seal of approval in accepted psychological terms upon me as a woman. It signified for me that my authority to think and write, speak and counsel, is equal to that of men, and is a gift given by God.

2/13/86

Dear Lord Jesus, help me know what to do today. I am exhausted and depleted physically and emotionally. I have a CARERS meeting at 9:30 and a Hunger Task Force meeting at 1:00. I don't think I can make it. Norm and Jim are going to the auto show—I could make this a retreat day. I NEED that.

Am I just wallowing in my tiredness and my weakness? . . . Can I admit I am tired (not in control)and let someone think that of me?

Believe it or not I took that day off for a retreat! I called the leaders of the meetings I was supposed to attend in Chicago and told them I couldn't come. I was home alone all day and had as good a retreat as if

---

2 Sandra M. Gilbert and Susan Gubar, eds. *The Mad Woman in the Attic, The Woman Writer and the Nineteenth Century Literary Imagination* (CT, Yale University Press, 1984) 3.

I had gone to a special place. As I meditated, I kept my prayer journal handy.

This day is Yours, O Lord. Do with me what You need to do. What am I anxious about? My first answer would be nothing. I know God is in charge of everything and I try always to be at his disposal. But if that is true, why am I such mess?

The woes I enumerated were that I was physically tired—and that was the truth! The months of CPE added to my regular life had worn me out but I concluded I would get over that. I was concerned that my exhaustion might be caused by something wrong with me physically, just as I was concerned with the health of my husband and children. Besides praying and writing in my journal that day, I went for a walk, slept for an hour, finished reading a book and played the piano for half an hour. At the end of the day I wrote:

O my dear Lord, You are so good and loving and patient! Thank You for this day. I still have much to think about, but you have made me strong again.

It is okay to stop what we are doing and take time for ourselves. It is more than okay, it is life-saving.

3/10/86

Father, as I think about Jim and Nancy and the things I would have done differently in raising them—no I couldn't have because it wasn't in me to do it differently—I am so grateful that you have known each one of us from the womb and that You know them better than I do. And that You have a plan for their lives. Keep them safe and keep them in Your love.

3/31/86

Lord God Almighty, Creator of heaven and earth, Sustainer of all that is, and Redeemer of humankind, You are great and wonderful and powerful beyond description. There are no words nor any sound that can describe You. Accept then my humble and inadequate words of praise that only begin to describe You. And also accept my feelings that more than words attribute to You all honor and glory and power and praise. Accept my swelling and full heart as praise and thanksgiving and honor to You. It is You who makes it so as I praise and adore You! And please accept my life as the ultimate that I can give for You, to You—the very ultimate. It is the most that I have to give to You.

O Father, during these past dark days I felt You in my heart and knew that You still dwell with me, but I was so overcome by my tiredness and depression that it almost took me over. Please don't let that kind of self-centeredness happen to me again. Guide me and direct me so that I will act wisely in what I choose to do so that it may always be for Your service and Your glory.

Lord Jesus, I love You! Make me Your friend and companion. Holy Spirit, dwell in my heart always.

4/4/86

Jesus came to me and we sat on a bench—His arm around me and His strong hand holding mine in my lap. I asked, "Where are we going?" And He said, "Can't you see, we sitting still. We aren't going anywhere right now." No forward progress right now, don't push, just do what you have to do, enjoy it, and sit down as often as you can and want to.

4/5/86

Be with Norm today as he writes his sermon. Speak to him and through him the words You would have him and the congregation hear.

Having my husband, Norm, as my preacher was a great blessing to me. He was an excellent preacher with a deep understanding of the love of God for all creation. When we were newly married he was called to his first churches, a yoked parish of two churches in northeast Nebraska. We served these churches from 1961-1966. He would "practice" his sermon on me on Saturday night. So by noon on Sunday, I would have heard the same sermon three times. Even at that, or maybe because of repetition, his words proved helpful to me. In fact I still remember one of them in which he said that we can act ourselves into a place we resist being. If we feel we should be doing something because of God's love, but we don't want to do it, we should do it anyway. We will act ourselves into a place of service.

As a result of that sermon, a friend and I decided to volunteer at the boarding school for Indian children that the Dutch Reformed Church operated on the Winnebago Indian Reservation where we lived. Shirley and I felt that we needed to be doing something for the Indian people, but we were both busy—she busy with being a farmer and mother of four children and me with being the wife of the minister. So we volunteered at the school. I don't exaggerate when I say they were overjoyed to have our help. Our two jobs were to sort donations of clothing and to bake cookies—dozens and dozens of cookies!

Sorting the donations was funny and irritating. It was funny because people would donate girdles and bras—useless items to school children. And equally as useless were the two cases of suntan lotion—not sun screen, but suntan lotion!—we opened one day. Sun tan lotion for Indian kids! It was the beginning of my certainty that quite often people donate to charity whatever they want to get rid of, taking pride in their generosity.

Baking the cookies was sheer delight! We baked them in a kitchen in which everything was industrial size. The recipes we used called not for cups of flour and sugar but for pounds. We always timed the cookie baking for late afternoon when the children were dismissed from classes for the day. The smell of those cookies drew them to the kitchen like a magnet draws metal. We felt as if we were giving these abandoned children one of the joys they might have had if they were living with their mothers.

Shirley and I kept volunteering at the orphanage for a couple of years until we moved to another parish. Norm's sermon is for all people: When you feel you should do something and don't want to, give it a try. It could well be that you will act yourself into a place of service where God needs you.

4/17/86

Passages, life's passages are real. Sometimes a person goes through them without even being aware that change is happening. But anyone who has kept a diary, anyone prone to writing things down, can look back over their writing and see these changes. People talk about the passage of life called the "empty nest syndrome." I didn't think I suffered from it when my children left home, but listen to this:

Thank You for my "new" life. Help me not keep looking back to the "old" one and wishing things were the same. What I am doing now is good and You have called me to it. So take away the longing for the "old days" when it comes. But also help me take time to rest and do some things that renew and refresh me. Thank you for this precious time that does that.

Being a homemaker had always satisfied me. I truly enjoyed cooking and sewing and keeping the house clean. Through the first twenty-five years of our marriage, I was happy being the minister's wife and my children's mom. I had enough outside activity such as preaching and teaching and playing the organ and studying the Bible. But in the middle 1980's, things began to shift. At this point I was trying to do it all—trying to be a full time homemaker and doing what might just as well have been a full time job for the presbytery.

When I wrote the above prayer, I was looking back on days when I didn't have to go somewhere every day, when I could be at home and decide my own priorities and activities. I was looking back to when Jim and Nancy needed me and when we did things together.

At the same, time I truly enjoyed my work as Hunger Action Enabler and then as an organizer for Bread for the World. It was so enjoyable that sometimes I felt guilty for having so much fun at my work. I felt this especially when I talked with others who were miserable in their jobs.

Change is what life is all about. The changes in my life became more and more apparent as I read the journals. And yet some things stayed the same.

By the way

Something that stayed the same and is still the same today is the way I praised God in my prayers and the way I marveled at her care for us.

Dear Lord my God, how great Thou art! How great Thou art! You are so high and lifted up above us! You are so great and so mighty and powerful! You are Creator and Healer of the universe! All praise and honor and glory to be Your name forever and ever.

Thank You for caring so much about what happens to us here and now; what happens to each of us!

What a difference there is between thinking of God only as on a throne far above us and thinking of God as One who is involved in each of our lives. Both views—transcendence and immanence expressed in this prayer—are characteristics of God that need to be recognized and celebrated. As contradictory as they seem, they are part of the mystery of God. Either one taken by itself is a distortion of what God has revealed of herself.

We cannot help but fall down and worship at the foot of the throne of God who has created this magnificent, intricate universe! But if that is the only view we have, then God on his throne is distant from us. On the other hand, if we concentrate on God active in our lives, we are in danger of reducing him to an errand boy who exists to meet our every need and want.

To keep a healthy spiritual life, we need to worship and fully enjoy both God transcendent and God immanent.

7/19/86

When I was recovering from a hysterectomy, a friend gave me an inspirational booklet. I copied a poem from it in my prayer journal. The reason I think it may have been one of those little books that are geared to be carried along in a pocket or purse is because I didn't record the name of the book or the author. It is not fine poetry but it has a lasting message for all of us. We can stay in our well worn ruts or we can look for and accept newness in our lives.

> Give me wings, Lord,
> to soar as a bird in the wide blue skies.
> Keep my heart ever open
> to enfold new dreams, new friends,
> lest my way be narrow,
> my love measured.
> And give me courage, Lord,
> to begin new journeys, new ventures,
> that I may grow in all life's seasons.

to begin new journeys, new ventures,
That I may grow in all life's seasons.

This poem heartened me in 1986 as I was struggling to work out the details of being ordained to the position of Hunger Action Enabler and changing from being a homemaker to being a full time employed person. It inspires me just as much now when I think about the decreasing number of years I have left in this life. It seems there are two ways to face old age. One is to think in terms of it being almost over or one can embark on new journeys and new ventures, meet and make new friends. It is the contrast between living in a musty, darkened, closed up house and living in the whole world with eyes and hearts opened like windows to all that is going on.

9/27/86

We should be more careful in calling ourselves Americans. We, U.S. citizens, act as though that is the name of our country and our country alone. To be more specific we are North Americans just as the Canadians and Mexicans are. O God, Lover of the whole world, of all nations, forgive us our arrogance! And help us become one of the nations of the world, not a superpower. Is that a treasonous prayer? A subversive one?

This prayer was written twenty-one years ago. I didn't elaborate on why I was thinking those thoughts. Any number of things could have prompted such musings. Under today's conditions it could easily and quickly be called treason and subversion. In this time of fear and obsession with finding our country's enemies, it would at least be called un-American.

10/5/86

What a beautiful morning! The sun is shining and it is raining! There was an absolutely beautiful, perfect rainbow in the West! You are such a lover of beauty and perfection and yet you also love every part of Your creation that is not beautiful and perfect, even me.

11/16/86

Dear Lord, my Lord, yesterday I prayed for you to give me this sermon. I felt Your power and I praised and thanked You as it came. Last night I started feeling uneasy about it and this a.m. I don't want to preach it at all! If the title and Scripture were not already printed I would change the whole thing! Lord, forgive me. Forgive me for praying for and accepting a gift from You and then denying its value. I prayed that this message would be what You want the people to hear and to use me as the messenger.

To this day that pattern of praying for a message, receiving it and then doubting it is repeated almost every time I preach. My habit is to pray that God will give me thoughts and words that she wants the congregation to hear and then to write only an outline. The outline keeps me on track but doesn't restrict me to written words as I speak. Usually I have the outline done a day or two in advance of the preaching and that leaves plenty of time to worry about it.

Most recently I followed this procedure with a memorial service sermon that I was asked to deliver. When it was on paper I put it aside and as usual worried about it. But God is always faithful, always sure! I delivered it well and it touched the hearts of the family and friends in attendance.

Wouldn't you think that after all these years, after all these sermons, I would know the drill and when the outline is on paper rest easy in the assurance that God will speak through me. God is not only faithful and sure. She is also patient. Which is a very good thing for me!

1/4/87

Thank you for giving me the reassurance this morning that I am <u>not</u> a victim. I am a smart person. I am a talented person. I am a loving person. I am a person of worth. Thank You Lord for creating me so! Take me and use me in whatever ways You intend. Help me be obedient. Help me be wise and strong in my faith in You!

1/28/87

Dear Lord, my God and Father, You take such good care of me! You meet my physical needs. You keep me safe. You guide and direct me. You lead me in pleasant paths. You send me among pleasant people. You dwell with me and let me feel Your Presence even when I have not taken time to be with You alone.

It had been three days since I had written my prayers in time set aside for God, so I was feeling this absence deeply in my spirit.

Dear Lord, I am sorry that I haven't taken time to <u>sit</u> with You and write my prayers. You fill my heart so frequently during the day and that is wonderful and I thank You and praise You! But I know I need to keep this special time as well. Guide me to growth through this special time.

My spiritual life can only grow at the speed with which I let it. Not if I am "too busy," or if I am too tired. "Therefore the Lord waits to be gracious to you! (Is. 30:18) Thank You, Lord, for waiting for me. Please never give up on me! Please!

My image of Jesus waiting in the living room for me to come and sit down to talk was certainly in keeping with this passage from Isaiah. God is waiting for us. God wants our company. After my mother passed away, I went to visit my dad a couple of times a year. I took the AMTRAC train from Chicago to Hastings, Nebraska where my dad and my sister, Sharon, lived. The train ride was always a precious time because I was alone. I avoided conversation with anyone as much as I could. I realize I probably missed many good opportunities for interesting conversation, but I needed and wanted the time for renewal. In effect, I pampered myself. I usually had a seat by myself and I read books and listened to Mozart as the train sped across the fields of Illinois and Iowa and into Nebraska. Those train rides were refreshing and strengthening times for me.

By the time I got to Hastings, I was calmed from my daily life at home and ready for time with Daddy and Sharon. One morning in particular, he was up and out so I spent some time writing. The kitchen table was the best place for that. We always used the back door at our house so he had to pass by me in his comings and goings. I wanted him to sit down and talk with me but he was too busy. He would pass through the kitchen and we would exchange a few words, usually because I asked him a question. Then he would be out the door.

I realize he may have thought that he was interrupting whatever it was I was doing or maybe what he was doing was of great importance. There is an incredible similarity between what was happening with Daddy and me with what happens between God and us. God wants so much to have us sit down and spend time with her, just like I wanted Daddy to sit down and talk with me. Instead, we rush in and out of conversations with God as Daddy did with me that day and as I too often do with Norm.

5/10/87

It is weird and unbelievable how cleaning house can refresh one's spirit:

My four days of house cleaning have been a wonderful respite from meetings etc. and it feels so good to have the house in such good shape. Thank You for making these days possible. But now, Lord, help me turn my thoughts and my energies back to my spiritual growth and to the problems of the world that you have called me to chip away at.

6/13/87

"Write a paper to show me that the job of Hunger Action Enabler is an ordainable position." The man who said that to me meant that he doubted that the work I was doing in the presbytery was worthy of ordination. The Presbyterian Church has always held the office of Minister of Word and Sacrament in high esteem and has, rightly I think, tried to protect it from being trivialized by bestowing it too freely. I was ready and qualified.

Having an educated clergy is and has always been a hallmark of the Presbyterian church. I had the education and had even passed the ordination exams with flying colors even after twenty-seven years since I graduated from seminary. I was serving in a position that used all the gifts of ordained clergy. It took about four months of staring at a blank sheet of paper for me to write the paper he was requiring and then it happened only because Norm brought home from a Presbytery meeting papers about ordaining people to part time ministry. In a matter of a few days I had written eight pages on why the job of Hunger Action Enabler is work that merits ordination. So that the information would not stop with him, I put a copy of what I had written on the desks of seven or eight people around the Presbytery office

Shortly after that I met with the candidates committee of the Presbytery for my annual consultation. The four people who met with me were aware of my struggle to "justify" my being ordained to be Hunger Action Enabler. One man said, "Who better to serve the sacrament than someone who feeds the hungry." One of the women said, "Feeding the hungry is a sacrament." Everyone who donates food for the needy, works in a soup kitchen, raises money to buy food for hungry people, advocates in the halls of power is performing this sacrament. Feeding the hungry is a sacred act.

8/29/87

Thank you that You have given me so many gifts and talents. Help me recognize them and act in accordance. Not that I should be proud or arrogant but that I should acknowledge that I am a person of worth. Especially, most obviously right now, I should recognize this when I am at the Presbytery office. According to those tests I took at the Midwest Counseling Center, I may be smarter than some of the people at the office and yet I act like they are gods.

Forgive me for that, O Lord! You made me who I am for a purpose and if I treat my gifts and myself as inferior I will miss that purpose. But I should not think more highly of myself than I ought to think. Lord Jesus, You be my guide as You are my strength.

9/11/87

Dear Lord Jesus, protect Hattie! Heal her of those brain tumors. O Lord, thank you for the people who pray with such great faith for her! Bless us all and keep us strong and faithful. Help me in my weakness and my fear of losing her—help me remember always that she is in Your loving care, that she always has been so close to You in sickness and in health. She called me her foundation and her comfort and here I am crying. And I lost a lot of valuable time yesterday feeling depressed over her illness. (She was on her way to the Holy Land and got sick on the flight to New York—another brain tumor, besides the one that was already there.)

I want to say that there is no one else in my life like Hattie. That is true, but I am also sure that it is also true that there is no one else in the world like Hattie! We are each one unique and special to You. Praise be to You for Hattie and praise be to You that You brought her into my life, into our lives!

It is still true—there was no one else in my life like Hattie, neither before nor since. She taught me how to pray, really pray. In a way I hesitate to say this but she always got what she prayed for. I hesitate to say it because getting things is not the purpose of prayer and also because many devout people don't always get what they pray for like Hattie did.

It was a given that when you went to Hattie's, you would be involved in prayer at least once during your visit. Her living room was small. To an interior designer it would have appeared to have way too many chairs. It was Hattie's design. It was possible, in that room, for a group of people to hold hands in a circle of prayer without reaching or straining. The very minute she started praying, something similar to an electric current flowed around the circle. The Holy Spirit flowed from person to person around the circle uniting us in God.

Even when just she and I prayed together that great Power moved in us. Once when we were praying her baby canary began singing. The bird was too young to be able to sing like that. The notes tumbled from the heart of that bird like the notes Mozart wrote rushed forth from his soul. We stopped our human praying and listened to the voice of God in this tiny, yellow, baby bird. God's presence filled Hattie and everyone around her, including birds.

9/12/87

Thank You that You are active in the process of my ordination, indeed, that You are the "Caller" and I am the called. Help it always be for Your glory and honor and for the sake of Your children some whom I meet and some whom I will never meet.

10/2/87

Please fill Hattie with Your healing power. May Your power fill her brain and clear out every tumor. May it flow through every nerve and muscle to her eyes and her voice box. May it flow through every vein and nerve and muscle to her arms and her legs and her hands and her feet. Her body and her mind and her spirit are prepared for such a power, for Your power because you have done it for her before. . .three times You have done it for her before. Is it any wonder that she should have such faith! That she should so easily abide with You! Oh, Holy Spirit, I feel such power as I pray for Hattie. I know it is Your power! Fill me with Your power whenever You will for the sake of others and for the glory of God!

10/5/87

If a busy career woman and/or wife and/or mother wants to pray she can always make the time. The best example I have ever heard was Susanna Wesley (1669-1742). She was the mother of the famous preachers and founders of the Methodist Church, John and Charles Wesley. She gave birth to nineteen children only nine of whom survived. Her way to have time alone with God was to put her apron over her head. When she did that her children knew not to bother her.

Her preacher husband was away much of the time at church meetings or in debtor's prison. Managing the few financial resources they had and caring for and educating the children was left to Susanna. She had a list of sixteen rules to be followed that gave consistency to the lives of her children. Among her prayers is this one.

> O God, I find it most difficult to preserve a devout and serious temper of mind in the midst of much worldly business. Were I permitted to choose a state of life, or positively to ask of Thee anything in this world, I would humbly choose and beg that I might have daily bread with moderate care and that I might have more leisure to retire from the world without injuring those dependent on me.

Yet I do not know whether such a state of life would really be best for me; nor am I assured that if I had more leisure I should be more zealously devoted to Thee and serve Thee better than now.[3]

Susanna Wesley is a prime example for us to follow as we seek a life of prayer and dedication to God.

10/22/87

Praise be to You!

Let the mountains and the hills say, "Praise be to God Almighty, the One and only God!"

Let the oceans and the rivers say, "Praise be to God Almighty, the One and only God!"

Let the rocks and the stones say, "Praise be to God Almighty, the One and Only God!"

Let the trees and the grass say, " Praise be to God Almighty, the One and Only God!"

Let all women and children and men say, "Praise be to God Almighty the One and Only God!"

Praise be to You Lord God, Creator, Sustainer, Redeemer of the whole universe!

Praise be to You!

3　W. L. Doughty, ed. *The Prayers of Susana Wesley,* (Grand Rapids, Zondervan Clarion Classics,) 1984, p. 17.

Chapter Six

10/25/87

I didn't know my mother was having any physical troubles until she called to tell us that she might have to have surgery.

Bless my Mom as she contemplates surgery. Oh, Lord, I have no idea what this can be, but please, please, please help it not be cancer. Help it be something they can fix and heal her.

She was seventy-seven and had always been strong and healthy. She hardly ever had even a cold or the flu. For two years she had been having physical problems that the family doctor described as a "floating kidney." When she reported having been to see the doctor, I knew whatever it was serious. Neither Mom nor Daddy ever went to the doctor except under the most extreme circumstances, like when Daddy fell off the roof of our two story house onto the concrete driveway.

10/27/87

Please be with my Mom. I am afraid for her because of the way Grandma died of colon cancer, although she had no pain. But Mom must be afraid too. Comfort her and help her not be afraid. Be with the doctor and give him knowledge and skill as he does her surgery. Help it not be malignant, please, Lord! Please.

Her doctor was the son of the doctor who had delivered two of my sisters. My folks had unbounded confidence in the doctor/son as they had previously in the doctor/father. When we found out what the problem was we wanted to blame the doctor because he should have found it sooner, but we also realized that he needed to see Mom to make a diagnosis. It had been seventeen years since Mom had been to a doctor!

At this time I was praying for healing for Nancy's sore throat, Hattie's brain tumor and Tonja's breast cancer. I prayed and prayed that God would lay his healing hand on these dear ones of mine. That he would restore wholeness to their bodies. Over and over again I prayed that Mom did not have cancer.

I was also praying for Daddy. He was afraid for Mom not only because of what they might be facing but because his philosophy had always been that anyone who went into the hospital didn't come out alive.

11/4/87

May my Mom's trouble be something that can be cured with medicine not the surgery. If she has to have surgery may it be easy and totally successful. What I really want is the strength of Your healing power to flow over her and in her and through her and to clean out whatever infection or abnormality is there. I believe You can do that. Help my unbelief.

Later in the day, Mom called and said she would be having surgery only two days later. They were going to remove part of her colon. The doctor said there were adhesions on it that were causing pressure on the kidneys and the hernia. That night my sister, Cindy, a critical care nurse, called and said she had talked with the doctor. He told her what Mom really had—a malignant tumor the size of a grapefruit in her colon.

The word "devastated" took on a new meaning for all of us. My Dad cried a lot but Mom seemed unaware of the details and towards the very end of her life said that she didn't know it was so serious. On the Amtrak train on the way to Hastings the next day this was my prayer:

Dear Lord Jesus, I can hardly believe it. Somehow I believed that Mom would always be well and would one day just fall asleep and go to heaven. I never thought—or if I thought about it—never believed that she would have cancer. Mom Phillips says her body is strong and always has been so maybe she will overcome this.

Lord, my aching, crying heart continues to ask for healing for her. May the doctor lift that tumor and the malignancy out of Mom's body "en toto." May it be as contained as a grapefruit in its peel. May all the malignancy be drawn into it and removed!

In reading one of many books about prayer and healing, I had come across the idea that one needs to imagine the healing. So I drew a diagram of the tumor, contained and removed. It was like a grapefruit with an opening in the top and arrows representing the cancer cells going into the grapefruit. Right beside it I drew another one closed and containing all the cancer cells.

11/6/87

"The tumor was too pervasive." He couldn't remove it. He did a colostomy. That will relieve obstruction and discomfort. She talked to him last night about her pain. Daddy cries and cries. He showed me around the yard and told stories about how she loved each plant. Says this isn't home any more. She was home!

The doctor met with us the next day at the hospital to talk about Mom's condition. He had said he would talk to us all, including Mom, but he gathered us in a little sitting room in the hospital without her. He said we shouldn't tell her about her impending death. He said she had just a few months to live but that we shouldn't tell her! My Dad agreed with him. The doctor said he needed her to have a positive attitude so she would get well. What a disconnect that was! He had just told us she wasn't going to get well, that she was going to die in a matter of months and there was nothing he could do about it. Within eleven months he served as one of the pall bearers at her funeral.

If I knew how to spell a word that makes the "wrong answer" buzzer sound, I would write it here. It would be loud and jarring. I had some wisdom and experience on the subject of death and dying and how the family should be united in facing it. And I knew that Mom should be told that her tumor was inoperable so that she could say to us the things she needed to say and vice versa. Her mother had died of colon cancer so she would know what lay ahead of her. About two months before she died, she told me the doctor had told her that her illness wasn't serious. I believe that through the whole ten months of her dying she knew better.

That we didn't tell her is one of the greatest regrets of my life. If I had it to do over again I would tell her.

11/7/87

Dear Lord our God, how great You are! I thank You and praise You for the gift of faith in You that You have given my family. Increase our faith, O Lord! Increase our faith!

O Lord, may Mom put herself completely in Your hands. She is so strong and so determined and so stubborn, but I think this is something she cannot do by herself. But none of us can do it for her either. O Lord, I don't want her to suffer. I don't want her to be confused. I don't want her to be afraid. But this is part of her life, part of her journey, isn't it. She has to do it herself—and yet she is not alone, for You are with her to comfort her and strengthen her and protect her.

She bore the knowledge of her illness by herself but she had the love and support of her whole family, especially my sister Sharon, who lived across the street. Daddy took care of her in tender ways we never could have imagined. After the surgery, while she was still in the hospital, Daddy learned to change her colostomy bag. She insisted that he was the only one who could do it for her. He had always gagged at nasty smells. In fact, when we were little and were sick in the night, Mom made him stay in bed so that she didn't have to clean up after a little girl and him too. But he changed her colostomy bags and took care of the site with loving care. A tenderness that I had never seen before grew between them.

11/9/87

Her surgery was on Friday. On Sunday Daddy and my sisters and I went to worship. The closing hymn was "How Firm a Foundation."

> How firm a foundation, ye saints of the Lord
> Is laid for your faith in His excellent Word!
> What more can He say than to You he hath said,

You who unto Jesus for refuge have fled?
You who unto Jesus for refuge have fled.[1]

The first verse was a comfort to us, as were many phrases from the other verses: "be not dismayed," "I'll strengthen thee and help thee to stand," "And sanctify to thee thy deepest distress." We were in deepest distress and the Lord did comfort us and strengthen us.

11/11/87

At my Mom's bedside was the first time I ever heard my father pray. I can still see him standing by the head of her bed, bent over with his hand on her forehead. What a powerful witness that was to me not only of his love for her, but of his faith in God. Somehow his faith gave a new dimension to my own faith. It seems that knowing that my father could pray gave me a sense of continuity. My faith was fed by his faith and by that of my forebears.

11/13/87

The trees are bare and the grass is covered with dead leaves, the weeds are brown. Some fields are covered with stubble, some are plowed and ready for spring planting. The seasons come and go and come and go and we all move through the seasons of our lives.

11/21/87

Thinking back over the week spent in the hospital with my family at Mom's bedside I wrote a prayer about how strongly I felt God's presence. I had the feeling of being full of God's presence and that somehow I needed to be the conveyer of it to others.

O Lord, during that time in Hastings—especially Friday, Saturday and Sunday, I realized how deep my spiritual roots go. Mom and Daddy and the girls don't know the Bible or theology like I do and in my view they have not served You like I have, but their roots in You are there and they are deep!

---

1   *The Presbyterian Hymnal,* 361.

This prayer was true except for the part about my serving God more than they! That was as sanctimonious a statement as I have ever made! Five weeks later I wrote in the margin of that prayer:

Pride!

Yuk!

When I am with other people and am so filled with God's Presence how do I know but that it is the prayers of one of them that are making it possible for my heart to be so open to God!

11/26/87

O Lord, why don't You
> *Why don't You prevent the displacement of poor people*
> > *from their homes, shabby as they are, in Chicago?*
> *Why don't You wipe out apartheid in South Africa and*
> > *all its forms all over the earth?*
> *Why don't You open the minds of all narrow minded,*
> > *cement-headed Christians who are only against things*
> > *or for an ugly ideal.*
> *Why do You let someone like Harold Washington[2] die*
> > *and someone like (a certain alderman in Chicago) live?*
> *Why do You let innocent children suffer hunger*
> > *and death and torture and anguish?*
> *O Lord our God, You are so great and so mysterious!*
> > *You must agonize over these things more than any human being does!*
> *Lord, God, may You soon be comforted!*
> > *May we soon be comforted.*
> *Not by words but by actions that wipe out these injustices!*

1/4/88

In a cynical tone of voice, people ask, "What meaning can there be in ritualistic words repeated over and over?" They say that old forms should

---

2   Harold Washington was the mayor of Chicago from 1983-1987. He was a man of integrity who worked for the best interests of the people of Chicago. He was the first African-American mayor of that city. He died unexpectedly on November 25, 1987.

be replaced by new ones if they are to attract people. We do need new words, such as feminine names for God, but old ones connect us to the great cloud of witnesses that has gone before us and surrounds us now. The living God is in living words. *In Christian Prayer: The Liturgy of Hours* the Lord's prayer is prayed, after the intercessions, twice a day every day.

At first, saying the Lord's prayer twice every day seemed like it would just be mechanical but today it was like little sparks coming from it. O Lord, Your Power and Presence in these words written down and repeated—maybe, instead, it is Your power and Presence in me—are marvelous to be a part of. I never thought of this before. That maybe these are just written words on a page and the life they have is the life You give me to take to them.

Is that why the Bible has such power? Does it or the liturgy or the Lord's Prayer have power for someone who reads but doesn't know You and doesn't care to?

1/8/88

Somewhere, probably at a Call to Action[3] meeting, I discovered the Catholic prayer book, *Christian Prayer, The Liturgy of Hours*. It is like a rich feast, a hearty bountiful buffet. God speaks to me through it. Ancient and beautiful words have the power to touch our hearts with new life.

The Word of God existed before the creation of the universe
> yet was born among us in time. We praise and worship him as
> we cry out in joy:
> *Let the earth ring out with joy for you have come,*

You are the unending Word of God who flooded the world with joy at your
> birth,
> fill us with joy by the continuous gift of your life.

You saved us and by your birth revealed to us the

---

3   Call to Action is an organization that advocates for a variety of causes within the Roman Catholic Church. Their goals include women's ordination, an end to mandatory priestly celibacy, a change in the church's teaching on a variety of sexual matters, and a change to the way the church is governed.

covenant faithfulness of the Lord,
    help us to be faithful to the promises of our baptism.
You are King of heaven and earth who sent messengers to
    announce peace to all,
    let our lives be filled with your peace.
You are the true vine that brings forth the fruit of life,
    make us branches of the vine, bearing much fruit. [4]

3/23/88

Dear Lord, thank You and praise be to You that the certification committee voted to validate the HAE job as ordainable. It was so easy! I didn't have to convince them of anything—You had done that already! You are so great and wonderful.

One member of the committee was so enthusiastic about me and the job. He kept saying how exciting it is. And then he said he liked my spirit about the whole thing. I am sure that what he was feeling was Your Spirit and again I praise You and thank You! You are so great!

The meeting with the committee was easy, but the whole process of being approved and then ordained was not easy. There were so many papers and letters to write and so many committees to work through. I am not sure I would have made it if it hadn't been for Earnestine,(then an administrative assistant, now Mission Network/Personnel Services Administrator of the Presbytery of Chicago. She made sure I knew the dates that every paper or application was due, that what I wrote got to the right person, that the minutes of each committee showed what had been done and what the next step was. She had been that kind of a help to me the whole nine years I had already been Hunger Action Enabler and her passion for social justice matched my own. Whenever it looked to her like I was missing a deadline or needed to do something she gently and quite often humorously reminded me of what needed to be done. One day when she reminded me of a task, I said to her, "You're a slave driver!" I said this to my loving, efficient African American friend. After our astonishment at the irony of my words subsided, we had a good laugh.

---

4   *Christian Prayer, The Liturgy of the Hours* (NY, Catholic Book Publishing Co.
      1976), p. 202.

Earnestine and me, 2005

4/2/88

Dear Lord, my God, the service of shadows last night made me realize all over again my guilt and sin and unworthiness to be loved by You. There is <u>nothing</u> in me that can earn or merit Your love! Yet You give it freely! You give it abundantly! You give it sacrificially.

Oh, Lord God, may my ordination never be a badge of pride, but always a mark of servant-hood. I want only to serve You in every possible way.

Because You love me so—not because I am good but because You love me so—You have given me gifts and talents. Use them always for Your own ends and purposes.

By the Way

Our yearning for new ideas is a response to God's call to us. Reading the words of Julian of Norwich, who lived in England during the fourteenth century, exposed me to many new ideas. On May 13, 1373, when she was thirty she reported seeing sixteen showings, or mystical visions. She wrote her visions in a book entitled, *A Book of Showings*. The story of her life is sketchy, but at some point she became an anchoress which meant that she entered a small cell whose door was then bricked over. Her cell had a small window opening to the outside so that she could receive food and speak to those who came to seek her wisdom. The point of this kind of discipline was to keep her focused on meditation undisturbed by any need to do worldly work or activities. I recommend reading her words because they speak so vividly to one's search for relationship with God.

> To seek
> is as good as
> seeing.
>
> God wants us
> to search earnestly
> and with perseverance,
> without sloth
> and worthless sorrow.
>
> We must know
> that God will appear suddenly
> and joyfully
> all lovers of God.[5]

3/23/88

We were on vacation at my parents' when the news came that I could set my ordination date. I had jumped through all the hoops and now we could do it!

Praise be to You for the wonderful news we got Thursday night that I am supposed to get my ordaining commission selected! You know how right away I got to thinking about how I needed more time with You to talk about this ordination and You reminded me that "we have been on this path for a long time." And we have been! You have nurtured me and inspired me and caused me to grow all these years!

---

5   Brendan Doyle, *Meditations with Julian of Norwich*, Santa Fe, NM, Bear & Company, 1983, p. 36.

I guess what I want is constant reassurance that I am doing what You want me to do. And I think (right now it came to me) that deep core of self-doubt that I have enters in and I think why should anybody think that what I want is worthwhile and worthy of official approval and action—in essence official approval of me.

When the phone call with this news came, Mom, Daddy, my sister Sharon, Norm and I were sitting in the living room. We discussed the news excitedly because we had been waiting for this news for so long. After a little while my Mom, who had now had colon cancer for over seven months, got up and went into the kitchen where she sat down and cried. She said, "You will all be there, but I won't."

Sharon comforted her by laying out a plan for installing a makeshift toilet and bed in her old van in which they could travel to Chicago. Mom, who always believed you could do whatever you set out to do, stopped crying and began to enter into the plans for my ordination. The next morning she mixed a batch of mint candy dough and began making mints for the reception, which would be held after the ordination service. From then on she continually had a bowl of mint candy dough on the counter and shaped it into forms whenever she had the strength. We didn't count how many of these delicious mints she made, but we were eating mints for weeks afterwards.

4/15/88

Thank You for Hattie! Thank You for all that she has taught me about prayer and about waiting upon You! Oh, Lord, teach me how to be like her. Not that I can be a carbon copy of her because we are so different in where we live and where we are, but help me be like her spiritually. Use me in other people's lives the way You have used her.

I could not have served God the way Hattie did. We were two different women from two different worlds, with two different sets of gifts. The world she lived in was a place of discrimination, poverty, overcrowding, and oppression. When she survived her first surgery for a brain tumor she vowed to make her neighborhood a better, safer place for her children and for all children who had to live there. She said many times that if she did not work to make things better in her neighborhood, Satan would take over.

The world I lived in was a world of plenty and of power. I worked among people who had every material thing thought to be necessary for life. My calling was to change their hearts and to open them to the needs of the people with whom Hattie lived.

One day, Hattie and I decided we wanted "her" women to meet "my" women. As a result, the circle I belonged to at Christ Church invited Hattie and her friends to come to a coffee in my home. We were excited about the refreshments and the plans we had made to get acquainted with these women from the ghetto. As the time approached, I became very anxious. I was worried that these two groups of women who were from such different worlds would not know what to say to each other. The worry was all for naught. As soon as our guests walked in my front door the chatter began. It didn't end until they walked out the door at the end of the morning! It was witness to the truth that all people are children of God.

4/22/88

You want to be with me and guide me and give me peace and joy! Thank you, Lord! Thank You! Without You I would be an empty shell—I would be a creature trapped in fears and insecurities. . .and I still have plenty of them that You seek to free me from.

4/25/88

A prayer that I have repeated through all the years and continue to pray is:

Never leave me, Lord! Never leave me! Never let me leave You! Never let me leave You!

There have been many people in my past who have been faithful and dedicated to God and to the church and then suddenly—suddenly it seemed to me, but maybe gradually for them— they turn away, turn cold. Some have told me they were burned out, some that they didn't believe in God any more, some that they were angry at someone in the church. People do get overworked in the church. People do go through phases in their lives. While I can't believe that I would ever burnout, I pray this prayer frequently.

5/21/88

Dear Lord, thank You that I get to go see Hattie today! I thought I had so much to do, but this morning all of the things I can think of I can do before and after I go there. Thank You! She must really need to see me. . .no, not to see me, but to have the kind of prayer You give us when we pray together. She does need me. I need her too.

O Lord, I wish she wasn't going to die. There is no one like her. It would be so good to share things with her the rest of my life. She has been one of the finest gifts You have given me in my whole life. Praise be to You for all Your good gifts! Praise be to You!

5/26/88

God's journey from heaven to my heart advanced by leaps and bounds during the final days of my mother's life. Prompted by the knowledge that I would soon be motherless, I thought deeply about what it means to call God "Father." It seemed more and more clear to me that if God could be described as father, God could also be described as mother. I chose to read things that would help me understand this. Again, Julian of Norwich offered me great wisdom. I was delighted to discover that feminine language for God was being used long before the beginning of the movement of the 1960's, called "women's lib" and before modern Christian feminist theologians.

> And Jesus is our True Mother
> in whom we are endlessly carried
> out of whom
> we will never come.[6]

> Just as
> God is
> truly
> our Father,
> So also
> is God

---

6   Doyle, p. 99.

truly
our Mother.[7]

A Mother's service is
nearest,
readiest
and surest.

This office
no one person
has the ability
or know how to
or ever will do fully
but God alone.[8]

6/12/88

Finding a place to meditate is of primary importance to me when I am away from my usual prayer place in my home. The week before my ordination, on my first trip to Washington D.C., the special place I found was a bench outside the Basilica of the National Shrine of the Immaculate Conception on the campus of American University. It is an important Catholic minor basilica dedicated to the patron saint of the United States. Having no idea who the patron saint of the United States was, I googled it. She is the "Blessed Virgin Mary," under her title of the Immaculate Conception. She was chosen in the nineteenth century by the U.S. bishops and confirmed by the Holy See. Thus, this basilica is a Marian shrine which took over one hundred years to build. The Shrine is a magnificent cathedral marked by both a spire and a dome. Millions of pilgrims visit the Shrine each year.

In the shadow of this cathedral built to the glory of God, I prayed:

Lord, You saw me yesterday—not going beyond my face! It felt like all I had was a face. Last night at the reception it started to change and I started to become a whole person. This morning I am a whole person (or nearly as

---

7   Ibid., p. 103.
8   Ibid., p. 105.

I am that ordinarily) Thank You! Help it be to Your glory and for the sake of Your children here who are lonely and maybe feel like only a face. And for the sake of Your poor and hungry children everywhere.

I feel a strong need to be able to express myself better in conversation. This will be a good place to practice. Sometimes when I talk I feel like the gears aren't meshing. Help me get it together. Always for your glory!

6/25/88

Dear Lord my God, how great You are! Your timing for our lives is excellent and makes everything work together for good. Look at Hattie—only she would say, "Look at God!" See what He has done. That her illness should come at a time when her beloved neighbors and neighborhood are being destroyed and no one can stop it. . .and that her illness is brain tumors so that for months she has been unable to worry about or fight against the inevitability of the takeover of her area by rich, white people. How great You are! Your timing in our lives is excellent and makes everything work together for good. If Hattie is suffering now in the ICU, give her glimpses of the glory she is about to enter. I want her to know that I was there yesterday.

May Mom be assured in her heart and her mind of the same glory that she is about to enter. Lord, help her not be afraid and help her not suffer long. May she see Grandma and Grandpa and Ben and Edward and all the rest of her family waiting for her so that it will be easier for her to go. Help Daddy be assured of his place in heaven as well so that he can have hope.

6/28/88

Dear Lord, the two women who have meant the most to me in my whole life are dying and You are giving me the strength to bear it. Praise be to You! You are so steadfast, so loving and true.. . .Protect Hattie, dear Lord. She is afraid of Satan. Protect her and keep her safe. Help her to see some glimpses of heaven and reassure herself of its glory.

7/16/88

Now I use feminine names for God in my conversation and when I feel brave in public settings. People often say to me, "I just can't use mother in place of father for God. It is too hard to do." My reply to them is that I know it isn't easy. It is such an unknown way to think and to speak. It doesn't come easy. After hearing a woman theologian speak about using feminine names and pronouns for God, my heart cried out to God.

One step at a time, Lord. Help me take one step at a time! I can hardly, I can't, comprehend this. Hold me back. Reveal it at Your pace, oh my God! It is literally mind-boggling!

7/24/88

Mom was taken to the hospital the day after they got home from my ordination.

When I got home from a Bread for the World gathering in Washington, I boarded a train and went home to Hastings to help celebrate Mom's seventy-eighth birthday.

When Daddy and I went to the hospital after church, he said to her, "Mother, shall we get a different God, this one doesn't seem to be listening."

Mom looked at him for a minute and said, "No, let's give Him another chance."

O Lord, You are so great and so wonderful! You have known Mom since before she was in her mother's womb. You have known all her pain and suffering, all her joys and satisfactions over the years. And now You know her dying just as You have always known her living.

My ordination service, June 19, 1988.

The newly ordained Reverend.

Mom and Daddy after my ordination.

8/14/88

Sharon said that Mom is really failing. Things that are happening to her body indicate that the end is near.

Oh, Lord, I need to know where I belong next week! I want to be at Ghost Ranch so much but I also want to be with Daddy and Sharon if that is where you want me—and with Mom. . . . I know You will give me peace about whether to go Ghost Ranch or to Hastings.

I wanted to spend the last days of her life with Mom! My sister, Sharon, lived across the street from my folks. My sisters, Peg, from Colorado, and Cindy, from Indiana, made trips to spend time with her and Daddy. I went to meetings. I had registered and paid for a trip to Purdue, Indiana, for the Churchwide Gathering of Presbyterian Women. While I was there I talked with Mom on the phone every day and grieved that I was not with her.

After the Churchwide Gathering, I was scheduled to attend a meeting at Ghost Ranch in New Mexico. Norm and I were planning to go to Hastings on vacation after the Ghost Ranch meeting. Peg told me to come home. I struggled to make the right decision.

It was the first meeting of the Eco-Justice Task Force of the General Assembly of the Presbyterian Church (USA) on which I was going to serve for three years. I felt I needed to be there to get in on the beginning of the work. After all I would be at Mom's the very next week. In the course of our pastoral ministry we had known many people who lingered for months and even for years after family had been called home to be present at their dying. We would be there with her the next week. So I made the decision that has caused me deep regret ever since.

8/13/88

In a dream:

I was taking care of Mom and was able to hold her in my arms on my lap. But she kept getting smaller and smaller and then I was holding a dead canary.

8/16/88

I arrived at Ghost Ranch on Sunday evening. My mother died Monday at 5:00 a.m. Getting in touch with me was difficult because the ranch is remote and no one was on duty with the phones when Sharon first started calling me. When the staff at the ranch did get the message they came right to the bunk house where I was staying. As soon as I had gotten dressed and repacked the suitcase which I had just unpacked, one of the ranch hands drove me to Santa Fe where I caught a shuttle to Albuquerque to board a 2:30 p.m. flight to Chicago.

Albuquerque airport. Mom died at 5:00 this morning. Thank You, Lord, that her illness is over. Thank You that she is with You! Thank You that I came to Ghost Ranch! Thank You for Norm's thoughts that helped me make the decision to come. It was right. Thank You for Fern Norris! Thank you for Joan and Joe Keesecker and for all at the ranch who hugged me and cried with me. Thank You for American Airlines getting me on this return flight.

The thankfulness must have stemmed from my relief at having her suffering over and from my sure knowledge that she was in a better place. That sure knowledge came not only from my faith, but also from the fact that on that long trip I could hear my Uncle Edward laughing! He was her older brother and had died many years before. He had a laugh, a loud bubbling laugh, that he used often. No one could forget his laugh. I believe he was glad to see her!

8/17/88

How relieved she must be! How relieved she must be! Sharon, told us about your dying. Mom, you did it and you did it well! But God has already told you that: "Well done, good and faithful servant. Come into my Presence and rest." Thank You, dear Lord! Thank you!

8/19/88

"I'll see you in the morning of the resurrection." Daddy's words beside Mom's casket last night as he stroked her face and kissed her. "Wait for me. I'll be there before too long."

Oh, Lord, grief rips and grabs at my body. It doesn't just make me cry and feel sad. It makes me feel sick to my stomach and my head aches. As I lay awake in bed it makes me twitch and sigh. Oh, God, how grief must pain You! How much grief You have to bear.

Daddy tried to pray during the time the minister allowed for prayer at the service last night—Norm and I did because Daddy asked us to and because we wanted to—but he could only get out Your name—You heard the cries of his heart too deep for words. Then he gathered the four of us and Patti around Mom's body and prayed a beautiful prayer of praise and thanksgiving for her and for us and for our husbands and children. His prayers are wonderful! Thank You for letting me hear him pray! Thank You for moving him to prayer.

There hangs Mom's purse on the door knob (apron on the pencil sharpener)as though she is going to need something out of it!

She doesn't need any of these things that she loved so dearly and took care of so meticulously. They mean nothing to her now and they mean so much to us!

8/20/88

We went to the cemetery this morning. Mom has completed her time here. She is resting in the same place she was born, grew up, worshipped and went to school. It is a beautiful place to be. We walked through the cemetery and Cindy said she envied all those people their connectedness.

We took flowers to Mom's grave and then we walked back and forth between the headstones in this country cemetery. So many of the people buried there are Mom's relatives—parents, brothers, aunts, uncles, cousins. They are all connected by blood and by land. From where we stood we could see the church, the school, the house where Mom grew up and the fields of the house where she was born. Those few acres of land hold her roots. The graves around us also hold her roots. Ten years later, Daddy's grave was added. Her whole life came together in that rural Nebraska landscape. She was connected. We were all connected.

Hanover Church Cemetery where both my parents are buried.

Hanover Church, Glenvil, Nebraska where my Mom worshipped as a child.

Chapter Seven

5/19/89

The biggest adventure of my high school years was a trip to Allenspark, Colorado to church camp. My best friend and I rode the train to Denver and slept one night in a hotel. We were picked up by the two boys we loved, but who did not love us. They had driven to Colorado so they met us at the hotel in Denver and gave us a ride out to the camp. My family had vacationed in the Rockies several summers so the area was not new to me but being there in rustic cabins in the mountains with my old friends and making new friends was a great experience!

The highlight of each day was the morning time for meditation alone. We each went to separate places for thirty minutes. I went to the same place everyday where I had a wide view of the mountains and valleys. That may have been the beginning of my realization that I truly need time apart.

Thirty-some years later I returned to that camp for a Hunger Action Enabler conference. I went to that very same spot for meditation.

Thank You for this absolutely beautiful, breathtaking place for prayer time! You are present with me here and then I can see You and feel You in the mountains! How great You are! Oh, how great You are!

I wish I had looked up pictures from when we were here during our high school days! Thirty seven years ago! What seeds You were planting! O God, it seems as though You have had a special part in my life—my whole life.

Whatever it was You were and are calling me to, don't let me let You down. Keep me in Your tender mercy and use me in whatever ways You will.

God is still calling me. Still growing me.

5/20/89

My part in one of the worship services of this Hunger Action Enabler conference was to be a clown. "Christian clowning" was something of a fad during those years. I had been drawn to it and began by creating a character named Cee Cee Clown, which stood for Christ Church Clown. I did several announcements in our church as Cee Cee—mostly for the One Great Hour of Sharing—and the people responded enthusiastically. As time went on three of my friends also became clowns. Together we conducted whole worship services without words. The point of being a Christian clown was that you never spoke. We would gather in whatever room was our "dressing room" and pray. From the moment we started applying the white face until our program was over and our faces were washed, we would not speak.

The organizer of the conference knew I had been doing this so she asked me to lead the worship service as a clown. I was so nervous about doing it I could hardly think straight! Always before, I had clowned in front of people I knew and whom I knew loved me and would forgive me any foolishness. But most of the people at the conference were strangers to me. I also feared that they would not be able to worship. Here is the prayer I wrote after the service:

Dear Lord, what a day! Please forgive me for not trusting Your gift of the clown worship today! You know how nervous and almost sick I was this morning. I just wanted to cry. The clowning was so good! But only because it was Yours! Help me trust You completely!

Christ Church Clowns. I am the one second from the right.

6/8/89

Even though the tickets were extravagantly expensive, Norm and I saw the musical, "Les Miserable," three times when it was performed in Chicago. The whole theme of poverty and justice and the bravery it takes to stand up for the right thrilled both of us. The power of the music still rings in my ears. "Les Miserables" replays the old, ever recurring struggle: the struggle of right against wrong.

Thank You for the wonderful day Norm and I had yesterday! Thank you for the thrilling production of "Les Miserables" and the GREAT talent that is assembled there. The message of that play is powerful and so needs to be heard by people today.

Dear Lord our God, You are so great! You have filled Your people with noble dreams and the courage to fulfill them since the beginning of human existence. Especially today I think of the Chinese students [in Tiananmen Square] who have started a revolution for the sake of dreams of freedom. O

Lord, bless them and strengthen them and stand with them. Norm and I both thought of them during the play yesterday as those students were killed for what they believed and what they were willing to fight for.

6/10/89

Dear Lord my God, how great You are! It has been a long time since I have let two days go by without having this quiet time—when I write and try to listen. Will I feel Your Presence again? Please forgive me, my dear Lord and Savior and help me feel Your Presence again! Always, every day, at all times and places, You are my life and my breath and my strength. You are my everything!

Without You I am nothing!
THANK YOU!
THANK YOU!
THANK YOU!

Just to bask in Your presence like a kitten in the sun or like the patches of Shasta daisies in Massachusetts that turn their faces to the sun and follow it from dawn to dusk.

If I could dwell in Your Presence like that the rest of my days I would be so grateful and all the glory and praise would be to You.

I want to be a tool in Your hand, O Lord, and whatever You can do with me, I would be most pleased and honored and all the glory and praise would be to You!

It was a year ago today that I was ordained. Praise be to You again for that blessing, for that honor. Take me and use me, O Lord!

6/21/89

We were on vacation in the Northeast and were in Vermont when I wrote the following prayer. The historical places of Boston impressed me so much and the beginnings of our country were much on my mind.

What a great heritage you have given our country! What great things the U.S. could do for the oppressed people of the world if we were willing to act out what we say we believe, what we say we stand for. Sam Adams' "preached" that wealth and materialism were dulling the desire for liberty

1   Sam Adams was a delegate from Massachusetts to the Continental Congress.

of the people of Massachusetts. Is that happening today? If someone wants liberty for themselves they must want it for all. What is the difference between liberty and freedom?

7/27/89

O Lord, when I feel the power of Your Presence with me so strongly and for several minutes I marvel at the power and rejoice in it but I also wonder why. Why me and for what purpose?

"Because of your faithfulness." --God

It is a gift to me, because I have been faithful in seeking You. Thank You Lord, and praise be to You that I have been faithful. Forgive me in my _unfaithfulness_.

"It's a gift, it's a reward, it's a result." --God

How long could I sustain it, if I tried?

"I am always with you." --God

I am afraid to try to feel Your Presence constantly because I am not sure how I would act or function if I was as open to You in daily situations as I am in this quiet time. That's pretty silly, isn't it! Think what would happen to people and to situations if I could be a bearer of Your Presence to them. I do sometimes but it is so erratic.

"Maybe I move in you more than you think I do." --God

I know You do, but I want more. Maybe You do it that way on purpose so that I won't become proud and arrogant. I just want to be useful to You, Lord!

"Right now, just enjoy!" --God

As I get better at practicing Your Presence will I know, recognize others who are practicing it?

"Yes, but you will also know evil." --God

I know the only way I can meet that and stand up to it is by more practicing Your Presence. You know that sometimes I am afraid of these feelings and insights that they may not be You but may be or become mental illness or possession. It is so good and You are so good—help me cling to You always.

7/28/89

The words of Joseph Campbell, the great student and teacher of world mythology, entered my spirit deeply by way of the conversations he had with the journalist, Bill Moyers. These conversations were originally filmed for a PBS special, "The Power of Myth," in 1985 and 1986 at George Lucas' Skywalker Ranch and later at the Museum of Natural History in New York. The twenty-four hours of film of the two great men in conversation had to be cut to six hours to fit the TV time. Betty Sue Flowers, with the blessing of both men, edited a book by the same name. She worked some of what was cut out of the original tapes into the conversation to be shown on TV.

> CAMPBELL: I think of mythology as the homeland of the muses, the inspirers of art, the inspirers of poetry. To see life as a poem and yourself participating in a poem is what the myth does for you.
>
> MOYERS: A poem?
>
> CAMPBELL: I mean a vocabulary in the form not of words but of acts and adventures, which connotes something transcendent of the action here, so that you always feel in accord with the universal being.[2]

These few words from their talk still have the power to puzzle me and to see my life and the lives of others in a new light.

I heard an echo of my reality in this but couldn't grasp it at first. It is just so beautiful! Now I think it does mean being a part of God's plan for the world, of being part of the epic poem that is acted out as You move in history to see Your will done. I am part of that. Everyone is part of the poem but not everyone one knows it. In fact very few know it. How sad! What wonderful knowledge and feelings they are missing.

Maybe that is an explanation, a way of explaining the peace You have brought and are continually bringing to my life. It gets to be less and less of a struggle, and a drive as I let You take over in the hope and the realization that You can and do work through me, that You do use me. And then is

---

2   Betty Sue Flowers, editor, *The Power of Myth, Joseph Campbell with Bill Moyers,* (NY, Doubleday, 1988), 55.

when I "feel in accord with the universal being," then I actually feel the power of Your presence.

You are so great and so wonderful! Thank You from the bottom of my heart and the depth of my soul for Your Presence with me. There is no greater Gift and I cherish it and fall down and worship You for it!

By the way

Since I don't know the source of this quote, I hope for grace and leniency if the original writer happens to read this book. It is just too good a quote not to share.

> As Christians who fail to tend inner stories, we increase
> the danger of a rift between what we believe and how we
> live. The challenge is to make theology autobiographical,
> be a story, not just to subscribe to one.

These words describe what I have found in my prayer journals, even though I would not have thought to say it that way. These pages describe my struggle to live my theology. Each day I tell God's glory and give thanks. Often I confess and always I am seeking God's way for my life. Each step of the way. More and more turning things over to God. Seeing God more and more in every aspect of what I do.

8/8/89

The TV news last night said that Mickey Leland is missing in a plane in Africa. Oh, Lord, help him be alive and safe. He is such a champion in Congress for hungry people. Oh, Lord, by Your grace may he be alive! Just now the news said that his plane took off in bad weather from Addis Ababa yesterday and hasn't been heard from since. Fourteen other people were on it. He was on his way to a refugee camp. Oh, Lord, protect them all and keep them safe. I feel like I know him, like a friend and an ally.

A close reading of the history of our country shows that members of Congress and Senators have often been held in contempt. Contemporary polls show that to be true today. Indeed, some of them are self-serving scoundrels. But there have been, are now and always will be great, self-giving men and women among them. People of great integrity and compassion. People who have the best interests of our country and the world at heart.

Mickey Leland, who was a member of the House of Representatives from 1979 until his death in 1989, was one of the great ones. Leland felt strongly that hunger could be ended. He lamented, "I cannot get used to hunger and desperate poverty in our plentiful land. There is no reason for it, there is no excuse for it, and it is time that we as a nation put an end to it."

In 1984 Leland (D-TX), Benjamin Gilman (R-NY) and Tony Hall (D-OH) authored a bill that established the House Select Committee on Hunger. The mandate of the Committee was to "conduct a continuing, comprehensive study and review of the problems of hunger and malnutrition." That work continues today in the Congressional Hunger Center whose motto is "Fighting Hunger by Developing Leaders."

8/9/89

Oh, Lord, help Mickey Leland still be alive. Protect him. The paper said that a small plane was seen circling over a remote airfield that doesn't have any communications. Oh, Lord, please may that be Your miracle for him, for us, for all the poor and hungry people whom he works so hard to help.

On August 14, it was confirmed that he died in the plane crash. He was leading a mission to an isolated refugee camp, Fugnido, in Ethiopia, which sheltered thousands of unaccompanied children fleeing the civil conflict in neighboring Sudan.

8/20/89

Dear Lord, You have taken me to some truly beautiful places and this place on Puget Sound is certainly one of them. Fern and I took "water side" rooms and the view from my window is fantastic. From the great open spaces of Ghost Ranch to the Colorado Rockies to the Maine Coast to Puget sound—Your handiwork is marvelous and mysterious and You are greatly to be praised! Your Presence with me is the same wherever I go! You are greatly to be praised!

Being at Highlands camp this summer reminded me of my high school days there. Being in this Redemptorist Retreat Center reminds me of my trip with Ann Goodrich to the convent of which she had been a part in Great Bend, Kansas. The crucifix is on the wall and one very Catholic picture.

O Lord my God, how great You are! O Lord Your wonderful Presence swells my heart, fills my body! Thank You! Praise be to You! I love You and want to be Your faithful servant always.

Here You have called me to be on this Eco-Justice Task Force for the General Assembly and it just dawned on me that the work we are doing will help save these very beauties that have meant so much to me spiritually.

O Lord, may Your filling of my heart with Your Presence not be in vain. Continue to fill me, increase my receptivity and make me brave and courageous and able to speak clearly and powerfully on the issues we discuss. You can do so much through me if I will cooperate. Help me cooperate—always for Your glory and the sake of Your creation! If only I could retreat in the middle of the discussions and feel Your Presence and think and speak from that.

9/1/89

Dear Lord, my God, my dearest friend and companion. I feel like crying this morning. I am so tired and my body hurts so much! Yesterday I drove to Hattie's, worked in my office, cleaned the small bathroom, played for choir practice, cleaned the lower kitchen cabinets, and made tomato juice and fixed one of the dining room chairs. I guess it is no wonder that I am tired, but that makes me want to cry. I feel like I need to work that hard to keep up with things. But I sure have to get over that.

Prayers of this nature constantly recur in my prayer journals, although the anguish and anxiety have lessened. Now, in retirement, I am finally learning that not everything has to be done right now and much of what I used to do doesn't have to be done at all. I used to clean my twenty-four hundred foot raised ranch-style house every week. Now I clean my little fourteen hundred square foot house a room a day, once in awhile.

There was always a counterbalance to the prayers of exhaustion, such as this one which I wrote shortly after the one above.

You have made my life so good. You have given me such a large measure of peace and satisfaction that things like that don't bother me nearly as much or eat at me like they used to. I praise You and thank You and ask You to continue to mold me and make me!

How great You are!

I love the things that You have called me to do that can rightly take precedence over the myriad details of housekeeping. Thank You that You have so gifted me—take me and use me.

9/14/89

Lord my God, how great You are! Every night You give us rest and every morning life anew. Praise be to You for Your great love and ingenuity in creation! The way the seasons come and go, the way Your marvelous variety of creatures are in tune with the seasons, the way You act in our individual lives and in the whole of creation is wonderful to behold!

You are great and wonderful beyond my ability to think or to say. Before all Your greatness and Your power I would dare to confess before You my sins, being sure of Your forgiveness even though I deserve Your wrath.

9/26/89

Dear Lord, my God, how great You are! You who created all things—plant and animal and mineral and sea creatures; You who set the seasons in motion and the sun and the moon and the stars to make their appointed rounds; You who down through history has moved in the lives of human beings and the happenings between nations. You are so great! You move with justice and compassion and love. You are great and greatly to be praised to the ends of the earth, now and forever more! Let every knee bow and every heart confess that Jesus Christ is Lord!

And yet You dwell in <u>my</u> heart. Oh, miracle of miracles and wonder of wonders! That You should care for me! That You should want me for Your servant, Your child!

Love so amazing, so divine!

10/18/89

Dear Lord my God, how great You are! You are steadfast and true and always dependable, even as I am flighty and changeable and sometimes dependable.

Forgive me that my thoughts this morning are all over my world of existence and that I didn't even wake up praising You or meditating on Your work in the shower. Feeling Your Presence, brings rest and peace to my soul and meaning and wholeness to my life.

10/19/89

Thank You for putting up with me.

"That would try the patience of a saint." I don't know where I have heard that saying but it struck me this morning as I wrote about my trying the patience of God. This praise of God "putting up with me" was occasioned by my prayers for healing for two dear friends. One was dying of metastasized breast cancer and the other was dying of colon cancer. Obviously, both of them wanted to be healed and I wanted them to be. I asked God for healing for both of them.

In the course of my reading about prayers for healing I read that you should visualize the diseased part of the body as healthy and whole. I had prayed that way for my mother and it didn't work. Now I tried it with Shirley's colon cancer and it didn't work for her either.

I wanted to believe that God would heal these two beloved women, but at the same time I knew it wouldn't happen. Look how I had prayed for healing for my children and it didn't happen. Look how I had prayed for healing for my mom and Hattie and they died anyway.

Some people believe if you pray for something your prayers will be answered unless you don't have enough faith. What a load of guilt that puts on you! So why do I keep praying? I was/am trying to be a righteous woman and yet if this is true I am not righteous enough. Some people suggest that healing depends on the righteousness of the one being prayed for. It becomes a gauge of their righteousness—if they are healed they must be righteous. If they are not healed they must be unrighteous.

The trouble with this theory about prayer is that it sets God up as a parent who makes his love and care of his children dependent on the behavior of the child. If his child does well this kind of father loves her and nurtures her. If she is disobedient he withholds his love. It doesn't take into account God's complete and perfect love for each human being. God is love.

"Thank you for putting up with me." God's great patience with my repeated prayers and pleas for understanding, helped me know that God is on a journey with me.

10/25/89

Heaven and earth are full of Thee! Heaven and earth are praising Thee, O Lord most High! And so are my heart and my soul! You are greater and more wonderful than my lips can say, than my mind can think, or than my soul can feel and yet I know a measure of Your Presence. I love You and praise You!

11/8/89

Dear Lord my God, how great You are! You are so great! You are high and lifted up! You are majestic and grand and awesome more than I can think or say! And yet You guard over us as a mother hen guards her chicks. You are worthy to receive all honor and glory and power and praise and thanksgiving! I adore You Almighty God! I love you, Lord Jesus Christ! I welcome and ask for You, Holy Spirit! You are my life and my breath and my strength! You are my reason for being!

11/11/89

Dear Lord, my God, how great you are! You are so great and so wonderful, so loving and patient and kind and just! Praise be to You, O Lord, God of Justice. Yesterday the East Germans opened the Berlin Wall! They let people pass into West Berlin even without visas. . .and most of them returned home! They let them stand on top of it, dance on top of it and to chop and dig at it. Praise be to You, O Lord! What wonderful things are happening even in the midst of all the pain and violence and ugliness.

Little did I dream when I wrote this prayer the day the wall came down that someday I would walk a path where it had been with a couple who literally helped knock it down. Manfred and Gudren had lived alongside the wall, enduring the hardships it caused for the twenty five years it stood there.

When we visited them in Berlin in 2005, they took us for a long walk on the path that marked where the wall had stood. They told us how they had taken hammers and picks and alongside their neighbors, tore down the odious thing. They told stories of the hardship its presence caused and of the difficulties its removal presented.

What good are walls? Today Israel is building a wall to separate Palestinian people from Israeli people. The United States is building a wall to separate Mexican people from people of the United States. Sometimes walls are invisible, but they are just as divisive as these ugly concrete symbols of fear and hatred. The Apostle Paul said Jesus broke down the dividing walls of hostility. So much for that piece of Scripture today!

1/23/90

Wintertime in Chicago, with strong winds and subzero temperatures, made prayers for homeless people part of daily prayer.

Oh, Lord, be with cold people today. Help them find warmth and shelter. Be with warm people today. Help them care enough about the cold ones to make some sacrifices.

2/10/90

When I saw the book, *Clowning in Rome,* on the bookstore shelf, I didn't hesitate to buy it. Henri Nouwen, the author of the book, is one of mine and Norm's favorite writers of spiritual literature. I knew this book had to be good, really good for Christian clowns. I didn't even read the table of contents or leaf through it. I just bought it. What a surprise it was when I sat down to read it! It was about celibacy! It didn't teach me much about clowning nor did it convince me to be celibate. It did teach me much about God's journey with me.

> ...solitude "is the place where God reveals himself as God-with-us, as the God who is our creator, redeemer, and sanctifier, as the God who is the source, the center and the purpose of our existence, as the God who wants to give himself to us with an unconditional, unlimited, and unrestrained love, and as the God who wants to be loved by us with all our heart, all our soul, and all our mind. Solitude is indeed the place of the great encounter, from which all other encounters derive their meaning.[3]

Nouwen helped me understand that my yearning for solitude and the accompanying search were not selfish and neglectful activities. The search for solitude is the search for God-with-me. It is the yearning for God who has created human beings for friendship with him.

4/7/90

Dear Lord, our God, go with us (Dave, Jan, Paul and me) as we go to talk with Congressman Hyde about the Harvest of Peace Resolution. He is reported to have said that he is in favor of it, but that it doesn't go far enough. Help us speak to him as equals. We are all four faith-filled people and we go in Your name. Use us in Your plan for fullness of life for all of Your children everywhere—including us and Henry Hyde.

Congressman Henry Hyde's home office was in a school building converted to offices in Glen Ellyn, Illinois, in his district, IL 06. As we drove into the parking lot there were no other cars there. When we tried the doors, they were locked. Four of us Bread for the World members had scheduled a meeting with Mr. Hyde for that morning. It was my first visit to a member of congress and I was very nervous. I actually prayed that he would not show up and we could just go home.

Finally, he and his aide drove up, got out of their cars and went into the building. We followed and were ushered into his office. He was a tall, barrel-chested man and he sat behind a huge desk. The other

3   Henri Nouwen, *Clowning in Rome (New York, Image Books, 1979) p. 27.*

furniture in the room was small—like that in model homes—so when we sat down on the couch we were looking up at him. We had met for breakfast and agreed on what part of the bill each of us would present. The meeting took on a strange, dreamlike quality when he began to argue our points with his aide who was saying what we thought he would say. It was like a bad cop/good cop routine with us as observers.

We visited him every year after that. Because of his co-sponsorship one of the bills for which we lobbied him passed the House of Representatives unanimously. An important part of influencing your Senator or Congressman is establishing a relationship with him or her. Sometimes we visited him in his office in Washington D.C. Once when Norm and I had an appointment with him there, he was on the floor of the House and his aide took us over to talk with him in the cloakroom/lounge just outside the House of Representatives' chambers.

Lobbying Mr. Hyde and other members of Congress was an intentional part of God's journey with me. Not only did I learn about the workings of our lawmakers, but through those experiences, God gave me bravery and a voice for the poor and hungry people I wanted to serve. God also taught me to treat opponents with respect and that, when you do, in most cases, you will receive respect in return.

4/9/90

Dear Lord, our God, You are so great! You are so powerful and so mighty, so strong and so patient! You have given us such a great, indescribable gift in coming to us as one of us! To live among us as Your Son, Jesus Christ. And then to suffer and die for us! How great You are! How full of love You are!

And then, O Lord, that You want to dwell with ME! Miracle of miracles.

Wonder of wonders! That You love ME and have work for ME to do. What I must understand is that what I do is not Your reason for loving me. You love me for who You created me to be. Help me know that in the depths of my being.

Even as I am learning that You make me more and more useful to You as I depend more and more on You.

6/16/90

Mother Theresa says she wants to be a pencil in Your hand—You do the writing. O Lord, that is what I want to be: a pencil in your hand.

6/19/90

This prayer is the story of the second angel God sent to me. The first was the man standing outside the Jewel store who told me I was divine. God sent him to show me my worth. God sent this woman/angel to comfort and bless me. It was after a presbytery staff meeting at which a young man who worked in a violent neighborhood had expressed his fears about the dangers that come to the inner city in the summer. He worked with youth on the streets, organizing softball teams and forming choirs. Summer was the most dangerous time in his neighborhood because the kids had nothing to do and many of them carried guns. It was a place of constant gang activity.

Peter's telling of the violence of life in his neighborhood made me want to cry and the whole self-centeredness of some of the staff added to it. I talked with Peter some more after the meeting and then went into an empty office and cried. I felt so helpless and inadequate to accomplish any change.

Usually I take the bus to the train but I decided to get out of the office and cry as I walked. So I did and I pleaded with You to let me know what I can do, where and how I can serve You better.

When I got to the corner of Adams and Green there was a homeless woman. She had been just standing there but then she started walking toward me. We said hello and commented about how hot it was. She was so sweaty that even her hair was wet. She asked if I would give her fifty cents for coffee or coke. I reached a five dollar bill first so I gave it to her. She was so surprised and happy! She hugged me and said, "God bless you!" and I blessed her too.

I told her I wished I could do more than give her money—like find her a job. Then she showed me the pencil drawings she had in her bag and the first one—unfinished—was the face of Jesus!

Lord, help me find her again! Please! I want that picture and I want to try to sell some others for her. Instead of thinking of that while I was with her I said how gifted she is and then some dumb thing about famous artists being poor. Forgive me, Lord!

"That's okay. It was still your blessing." --God

She was such a blessing to me. I believe that it was You hugging me. I do believe that! I want to be a blessing to her!

…She blessed me! She literally blessed me!

Several days later she was still on my mind.

I just got out a picture of Jesus that I love from a movie advertisement so that if I find her I will ask her to draw it for me. Am I crazy, Lord. There was a young man at the construction site on Adams and Canal who smiled and said hello to me. He was dark haired and bearded. At the time I thought how strange it was he spoke to me and that maybe You sent him to bless me as well. He looked just like this picture of Jesus. There were about five workers standing on the street where I had to walk to get into the covered walkway. None of them spoke.

Help me think about all of this and feel and learn what You want me to feel and learn and to grow in love and service to You.

I never saw her again. One of my friends was an ombudsman for homeless people so he knew most of them in that neighborhood. He said he didn't know about her right off hand, but that he would search for her. He never found her.

8/31/90

Hattie died yesterday.

9/1/90

Dear Lord our God, how great You are! Hattie has passed on to You, to be fully in Your Presence. I am sorry that I didn't get to see her again, but it is my own fault. If she had needed me You would have sent me. I don't feel bad about not getting her book written. If I should, help me know it. She and I were soul sisters, but she did more for me than I did for her, she for us more than we for her. She was truly one of the greatest gifts You have given me for my prayer life.

Please use me to bless others in the same way—not for my glory but for Yours and for bringing people close to You. She approached You in a very different way from mine. She came with such confidence almost demanding what she wanted and yet giving You all the glory and thanksgiving.

11/10/90

Guide and protect and prosper the people I met in the West Town area last night. Guide and protect and prosper that neighborhood and all its people. Mayor Daley says that the river should not be a dumping place for industrial waste, but that it should be lined with beautiful homes and neighborhoods and parks and communal areas. He is right in the first phrase, but Lord why can't he see that it can be made the second part of his sentence and still have industry that will provide jobs so that the people who work there can live there and the people who live there can work there. It is so unfair! It is so unjust! Soften the hearts of the people in power. Give them wisdom and a sense of justice and compassion.

11/12/90

When I sit here and seek Your Presence and Your Power in my heart it is not like I am begging You to come. I believe so strongly that You are already here and my work and my effort is to prepare my heart to receive You. Sometimes I feel You so strongly that I cry and feel so full and then I stop and wonder how much further I could go.

If I were able to open my heart to You completely, what would happen? What would it be like?

And then I wonder why You should visit me this way! For what purpose? Is it for some grand finale somewhere in the future or is it for what is happening in my life all along, day by day. I think secretly I hope it is for some "glamorous power" when You deem me ready. But what could be greater or more miraculous than what You are already doing in my life!

You have wrought such miraculous changes in me! Please continue to do so always for Your glory and for the sake of Your people who are in great need.

In Jesus' name and for His sake. Amen and Amen. I love You, Lord! I love you!

1/16/91

Dear Lord, thank You for each passing hour without war! By Your grace and Your mighty power may it never come! Hear the voice of Your people crying. Forgive us, Almighty God, for we have gotten ourselves into this crisis! Our actions and thoughts have led very certainly to this situation. Forgive us, Lord and save us!

The Arabs cry in the name of Allah. Is that You, God of Abraham and Sarah, God of Isaac and Rebecca, God of Joseph and Rachel? Is that You? Do we look as vicious to them as they do to us?

On this very day the air campaign against military leadership targets in Kuwait and Iraq, concentrating on Baghdad, began. This was the first Iraq war. George H. W. Bush was president.

1/17/91

Dear Lord our God, Almighty God, Creator, Redeemer and Sustainer of the whole universe, You are greater and more powerful than any of the men, than all of the men on the face of this earth. But You would not use Your power for death and destruction, for hatred, as they are doing today.

What have they wreaked without even a thought of its after-effects, without even a care for the earth or the earth's people. Their one goal is to destroy one man, Saddam Hussein and they will destroy every thing in their path to get to him.

Oh, Lord, forgive us and make us better. George H. W. Bush raves about Hussein's atrocities against the Kuwaitis, when in our recent past is our invasion of Panama and of Grenada and our covert war in Nicaragua.

You are our almighty, omnipotent, omnipresent, omniscient God and You are love and compassion, life and beauty.

Bring whatever good You will out of this great evil, whatever good You can.

1/18/91

Secretary of Defense Cheney was telling how efficient our planes etc. had been and he said Congress had paid for them and he hopes that when it comes time to pay for replacements, Congress will remember how efficient they were. Replacement! More billions! 1 billion dollars a day for this war!

Oh, Lord, where is the "new world order" that President Bush talks about. What is the new world order? This is only more of the same on a larger and larger scale.

2/11/91

Be with the leaders of our country and help them seriously want to end the war in the Persian Gulf. It is such a massive destruction of a place in Your creation and of people of Your creation! Forgive us, Lord, and make us better.

3/3/91

After hurting my back picking a newspaper up off the floor, I was confined to bed for two weeks. The muscle relaxant that was prescribed for me made it easier to bear the pain, but it made me silly. Several times I called the office to tell Earnestine what I needed her to do. I thought I was thinking clearly and keeping on with my work, but after I was back in the office, she said I told her so many strange things.

Where am I now and who am I now that I can't do so many things? I like being home most evenings and resting during the day. But I don't want to get lazy. Oh, Lord my God, who am I and where am I? I know I am somebody—but who?

Maybe this is the Feldene making me nutty.

Is it a matter of just getting through each day and not asking any long term questions until something is settled with my back?

I don't like things the way they are with me.

What am I good for to You, Lord? What am I good for to You?

3/4/91

Oh, my Lord, please forgive me. If it is the Feldene and the pain, I want it to stop, to go away. If it is my wanting more than I have, more than I am, please, please forgive me!

Should I stop taking the Feldene or just go on and try to stay sane and keep from whining and crying for another two weeks.

I am a mess, Lord! You know what a mess I am!

Help me, Oh Lord! Help me!

I hate, hate, hate being limited in this way

What a whiner I was/am. Every one of you reading this book know people who are so bound by illness and pain that they can't leave their beds or their homes for months or even years. Maybe among you are people limited in such a way. Some wallow in their plight, but many others live their lives to the fullest and in so doing inspire hope for all of us.

4/2/91

Fifty-five years old today and I am still becoming somebody! Is that the way it is supposed to work! Whether or not it is, I like it! It is quite often painful, but I like it.

O Lord my God, You are so great! How great Thou art! Thank You for making me who You are making me. Help me cooperate! Help me work with You. My own birthday wish, prayer for this coming year would be that I spend ever more time aware of Your Presence and Your power.

I remember when I was fifteen, I thought when I got to be sixteen, I would have it made. When I was twenty, I thought when I got to be twenty-one, I would be an adult. When I was twenty-nine, I thought when I got to be thirty I would be full grown. That was full grown in the sense of being who I was going to be and knowing God the way I wanted to know God. Thus it came as a surprise that when I reached fifty-five, I still didn't know for sure who I was. I was still, and am still, becoming. That is the excitement of being on a journey with God!

Chapter Eight

7/18/91

The Sun Dancer said, "Here I am, Lord. Have mercy on me so that I may pray for the people." The sense of God's presence in my heart was incredible as I heard this Dakota Sioux, Presbyterian minister speak about the meaning for him of the Sun Dance. He was addressing a plenary session of the Churchwide Gathering of Presbyterian Women in Ames, Iowa.

The Sun Dance is an ancient ritual of the Sioux tribes in which men, and sometimes women, pierce the flesh on their chests with pieces of bone attached to rawhide thongs attached to a pole in the center of the arena. The ritual begins with the dancers close to the pole. As the days pass the men dance further and further out from the pole until their flesh is torn. They neither eat nor drink as they dance staring at the sun. It appeared to be such a barbaric practice that for a time it was outlawed by the government of the United States. However, it seems to me, it is similar to Christian practices in some parts of the world where worshipper flagellate themselves, especially during Lenten observances.

Does he have to hurt himself so badly in order to pray for the people?

Do I have to hurt myself so badly to pray for the people? I already hurt for them. . .I don't bleed...I don't give up food for them...Some people, most people don't hurt at all for the people.

Should I hurt more in order to pray for the people?
What is Your answer, O Lord our God?
 What is Your answer, Lord Jesus Christ, who was torn and bled
  and died on the cross for the people?
You who went to that "tree" willingly and set the pattern
 that the Sun Dancer is following.
What is Your answer, O Lord our Suffering Savior?
 Do You want him to hurt so badly?
 Do You want me to hurt so badly?
No! No! No! You don't want anyone to hurt so badly.
 You don't want starving people to hurt so badly.
 You don't want schizophrenic people to hurt so badly.
 You don't want torture victims to hurt so badly.
 You don't want anyone to hurt so badly.
But it happens.
 You did it for us.
 Now You do it with us.
 Here I am, Lord.
Have mercy on me so that I can pray for the people.

7/28/91

Dear Lord, forgive me for all my sins! Have mercy on me, stay near me stay in me even as I fall short of what You want me to be, of who You want me to be. I feel awful this morning and I know it is because I haven't given You special time. I haven't drawn from Your love in a consecrated way each day!

Oh, Lord, without You I would perish! Without You I would wither and die! You are my life and my strength and my breath! You are my reason for being!

When I let days pass without writing to You, without spending time with You, it is like injuring myself, like committing suicide! Forgive me, Lord. And please never, never leave me.

7/29/91

It is always good to have another person affirm my beliefs and my feelings. The affirmation is especially powerful when the person, in this case Ted Loder, says, in words far grander and more poetic than mine, what I believe.

> Thank you
> for the sharp senses
> of the timeless stirring in my time,
> and your praise in my heart;
> for the undeniable awareness, quick as now,
> that the need of you,
> is the truth of me,
> and your presence with me
> is the truth of you,
> which sets me free
> for others,
> for joy,
> for your grace...my life...forever.[4]

7/30/91

I have always been careful to be nice. I grew up trying to avoid conflict at all costs. I would not press a point theologically no matter how important it was to me, if I could see that there would be conflict over it. Expressing my political ideas as Hunger Action Enabler, sometimes produced situations of conflict. One man, in front of an adult Sunday School class, told me I was a liar. It was during a discussion which I was leading about the effect of budget cuts made to entitlement programs for the poor being made under President Ronald Reagan. My thoughts about God and women have also been sharply criticized. As I have expressed the need for feminine names for God, people have told me that what I say is wrong because God has no gender so we should continue to speak about him as male.

Again, Loder has good advice for me.

---

4   Ted Loder, *Guerillas of Grace,* (San Diego, CA., Luramedia, 1984), p.43.

Help my unbelief that I may have courage to dare to love
the enemies I have the integrity to make.[5]

As I try to put God's journey with me into words, this quote sums
it all up.

O God, make of me some nourishment for these starved
times, some food for my brothers and sisters who are hungry
for gladness and hope that being bread for them, I may also
be fed and be full.[6]

8/19/91

What do my prayers avail?
    "The power of my Presence." --God
    Yes, Lord! Yes, Lord! That is good for me! So good
for me! Thank You and praise be to You!
    What difference do my prayers make for Jim and his situation? What
difference do they make? You promise to answer prayer. I pray fervently and
faithfully. What difference do my prayers make?
    "Time." --God
    Does that mean that Motorola is going to hire him back when Your time
is right? I could live with that, provided it is soon. What would Hattie say?
She would go on praying, believing her prayers would be answered. But she
would also say that You make a way where there is no way. That You open
a door where there is no door. I wish I could sit and pray with her.
    Oh, Lord, I want Your will to be done for Jim, but I want it my way
and now. Thank you for Your patience with me. Thank You for loving me
and dwelling with me even when I am mouthy with You.

8/24/91

Dear Lord my God, I am such a baby! Please forgive me and help me to be
different. I went to the doctor for this cold or whatever it is and he told me
to rest so it doesn't get worse. I had to try hard to keep from crying when I
left his office! I don't want to rest. I want to do things—and already that
day I had practiced the organ, grocery shopped, washed two loads of clothes,

---

5   Ibid., p.53.
6   Ibid., p. 67.

been to the bank and the vegetable market, and washed the veggies! And I wanted to cry because I couldn't do things. Dear Lord, forgive me!

When I did get to the point of laying there in bed, I asked myself the question: What is the worst possible thing that could happen today if I didn't work at my job? I couldn't think of anything.

9/11/91

I slept so well and so warm last night. Thank You. My back still hurts this morning but it doesn't feel like a crisis. Thank You. As I thought about those gifts and fixed my breakfast in my nice warm, clean kitchen stocked with food, I thought about all the people who had to sleep on the street last night: how tired and stiff and cold and hungry and dirty they must be. Another day with nowhere to go stretches before them and then another night like last night. Oh, Lord, how can I ask You to keep them in Your care when it is our fault that they are there. How can I expect You to change it all when the rest of Your people have other priorities.

11/6/91

I didn't remember that I wrote about the Regional Organizer job before I called Bread for the World and found out—much to my surprise!! that the salary is an amount that would be good for us. Please guide me. I am hesitant because I am afraid that the whole hunger program will fall apart, that they won't hire a new Hunger Action Enabler. If they do I would pray that it will be someone who will do well the things I have neglected.

See, Lord, I seek and imagine glory and praise—I sit here thinking about what wonderful, glowing recommendations people would give me. Forgive me, Lord! I want to live for Your glory and to make a difference in the lives of Your hungry and hurting children.

It really is decided, isn't it. I would be foolish not to apply for the job. And once I have applied then I leave it totally in Your hands and trust that Your will will be done. I thank You and praise You, dear Lord, my savior and friend!

I haven't read prayers from Guerillas of Grace for weeks. I just picked up the book and opened it at random and this is what I read:

So, I believe, Lord; help my unbelief that I may have courage to cut free from what I have been and gamble on what I can be, and what you might laughingly do with trembling me for your incredible world.[7]

Lord, if I listen You are speaking to me in every movement, in every action! Help me listen!

12/8/91

O Lord, my God, You are so funny! That You should send—right out of the blue—this little lady who needed a ride to Chicago to erase my disappointment with my class at Wheaton First Presbyterian Church this morning, my feeling of failure. When she called I wished I hadn't answered the phone, then, I wished I had made up an excuse because I wanted to drive into the city to the performance of the Messiah by myself. I even tried to think of a way to get out of it, but I had to be there to make the announcement.

And how she ministered to me by talking about her life and her disappointments, old and new, and sharing her concerns and her viewpoints! And her listening to me and understanding me.

O Lord, You are so amazing and so mysterious. As I was getting ready to go, I had the feeling that that is what You had up your sleeve. You do indeed work in mysterious ways.

1/10/92

I am going to Washington D.C. today for a second interview. [I was being considered for the position of organizer for Illinois and Indiana with Bread for the World.] O Lord, You know how much I want this job! I do believe with my whole heart that it is what You want for me. But if it isn't, Lord, help me still be strong in my faith that you have a place for me to serve— maybe right where I am.

---

7   Ibid., 54.

1/23/92

I am to call the director of the organizing department this morning and I do believe that the job is mine. I also believe that you have called me to it. Oh, Lord, that by itself is overwhelming. But I know over these years You have grown me to be the person who will, for however long, do this work for You.

Please help me always rely on You! If I will be faithful to You in prayer and meditation, we can, by Your power accomplish so much that otherwise would be impossible.

I thank You and praise You for this new opportunity to serve You!
At 7:30 that evening I wrote:
THANK YOU, Dear Lord! Thank You! The job is mine! OURS!. You are so great!

2/18/92

I was hired for the position in late January. By the middle of February, I was in Washington, D.C. for a week of orientation. When I got to my room after the first day of orientation I sat on the edge of the bed and cried! Would the Presbytery take me back?

Oh, dear Lord, what have I done?! What have I done?! Everyone is so nice and they are pleased, even thrilled to have me working for Bread. What if I don't like it? What if I can't do it? What if I don't do a good job? What have I done?!

What have You done to me?! What have we done?!. . .

I have been up since 4 a.m. I need to go to bed. . . .

I love You, Lord. All I want to do is serve You. Please take me and use me.

2/19/92

"Truly, truly, I say to you, she who believes in me will also do the works that I do; and greater works then these will she do, because I go to the Father." (Jn 14:12)I looked for these words especially because I needed them to bolster me and keep my feet on the path.

Thank You, Lord, for the ten hours of good sound sleep and another other forty-five minutes of just lying there. I really did need that!

Please fill me! I don't even know what to pray for today.

What I think I need is the power to be who You want me to be. It is so strange to be among people whose lives and work are centered on the same things my life is centered on. It is good, but it is so new! It is so different. O Lord, I want to be GOOD at it!

Help me today to be the strong person You have grown me to be. Outward looking—not inward shrinking.

This is important work to be done and I can only do it by the power of Your presence. By You using me!

2/20/92

Still in D.C. It is such a change! They value me before they even know me! They want me to be good at it and successful and they will do everything they can to help me. They have the same concerns as top priority that I have. I am somebody here. But Lord, please forgive me when I think I am more of somebody than somebody else!

This is not an easy job You have called me to. It means being really outgoing and brave and articulate. That is really scary, but I have done really scary things before—always, always with Your help.

Let the little children come to unto me… (Matthew 19:14)

It really is for the sake of the little children that You have called me to this…and for the sake of any one whose life I can touch and through me You can change. Stay by me Lord. Never, never leave me nor let me leave You!

2/25/92

For all the promises of God find their Yes in him. That is why we utter the Amen through him, to the glory of God. But it is God who establishes us with you in Christ, and has commissioned us; he has put his seal upon us and given us his Spirit in our hearts as a guarantee. (2 Cor. 1:20)

Since I just opened to this and read it, I really believe it is an answer to the little nagging doubts and fears about my being able to do this work. I believe You have called me to it and that we are in it together. Indeed, I want to be Your hands and feet and legs and voice. I want to be Your heart and love as I work with all different kinds of people---always for Your glory and for the sake of Your poor and hungry children everywhere!

2/27/92

Dear Lord our God, my heart is full to overflowing! I just want to cry. This will be my first day in my office and I could literally cry over the feelings of excitement and anticipation and challenge and good expectations I have over starting this work. Norm prayed such a beautiful prayer for me and my work and my office yesterday when I asked him to bless it. I can't remember all of it, but I am going to think of it as being part of the air, the environment in my office and in my work.

6/12/92

The Marine Corps Memorial is located in Arlington National Cemetery in Arlington, Virginia. It is more familiarly known as the Iwo Jima memorial. When I was in Washington D.C. for a meeting of Bread for the World organizers my cousin, who lived near there, took me to see the statue.

The statue of five Marines and a Navy corpsman raising the American flag on the island of Iwo Jima during World War II is truly awesome! It gives the viewer the feeling that the men could step right off the memorial and walk away or sit down on the green grass to eat their C rations. All the major Marine Corps engagements since its founding in 1775 are inscribed on the base as a tribute to all the Marines who have given their lives in battle.

This memorial is so magnificent! But they have desecrated it by adding Grenada to the list of battles Grenada! No doubt some of the other battles listed there de-sacralize it as well. Soon they will probably add Panama and the Persian Gulf. And there is so much space left to add more! Oh, Lord, we are a sorry lot, we human beings!

Forgive us and don't deal with us as we deserve!

*Fill with the power of Your Holy Spirit all of Your children everywhere
who are the leaven in the loaf, the salt of the earth.*

Truly, all soldiers who give their lives in battle should be remembered
with beautiful memorials, but it is the soldiers who deserve the glory not
the wars. Maybe we can't name one without the other. The spin masters
of every generation are like magicians. They trick people into believing
what they want them to believe. It happens over and over again. War is
a trick perpetuated by magicians who seek to deceive the people.

For Christians there is never a good war. God says do not kill. You
serve the Prince of Peace. What are the reasons behind a war? What are
the motives for engaging in it? Maybe some can be justified more than
others. Maybe sometimes we choose evil in the service of good.

11/6/92

*Today I get to hear Matthew Fox! Thank You, Lord! I bought a tape of his
and it touches my heart and my soul so much! So deeply. You have truly sent
him to me—first was many years ago in his book,* The Musical, Mystical,
Magical Bear, *and now in person.*

From Heaven to My Heart as the title for this book seemed to come
out of nowhere. However, in reading my prayer journals, I discovered
that it didn't come from thin air. These words have been the description
of God's journey with me my whole life. One of the people who taught
me about God's nearness was Matthew Fox, a Dominican priest, who
eventually was dismissed from the order because of his teaching Creation
Theology.

> Many Americans are familiar with the definition of
> prayer as 'a lifting up of the mind and heart to God.'
> What is revealed by this definition? First, the word 'up'
> implies a total cosmology: We are below and God is
> up. ...The word 'lifting' not only carries on the upward
> direction motif (the transcendent is somehow above us
> watching over us, but it implies that we do the lifting.

It suggests that prayer is more our action than our reception.[8]

I marked this paragraph in the book with a star in the margin, but it took years and years for me to make the understanding my own. There were just fleeting glimpses of it over the years. My early prayers were to God on a throne in heaven, although I would have acknowledged that there is no place "up there." He dwelt in a far off, unknown place, entering our lives only when we asked him to.

I have come to believe, over all these years, that God dwells in the heart of each human being. We speak to and have fellowship with God when we look into our hearts. Things outside ourselves such as beloved people, beautiful sights in creation, sincere worship can inspire us to feel God. And, indeed, God is in them all, but God waits in our hearts for us to speak to her. She is continually inviting, coaxing, me into fellowship with her.

I would like to write more about the musical, mystical bear and Matthew Fox, but it will be more fun for you and more beneficial to your spiritual journey if you check him out for yourself.

11/23/92

Dreams about something in my throat choking me were frequent during the first years of my work for Bread for the World. Sometimes it was a big glob of bubble gum. Sometimes it was stuff that looked like clear blue jelly. One night it was crushed glass. I believe these dreams were reminders that I needed to get rid of whatever it was that was keeping me from speaking out when there was an opportunity or a need for me to do so.

In my dream my throat started filling up with something so I reached in and pulled out a really big piece of bubble gum, purple. I was embarrassed that I had so much gum in my mouth so I took only part of it at first and then more on a second try. By now we were out of the car and I was still pulling stuff out of my throat, but now it looked like minute steak meat. At first it was a healthy red but then it got darker like it was spoiled or spoiling

---

8   Matthew Fox, *On Becoming a Musical, Mystical Bear; Spirituality American Style*, (NY, Paulist Press, 1976.) xxxi.

I can still feel how it felt in my throat—so full like when the dentist pours plaster in my mouth to make a cast to make crowns for my teeth.

I had another dream of this nature in July of 1993.

This is only a small part of the dream, but it is all I can remember. I think I am remembering it because I have dreamed about this blue stuff before. I was in Sharon's bathroom and this stuff (like Blue Ice backrub in color but the consistency and stickiness of phlegm) was causing some trouble. I think it was in heaps on the floor. But it was also in my throat. I coughed and scraped until I got it out—a small glob but big enough to have made me feel like I was going to choke.

What is it that needs to get out of my throat, Lord? Is it something in particular that is choking me or is it the thing(s) that keeps me from being articulate.

For several weeks now I have been feeling that there is a change needed in me or is happening to me. I have even asked myself who I am now.

Part of what prompts this is how outgoing I need to be for this job with Bread and how outgoing I am! It's not who I thought I was, who I am. I need to accept this new understanding of who I am or who I am becoming.

Secondly, but also part of that—I need to be able to speak out and to speak clearly, truly and confidently. It always surprises me when people want to listen to me. Like at the bridal shower the other day when I was telling about preaching at the Unitarian Church in Crown Point. Other conversations stopped and the whole room listened. I can hardly believe when that happens.

I don't ever want to get to be the kind of talker that only stops for a breath now and then. But I do want to be able to share the really interesting things that happen to me—and the important ideas and understandings that You give me.

And still in July of 1995.

Night before last I dreamed that I had a mouthful of crushed glass. I think I have had this dream before because I remember the feeling of the glass. I wanted to swallow, but of course didn't dare. So I just held it.

Does this have to do with my having things to say and not saying them? Does it have to do with a charge You have laid on me to be outspoken and I just hold it in?

I want to speak clearly and freely and articulately. I want to make my ideas clearly understood--my ideas which I want to be Your ideas! Your words and Your thoughts.

2/25/93

O Lord, You are in my heart! I know that every time I pray even the smallest prayer. You are there to give me courage to teach and to preach, to feel what other people are feeling, to help me pray for myself and others. It is a sin that I shut You out when I am in situations where I might be strong and aggressive—situations when I shrink back and don't offer what you have given me to use for Your glory and for the sake of Your hungry and poor people everywhere.

Forgive me, Lord, and cleanse me of this sin! Help me know how to deal with it, how to change it.

7/30/93

Dear Lord our God, how great You are! You are so great! Those words are like a key that unlocks my heart and the door is opened to let You in. There has to be a better way to describe it.

It is more like they make my whole being aware of Your Presence. That You are always within me and around me, but that sometimes I am unaware. Oh, Lord, if I thought I could hold up under the ecstasy of it, I would pray that I could feel Your Presence that way all of the time.

I am aware now, more often, and in many different places initiated by many different things. I thank You and praise You and ask that You will fill me as full as You can and as often as You will.

It happens when I lay down in bed at night almost without my bidding. Praise be to You! My Lord and Savior!

8/12/93

I was visiting Sharon and Daddy in Hastings.

Daddy said yesterday that he is going to quit talking to You because You aren't listening anyway. I know about that. Please keep him close to You and strengthen and uphold him. Comfort him in his moments of despair. He was so happy after Nancy got here yesterday. He almost seemed not himself.

8/13/93

Daddy cries and prays to die. He cries and asks what he did to deserve this. He says if only the pain would stop for a few minutes. He says You are not hearing him. Maybe You aren't good, maybe You aren't there, he says. It breaks my heart to see him cry like that and I, too, want him to die. I am sorry, Lord. Forgive me for knowing that what I wrote in praising You is true, but then not acting like I believe it. There may not be a reason for his still being alive through all of this, but the point is, what is he going to do with it. How is he (and we)going to live it. It is what he has to do.

"I grieve at suffering too, you know."-- God

I don't know if Daddy can absorb such a concept, know such a reality. He sees You as above us, almighty, all powerful. Somehow looking down on us and watching. At times he sees You more as an opponent than a companion. Thank You for speaking to me. Thank You for Your Presence with me in this prayer and when I am sitting silently in his room. Help me say clearly to him what You have just shown me.

2/18/94

Dear Lord my God, how great You are! You are so great! My few and weak words that I write each day about Your greatness are so inadequate to describe or convey the sense of Your greatness! It really isn't so much what words I use as it is that I am sitting here and longing for Your Presence— which You so freely and abundantly grant to me.

5/3/94

O great and wonderful and mysterious God, what a glorious day is dawning! May the time come soon when everyone of Your human children can greet the dawn of each day with excited anticipation for what that day may hold! You have such beauty and wonder in store for us each day and we get so bogged down we don't see it. Forgive us, Lord. And then there are those who wake each day—if they have slept—to the fear of guns and bombs, to the agony of hunger and disease, to the boredom and hopelessness of a day with nothing to do.

Dear Lord, I don't know how You bear all the agony that fills Your awesome creation. Your heart must always be breaking and Your eyes always crying. Take me and use me in whatever ways You can to lessen Your suffering and that of Your children everywhere.

8/24/94

O Lord, how dare President Clinton and his advisors and the U.N. play with the lives of people the way they are doing in Haiti and Cuba. Starving the people in order to make the governments fall and when the people flee they return them or put them in concentration camps. They try to say there is a difference between a political and an economic refugee, but I can't understand that—they are being deprived of economic well-being for the sake of politics.

And the Bosnian government letting the people in Sarajevo suffer more than they need to because it wants to receive foreign aid money.

And Bob Dole et al making a mockery of a crime bill that might save lives in our streets.

And the "Christians" on Christian radio who live the works of the flesh but do it in Your name.

How dare they!

Take me and use me, Lord. If I don't learn to speak out and speak out clearly of what use will I be to You! I excuse myself by saying that religion and politics are topics that people don't want to talk about. We've been taught not to, but they need to be talked about. And maybe people, at least some people want to.

9/5/94

I am reading Ted Loder's *Wrestling With the Light* and Barbara G. Walker's *The Crone*. Loder's prayers are so beautiful and touch such a deep place in me—they are radical. So is *The Crone*[9] and I am not at all sure that I

---

9   Barbara G. Walker, *The Crone; Woman of Age, Wisdom, and Power*, (San Francisco, Harper, 1985).

want to be as radical as it might lead me to be. Walker claims and seems to prove that the Trinity before Father, Son and Holy Ghost was something like Virgin, Mother, and Crone or Creator, Preserver and Destroyer. Guide me, Lord, in the paths You want me to think and believe.

This was a frightening path to be on. History is liberally sprinkled with stories of people who have fallen into insanity and taken others with them over their religious thinking. Not that I think these two authors are insane, but at the time I read them I had misgivings about where all of this might take me.

9/15/94

4 a.m. At Chris's in Washington. I never call You Father except once in awhile in public prayers. But neither do I call You Mother. I talk about it: that God is Mother as much as Father, but when I pray in my heart, or in the book I don't say Dear Mother in Heaven, Dear Lord our Mother, Dear Lord and Mother, Dear Mother our God, something is happening to me, something is changing in me. Please let it happen. Make me open. Open me up. Help me keep thinking and feeling about this.

The old woman's face on the book, The Crone, keeps looking at me. Whenever I move her, she looks at me. Kindly, but strongly and firmly. Saying You are Mother does not make You less than You are—You are still great and Your greatness is unsearchable. Is this as far as I can go this a.m.?

7 a.m. Started another prayer with Precious Mother. It is almost as though over these past months and years I have been making progress (in terms of my personal growth and my appreciation of myself as a woman) and now I am at a real turning point. It is a revelation, but not like a great flash or flooding of light, but rather like I've walked right into a wall, an obstacle. That I need to do some really deep, difficult changing here. It is even hard to put into words, God my Mother.

I came from Your womb and You know me through and through, my future and my past, my here and now.

Are You still here? You, the powerful, warm, expanding, potentially overwhelming Presence who resides in my heart and around me and to whom my heart is opened when I cry "Oh, Lord my God, You are so Great! How great You are and Your greatness is unsearchable." Yes! Yes! Yes! You are! You are one and the same, aren't You! You are my great God and my Precious Mother—which only makes You that much greater than I knew before! That You should reveal Yourself to me in this way is wonderful beyond words.

10/4/94

Dear Lord, what a goose I am! Delusions of grandeur! And You are so great and so good and all-knowing! If only I would learn to pay attention to You! And to Your trustworthiness! The speech I thought was going to be to four hundred people in a large auditorium was to forty in a large conference room! And there I was with an hour long, finely tuned speech! What a goose I am! Please forgive me, Lord, and help me to go with Your flow more faithfully.

10/5/94

Dear Lord our God and Precious Mother, You are so great! How great You are! And Your greatness is unsearchable! I want to know about You as Precious Mother, but it certainly is scary and in a way upsetting. Take me a step at a time. That is the way You have brought me this far so help me be patient and not rush ahead. My main fear is that of losing You, Jesus! I love You and adore You! You are my Savior (what does that mean in the new terms?) and my Friend. You, Oh, Lord, Father/Mother, Son and Sophia are my life and my breath and my strength. You are my reason for being. Please never desert me or let me fall away from You.

Mother God/Father God: not separate but one; not one or the other but both together. Mother/Father God. If we can describe God as three persons all at once why can't we describe God as both sexes at once?

1/27/95

That little old lady sits at the train station every day (in the corner formed by the bridge and the wall). She is there every day that I go so, I assume, she is always there from early until late. In the good weather she sings, plays toy instruments and talks to passersby.

Yesterday in the wind and the snow she sat huddled on a little camp stool with her head down, holding her two pound coffee can to collect alms from passersby. People bring her bags of cast off clothing but she can't eat them or pay rent with them.

How much money does she get a day? If even 15 people gave her a dollar each that wouldn't be too bad—if she has a cheap room. Tens of thousands of people pass her.

Something audacious about her. Maybe she gets a hundred or two hundred dollars a day. That would be much better than I make.

But that is not the point actually. She has her soul to care for and I have mine. (If she gets that much, maybe she helps others.) If I look at her uncaring or turn my face away from her, it is trouble for my soul. Whether she is honest and is what she appears to be or not is not relevant at all. If I harden my heart against her my soul shrivels. Does that mean I have to give her money every day? It means I have to consider it every day.

1/28/95

Dear Lord our God and Precious Mother, You are so great! How great You are! And your greatness is unsearchable! You are great and greatly to be praised.

Why ever did You get involved in the lives of human beings? In our history? If we were just the way You intended us to be, I could understand it. We are beautiful when we are acting Your image, living Your image, but when we are not we are awful!

You never give up hope on us. I guess if You did what would be left? If you gave up hope on me I would die or go crazy. You are my life and my breath and my strength. You are my reason for being! Without You I am nothing. Please don't let me fall away from You---ever!

4/12/95

Dear Lord our God and Precious Mother, You are so great! How great You are! Your creation is so great and wonderful and beautiful, full of such variety and so good! And perfect! And we human beings have brought so much ugliness into it! I bought a "Soldier of Fortune" magazine yesterday because it had an article on citizens' militias. It is so ugly, UGLY. The whole magazine is about death and destruction. Mostly how to do it and what to do it with. They give away guns as prizes for sweepstakes drawings. Forgive us all for the sin that is in us that makes us want to hurt each other.

✓ 5/1/95

Worshipping in different churches of different denominations in my region of Illinois, Indiana and Missouri was one of the blessings of my work for Bread for the World. The policy of Bread was that organizers, when they were doing field work, stayed in the homes of members. When the work was leading an adult forum or class in a church on Sunday morning, I would go to worship with my host family. Most of the time it was a blessing, but once in a awhile it was heartbreaking.

I must write about how I was hurt so deeply yesterday morning. I went to mass with my hostess. I wanted to worship and not just observe so I did. It was an easy service to get involved in because there was a lot of singing. Just before the Eucharist we joined hands across the aisles even and sang Your prayer (it was beautiful) then we passed the peace. I felt so included. Then they went to Your table.

I felt sure I would be allowed and had thought about it during the worship and thought I would just pray and meditate while they partook. When it was time I asked Susan if I was allowed. She very hesitantly said she didn't think so. I cried. It hurt so much to be shut out from Your table, excluded from partaking of Your body and blood! I cried. I tried not to show it, but maybe someone saw. Susan acted differently toward me afterward—kind of sheepish. I wanted to say something to her and to the priest but I didn't because I would have cried. I didn't know what difference such a scene would have made because if it was up to them they likely would have included me. It was such a deep hurting, I could cry again. Thanks and praise be to You for never excluding anyone from Your table for any reason.

There should always be room at the Lord's table for all who want to share the meal. There should always be room at the table.

5/28/95

Thank You for Rhonda's talk on Africa last night! Oh, Lord, how my heart burns within me when the subject of Africa comes up in any form. I want to go there so badly! Norm says I will. I wouldn't go while Daddy and Mom Phillips are in the condition they are in although it would take some serious thought and prayer if the opportunity presented itself. I will leave it to Your timing—if You have put this burning in my heart then if I am faithful You will make it happen. I will start saving money and getting myself in good physical shape so that I will be ready and able when You are. Take me and use me, O Lord. It would be absolutely great if Norm could go too.

9/27/96

I read Psalms 96 and 147.1-11 substituting feminine pronouns for the masculine ones. It was beautiful! We are missing so much by seeing You only as male. Take me and use me, O Lord.

12/14/96

Dear Lord our God and Precious Mother, You are so great! How great You are! And your greatness is unsearchable! Just look at how You manage Your creation—seedtime and harvest, sunrise and sunset, life and death. What a mystery You are! More and more I think of You as in all of Your creation—not above or outside it. Maybe you did give birth to it all, to us all instead of speaking creation into being with words.

2/19/96

There are two new revelations about me, to me, that I need to, want to write about.

One, when I was sitting in the Presbytery worship service the other night thinking how boring it was, the power of Your Presence came over me so strongly and the thought came to me that it was because someone else was praying for me or "blanketing" the whole assembly from their own reservoir of the power of your Presence.

So often I do that on Sunday morning at Christ Church or in other places—pray Your Presence in the sanctuary from the fullness of Your Presence in my spirit. Every time I wonder what that does—it feels good and right to do it, but I just didn't know what good it does.

I believe You gave me a glimpse of what it does.

It might be You working in me directly, but I usually have to "open the door" of my heart, and You are right there to fill me. Maybe someone else praying in the Spirit can open my door for You—and I can do that for someone else.

To be able to do so would be in keeping with this greatest of all blessings, being used to bless others. Thank You, Lord, for showing me. Take me and use me.

Two, Sunday night as I was falling asleep I was thinking over the week and the variety of things I had done and people I had met starting with the Self Development of People visit to Northwest Austin Council on Monday night and ending with the feeling of Your Presence in the chapel at Fenwick High School as the African American gospel choir sang in that Dominican chapel under the eyes of the stained glass saints! What a thrill! What context!

3/30/96

I felt Daddy's room full of Your Presence! I thought I brought it there but then You helped me see that You are there and I just walked in!

God was already in my dad's room. I wasn't taking God anywhere. When we pray we are not calling God to a place from which he is absent. We are calling ourselves to the place where he is. Matthew Fox, creation spirituality theologian, describes it this way:

> Describing prayer as swimming implies immediately the indispensable reality of the field of God's love…A fish in water evidences a certain passivity in its natural habitat, a seemingly utter dependence and relaxation in the medium…to talk of prayer as swimming removes any quid pro quo connotations…Prayer is thus removed from the category of means and reinstated as an end… The fish does not call for water; it is there already. So the

praying person does not call forth God. God is already here. Prayer calls forth the person, in ever deeper levels of his personality, to break loose, to see and behold.[10]

7/25/96

We went to the passion play in Eureka Springs, Arkansas, last night. Forgive me for my irreverence toward that conservative way of thinking about you and expressing faith in You—the singing of Gospel songs mainly but the patter as well. My heart is so filled and so moved by the power of Your Presence within me and in all things, so that pointing to the sky at the mention of Your name seems so limiting.

The theology that says You can't have created this wondrous universe and all Your creatures through a process of evolution as expressed in truths You have revealed is so limiting of You and Your awesome power! Help me love the people and not be so critical.

The passion play wasn't as moving to me this time as it was twelve years go—except for the part where the friends and followers of Jesus were taking the body down from the cross. That feeling of having You dead and unavailable was so distressing. I think the first time we saw it, I was moved more by the scene of Your friends deserting You and denying You.

I love Jesus!! I love Jesus!! He is my Lord! But He alone is not my reason for being. He along with God the parent, and God the Holy Spirit is my reason for being.

One alone is not enough. One alone is not complete.

8/4/96

Every kind of religious art form possible lined the walls and filled every nook and cranny of the church where my friend was being ordained to the priesthood in the Roman Catholic Church. As I entered the old Polish church in Chicago my Presbyterian soul couldn't take it all in. There were so many altars, statues, grottos, paintings, candles. There was too much adornment for me to absorb. The priest and bishops were

---

10   Matthew Fox, *Confessions; The Making of a Postdenominationalist Priest*, (San Francisco, Harper, 1996), 84.

in the nave in all their colorful finery, but I couldn't see John anywhere. As my eyes adjusted to the dimness of the sanctuary, I thought I had found him among all the dignitaries, but it was his brother who was an official in the order of Claretian Missionaries in which John was being ordained. Finally, I spotted John. He was wearing a pure white robe and lying face down on the floor before the altar. A powerful feeling of God's glory filled me at the sight of a person prostrate before God. A more cynical person would say he was prostrate at the feet of the bishop, but I had known John for several years. He was paying homage to God whom he loved and served with his whole being. It was a sacred moment created by the age-old practice of an ancient church.

As the service went on, I was able to focus on one grotto near where I was seated. In it was a statue of Jesus praying in the garden just before he gave himself up to die. As I focused on it I felt a deep connection with Jesus and with what John was doing.

Then it happened! It was all spoiled, all ruined by the Eucharist.

How powerfully Your Presence filled me at John's ordination to the priesthood yesterday! It was so sacred until it got to the Eucharist and then with your Presence still strong in me, I started crying and left. I cried for some time as I left the church and drove away. It hurts so much to be at Your Table and to not be invited, to be shut out while others are invited to eat with You.

Do You turn away from a table set in Your name that does not include all of Your beloved children?

As much as this incident hurt, the sacredness of John's ordination remained with me as he worked weekly as a volunteer in my Bread for the World office. He did tasks beyond the call of duty of a volunteer. Not long after his ordination they discovered a melanoma on his back. After surgery he continued to come to my office. He gave himself the chemo shots and would time them so that he could be in my office on a day when he was not so sick.

What part did he play in God's journey with me? He showed me the meaning of self-sacrifice, loyalty and devotion. He showed me what it is to give yourself for others. If the day comes when I need to live knowing I am dying, I hope I will live it as fully as John did.

10/17/96

I include this prayer to show the struggles of the soul that sometimes occur on a person's journey with God.

There is something trying to overcome me. I want to have You first in my life but tiredness and selfishness and whatever else it is slowly creep in and try to overcome me. I don't want "it" to. I want to be positive and happy and productive and able to minister to people. I don't know if "it" needs to be defined or if it is enough just to recognize that "it" is there.

I know that naming an evil gives a person power over it. If I think I know what "it" is and don't name it, can I prevail over it?

The other night I watched a horror film (not my favorite genre) with my son. The producers and directors tried so hard to make it horrifying that it turned out funny. The part that this prayer reminds me of is the background of the hero and how he did not want to deal with his past. As a child he had watched while monsters killed his family. As a twenty-something adult he would fly into violent fits of rage. Even with the help of a psychiatrist he could not face the truth of the effect that witnessing such a terrible thing had on him.

This is an extreme example but it does illustrate what I was feeling—that there was something—maybe not only one thing—that was overshadowing my heart at the time and that I needed to name it.

Just so you won't stay in suspense, let me tell you what happened to the hero. He was freed of the rages when he faced several monsters and killed them all. If or when there are monsters in our lives we need to face them and get rid of them.

11/24/96

I woke up at 6:30 this morning and went to the bathroom. Then decided to go back to bed for about half an hour. As I snuggled under the covers the power of Your Presence filled my heart (as it always does each night and morning but then suddenly it felt like You had overflowed my heart and were outside me as well as inside. It was such a powerful feeling that my eyes came WIDE <u>open</u> and I looked for You. It was wonderful! It was miraculous!

Is this a new phase in Your growing me?! It is something—a feeling of power that I never imagined before. As I have asked You to continue to grow me I had no idea what it would be like. And still even with that momentary taste of you, I don't know what I am asking for. Only that I trust You and I want to be more and more faithful and dwell always—each moment of each day with You.

That was a "pure" moment this morning. There was nothing else on my mind. Now I try to do it again but I am crowded by all kinds of thoughts. That's why spiritual people talk about meditation and centering. If I would practice that kind of spirituality would You surround me only in the moments of meditation or would it be like it is now—that I can feel You in my heart many times a day. Indeed, whenever I want to feel my heart overflow with Your Presence.

3/16/97

Etty Hillesum was a young Jewish woman who lived in Amsterdam during the occupation of the Netherlands by the Nazis. She was born in 1914 and died in 1943 in the gas chambers in Auschwitz. Her friends encouraged her to go into hiding, but she refused, saying she wanted to share the fate of her people. For months she worked for the Jewish Council in Amsterdam, a group formed by the Nazis supposedly to take care of Jewish people. She hated that work, but in 1942 she was transferred at her own request to Westerbork concentration camp. She did social welfare work for the people there who were to be eliminated. On November 30, 1943, Etty and her parents and brothers were sent to the gas chambers.

Her diaries record not only the horrors of the occupation and the death camps but, also her spiritual journey.[11] They are a record of the joys and sorrows of a woman who was faithful to her people and did all she could to make the end of their lives easier. Her last written words were on a postcard which she threw from the train that was taking her and her family along with thousands of other Jews to Auschwitz. Farmers found it and put it in the mail. In it she said, "Opening the

11 Etty Hillesum, *An Interrupted Life, Letters from Westerbork* (NY, Henry Holt, 1996).

Bible at random I found this: 'The Lord is my high tower.' I am sitting on my rucksack in the middle of a full freight car."

In God our lives are intertwined. It is the love and energy of God that draws together people like us with a woman like her. Her story, as different as it is from ours, resonates in our search for fellowship with God. Reading her diaries will lead you to a deeper faith in God. I wrote in my prayer journal:

She talks about the deep well inside her where You live. That sometimes she is there too. But more often stones and grit block the well, and God is buried beneath. Then he must be dug out again.

There are times when all of us need to dig out the things of the world that block our feeling the presence of God.

4/2/97

A Deepening Love Affair sounds like the title of marriage enrichment book, but the subtitle clarifies the title: *The Gift of God in Later Life.* In it the author, Jane Marie Thibault, writes for older people who yearn for a more intimate life with God.

This book is so perfect for some thoughts I have. It is truly, truly a timely gift from You! She suggests looking for threes everywhere to become aware of the Presence of the Trinity. That is similar to the way my prayer life got off the ground way back in Hiawatha—a leader told us to use visual sights as triggers for prayer.

This book is an affirmation of so many things that I have been thinking about You and me and sometimes thinking that I was getting a little crazy or having a false opinion of myself. Thank You and praise be to You that You led me to it!

A couple of months ago, I asked what my purpose in life will be when we retire. "Have confidence that in the creative efficiency of God you will always be magnificently well employed."[12] Thanks and praise be to You!

She also says "…God will put in Your presence those who desperately need to be loved by God through you." Thanks and praise be to You!

Show me ways to use this book.

---

12 Jane Marie Thibault, *A Deepening Love Affair, the Gift of God in Later Life* (Nashville, Upper Room, 1993), 95.

4/18/97

The Self Development of People Fund (SDOP) is a program of the Presbyterian Church (USA). It is funded by the One Great Hour of Sharing, an offering taken yearly in Protestant churches all over the United States. The Self-Development of People program affirms God's concern for people by working to empower economically poor, oppressed and disadvantaged people by establishing partnerships with low-income community groups. The basic rules for giving the grants is that the group requesting the money be the ones who have planned the project, who will benefit from it and who will carry out the project. The philosophy underlying it is that the people themselves know best what they need and that they have ideas for satisfying those needs. All that is lacking is capital to realize their goals.

For many years I served on the SDOP committee of Chicago Presbytery. Each year we were given a set amount of money by the national office and it was up to us to decide to which groups we should grant the money. After advertising the availability of the funds, we would wait for applications to come in. As you would expect, there were always more requests than we had money to grant. Visiting the sites helped us decide who qualified and who didn't.

We received applications from such groups as African women abandoned in Chicago by husbands who came here to study; a group working to help to ex-convicts make their way after release from prison; a group that wanted to clear drug dealers out of their neighborhood. The programs we chose were inventive and doable. This last group's plan was especially innovative and dangerous. They, with the approval of the police, had picnics on the streets in front of a drug dealer's home on Saturdays—when they would have had the most customers.

Talking to these people was a blessing to all of us on the committee. Their hope and confidence in their success was inspiring. But it could also be depressing. The strength and power of the opposition they faced was overwhelming.

What chance do any of the SDOP applicants that we visited and granted puny amounts of money to have? What chance do they have in the face of the wealth and greed that they face! What chance, indeed. Their power is great because You are on their side! Help me keep hope. Yesterday's visit to the Coalition to Protect Public Housing in Cabrini Green made me want to cry. I did cry. It's all right to cry, but it is not alright to mope about it. You have made great and powerful promises to Your poor and oppressed children and You always keep Your promises. Help me help You keep Your promises. Take me and use me, dear Lord.

Chapter Nine

7/30/97

Dear Lord our God and Precious Mother, You seem different to me since I started reading Prayers to She Who Is. You are still great and your greatness is unsearchable. But You are very mysterious and like someone I have not known before. The power of Your Presence is still very strong in my heart—thank You and praise be to You.

It seems like this book has created a distance. No, it has made me feel a distance between You and me. You are for sure a Holy Mystery.

9/16/97

Something is growing in me. Even though for a couple of years now I have been addressing You as Precious Mother, You still remain masculine in Your Presence with me, in my sense of You with me. What will happen, Holy Mystery, if I can overcome the blocks and know You as Sophia?

I went for years valuing the wisdom and conversation of men more than that of women. Now I value those things in some women. I value most my solitude. In my solitude You are a powerful, powerful Presence, pure power without gender in my heart, but male in my mind.

What would happen, what would it feel like if in my mind You were female? I want to know; Holy Mystery Sophia, I want to feel. Such a knowledge of You would certainly elevate women. What would it do to and for me?

The something that was growing in me was a sense of incompleteness in the way I was addressing God. There was something missing from a true description of the divine. I know that it is impossible for human beings to know God's name and understand God fully, but I had a sense that we have to try more names to expand the language we use about God. William Cleary prayed, "What little we know of you is dwarfed by your endless unknowability."[1]

In another prayer in the same book he wrote,

> Holy Mystery, beyond naming or understanding whom our forebears in profoundest awe, gave an unpronounceable name—YHWH—sometimes we shall call upon you as 'Sophia,' the scriptural name meaning Wisdom.[2]

God, coming into my life through these prayers brought to my faith and prayer life a new liveliness and greater joy. The names I had been taught to use for God were restrained, bound by masculinity. The possibility of inclusive names opened up pathways to God that made her more real to me than ever before.

A prayer I wrote in this same time period expressed how difficult it was to read the book that inspired Cleary's prayers, *She Who Is; The Mystery of God in Feminist Discourse.* This book by Elizabeth A. Johnson, Distinguished Professor of Theology at Fordham University in New York City, was about to change my life. In 1997, I was only able to read four chapters—it was so hard to understand. A year later I picked up her book again and not only read it all the way through, but studied it two more times and published my own book about her theology. Her work changed my whole life.

10/20/97

Timidly, I tried to speak in public about feminine names for God.

---

1   William Cleary, *Prayers to She Who Is,* (NY, Crossroad, 1997), 22.
2   Ibid., 15.

You know that some of the evaluations from this sermon about using feminine names for You were opposed and that is bothering me, but I do believe that what I said came from You and that You are working in the hearts of all of the women who were at the retreat. Thank You for each one of them and please bless them on their journeys.

10/25/97

Daddy died at 2 a.m. Sharon called me at Helen's in Rock Island at 6:30 and I came home instead of going to the conference.

Holy Mystery, Loving God, Peg says You and Daddy finally made a deal. . . If You did, I know it was good for him and I praise you and thank You. I know what conditions some Christians would say were required for entrance into heaven and I don't know if Daddy met them—I don't know if I meet them.

What I do know is that You are loving and gracious and full of compassion! And that You have mercy on us all. And that we all need Your mercy.

It sounds like he passed peacefully and alone. . .as far as we know, alone, but I can barely imagine the joy with which he greeted Mom and Grandma and Henry and all the others. And, You know, if it doesn't work that way then the way it does work is even more glorious because it is Your loving provision for Your beloved children.

10/29/97

This is the day the Lord has made. Let us rejoice and be glad in it. This is the day Daddy has been longing for—to be placed in the ground "right next to Mother." Rev. Utley used the words "joyfully surprised." I am sure that he was joyfully surprised when he found himself not in the ground or in some dark place of punishment, but in the light of Your love!

Jim suggested that we all eat breakfast at the OK Café [a favorite eating place of our family] so we did. It was great. The waitress was the one who always waited on Daddy. She said she thought he had died long ago since he hadn't been in for years. She said how nice he was and always had a kind or funny word for her.

From Heaven to My Heart

1/27/98

Disgust and sorrow are two words that describe the feelings I had when the news broke about President Clinton being involved with Monica Lewinski.

Be present with the Clintons and all who are involved in this mess! Again, I ask that the liars will be exposed and the innocent vindicated!

Forgive us all, Lord, that we are willing and eager to spend time on an issue like this and that hungry children don't even cause a ripple in our lives. Forgive us, Lord. And help us be better!

3/29/98

We were beginning to think about retiring to Arizona.

I keep thinking that I will stay in this house for awhile after Norm leaves Christ Church—I think I do that because I don't want to leave this place where the kids grew up but even more this place in this living room that has become a sacred place, a holy place for me. You will make another for me and I look forward to that, but I also want to stay here, a part of me wants to stay here. Help me give up control and turn it all over to You.

4/27/98

When I think that my life will be over at retirement, I know it is not true, but I think it anyway. Whatever else is happening to me I know that my life in You, my spiritual growth will never be over. You are my life and breath and strength. You are my reason for being!

5/4/98

We went to the Zion Passion play in a high school auditorium with the some friends. It was wonderful—not perfect, but wonderful. And I cried and cried. My eyeballs are still swollen! Every time I hear Your story, see Your story done by real people I am so moved. Lord Jesus, all I want from my life is to serve You faithfully even to death. In this play the disciples

219

gathered around Jesus and comforted him after the Supper. I'll bet it really happened that way.

I was not the only one who felt as though these actors were the real people. A mother and her little daughter, who was about seven years old, came in late. Jesus was sitting on the edge of the stage talking to his disciples who, at that point in the story were in the front row of the auditorium. Before she and her mom were even seated the little girl, who obviously knew the stories of Jesus, said, in absolute amazement, "What is he doing here!"

6/9/98

Thank You for John Cirone. Yesterday in prayer in his hospital room he offered up his sufferings for all of us at Bread and for the work we do. He said something like, "may we change the spirit of Congress." Thank you for bringing him into our lives.

6/20/98

We were in Missoula, Montana, when Norm's mom died. A young man, part of a group of boys who grew up playing games in our home with our son, had asked Norm to officiate at his wedding in Missoula where he and his fiancé were attending the university. His family was an important part of Christ Church and we were close friends with them all. We knew that Mom Phillips was failing, but this family meant so much to us. Feeling certain that Mom would not even know if we were there or not, we decided to go to the wedding.

It was another decision like the one I had made when I went to Ghost Ranch instead of going to Nebraska to be with my mother in the last hours of her life. Norm did talk to her on the phone the night before she died, but she was not able to respond.

Mom Phillips passed over at 11:30 this morning. . . .It is strange because Norm and I agreed Thursday evening that if it happened before the wedding we would not tell anyone until after. So we are grieving on the inside and rejoicing on the outside—although the grief is not displacing the joy we feel at being here for Mike and Kandyce and at being part of this family—it is an honor and we are proud of them.

Thank You that Mom did not linger long here after she became ill. I rejoice with her that she is now in Your eternal presence. And united with her loved ones who went before her.

Nancy, David, Me, Norm, and Jim at a friend's wedding, 1998

Norm's brother, Ken, me , his wife, Donna, and Mom Phillips.

7/3/98

Tertullian says the Trinity is like a plant "with the Father as a deep root, the Son as the shoot that breaks forth into the world, the Spirit as that which spreads beauty and fragrance, 'fructifying the earth with fruit and flavor'."[3]

8/6/98

I feel so sad that Mom Phillips is gone. Our lives are so full of such a variety of emotions that it seems like each one has to take its turn to surface. And now it is time to grieve again. I do miss her so much. She was a blessing in my life. No one could have asked for a better mother-in-law. Although many were the times when I wanted to shake her for her worrying and when I made fun of her for the strange, compulsive ways she did things. Forgive me. I loved her dearly. And we had such good times with her. How Norm could make her laugh! And how she loved Jim and Nancy. Thank you for her and that her passing was so "easy" compared to what she was afraid it would be.

9/5/98

I'm trying to think through something about myself and my purpose in life and I seem to think in circles. It is about what retirement means for me and where I will find my value—it seems somehow to hinge on where my value is now. That won't change. It will improve and grow, but not change. In reading She Who Is, I have a burning desire for other women and men to understand what Elizabeth Johnson is saying. As I have been reading other things I have had the thought: why should I read and remember?—always I will read, because I love to—but why should I remember—I won't have anyone to teach. That is where the circle starts over again.

Trying to back out of the circle: I am a teacher. I am a leader. Not only because I love being a teacher, because it is good for me, feels good for me but also because my teaching and leading has been good for others as well.

---

3   Kathleen Norris, *Amazing Grace; A Vocabulary of Faith*, (NY, Riverhead Books, 1998), 291.

9/8/98

Dear Lord, Sophia and Precious Mother, what new meaning, what liberating naming the name of Jesus Christ has for me in the context of the book, She Who Is. Even while You were God in person among us, You were still Sophia who is also God and Spirit throughout the earth, throughout the world's religions. That You are the only true God of all the earth—that it is Your human creatures who divide You up, divide themselves and set one against the other—all in Your name. Forgive us, Lord and help us stop that.

10/17/98

Thank You for the time I had, You gave me, last night to work on She Who Is. As I was falling asleep, I tried to pray prayers, word a prayer that would express the new, powerful thoughts that come to me as I outline this book. The power of Your Presence with me was glorious. If these ideas are good and true and helpful then I need to start using them. I realized last night that it won't just happen—I will need to practice. May it all be for Your glory.

12/23/98

It is hard to get started using inclusive names for God. We are so bogged down in masculine names and pronouns. Most of the time I use the word expansive for new language about God because there are names we use that have no gender: rock, foundation, fortress. Names that come from nature have great power to move us, but it is of the utmost importance that we broaden our language about God for the sake of the well-being of women. If God is always only seen as Father, King, Judge then only masculine traits are honored and to be sought after. When we begin to see God as mother, sister, aunt, we will be able to honor women equally with men. Having a list of expansive names at your fingertips is helpful. Here are a few that first connected me with God in new ways.

Insight-giver, Divine Planner, Trustworthy Guide,
   Precious Mother, Holy Savior, Guardian, Guide and Stay,

Baker,[4] Eagle,[5] Mother Hen,[6] Mysterious God,
Generous and Kind One, Ever Present Friend,
God-Sophia, Christ-Sophia, Holy Spirit-Sophia,
God of the Sparrow, God of the Poor, Spirit and
Mover of my life.

12/29/98

After twenty-seven years Norm resigned from being pastor of Christ Presbyterian Church in Hanover Park, Illinois. He accepted a position as interim pastor in the Presbyterian Church in Kouts, Indiana.

My last prayer time in this hallowed space, place. I know You will make for me such a place in our Kouts home. Dear Lord, my Teacher, Guru, Friend and Companion, Precious Mother, You have always been so faithful and true to me, to us. And how You have grown me through these twenty-six years. . . .How You are growing me now through this move, all these changes and experiences….Thank you! Thank You! Thank You for the power of Your Presence with me! During these prayer times and at increasing numbers of times throughout the days.

1/2/99

In our new home in Kouts, Indiana.

Thank You for this very nice place to live. It feels good here. When I got up this a.m. I went into the kitchen to make coffee and on the way pulled up the mini blinds so that we can watch the snow storm. As I looked around me I knew that this place will be hallowed too—in a different way from "home" in Hanover Park. Thank You and praise be to You!

We moved from a large raised ranch house in suburban Chicago to a very small duplex in a small rural town in Indiana. Because I didn't want to go to the work of having a garage sale, we gave away all our furniture except for two beds, two dressers, two desks, two rockers, my piano, a TV and a dining room set. The things we couldn't part with and those that didn't fit in our very small, new home were in a rental

4   Matthew 13:33;Luke 13:20-21.
5   Deuteronomy 32:11-12; Exodus 19:4.
6   Matthew 23:37; Luke 13:34; Ruth 2:12; Psalm 57:1; Psalm 61:4; Psalm 17:8.

storage shed waiting for the move to Arizona. The time spent in Kouts was short, eighteen months, but our little home was just right for what we needed at that point in our lives. The people in the church were gracious to us and loved us and we loved them back.

1/12/99

Dear Creator, Sustainer and Redeemer of the universe, You are so great! How great You are and Your greatness is unsearchable! How mysterious You are! That You can love and care for the whole universe and at the same time, all the time, care for me! Your awesomeness is diminished when human beings confine You with our names for You and definitions of You. Your awesomeness is expanded when I sit here and open my heart to You and know that the same Power that floods me is the Power that gives life and breath and meaning to all things.

1/29/99

What a strange thing! For at least two years as I walked by the flower shop in the AT&T building I have wanted a pair of bookends that have been in the window. Together they form a green apple with a brass stem. I wanted them. Thinking they were wooden I went in one day and asked to see them. They are brass and cost $84.95. I never would spend that on such an extravagance, but I still wanted them. Thomas Moore[7] wrote in one of his books about having things in your home that have spirit. For awhile I tried to make myself believe that these must have an evil spirit because I wanted them so much.

Moore talked about how good it is to have real not plastic things surrounding you. So I still wanted them—every time I walked past the window I wanted them. For awhile they had a couple of Beanie Babies draped over them—it was humiliating enough that they had to share the window with the Beanie Babies let alone be used as a display prop for them.

Rich and Cindy gave me $50.00 for playing at their wedding in October so I went into the store and asked if they would lower the price.

---

7   Thomas Moore, *The Re-Enchantment of Everyday Life*, (NY, HarperCollins, 1996).

The guy said he couldn't do it but gave me the phone number of the owner. I never called. But I still wanted them. Norm gave me money for Christmas to pay the $34.95+tax to go with Rich and Cindy's $50.00.

Finally, yesterday I went in to buy them. As I walked to the store, I told myself how foolish and extravagant it was to buy them. The lady gave me a twenty percent discount—her idea, I didn't ask for it! So I paid $73.91 for them! They are mine and they look really good with my Bible and meditation books on top of the bookcase Dad Phillips made for us!

Their spirit is good. I feel like their spirit was crushed and defeated but defiant in the window. Now they are owned and loved and doing what their maker intended, what was put into them as the Korean artisan worked on them. They look more relaxed and fulfilled this a.m. Am I crazy or what!?

3/6/99

Thank You for the time I had last night to read and take notes on She Who Is. How amazing her ideas are. What a revelation! A turning upside down of all that has been presented as absolute truth for centuries. How much greater you are with these new ways of speaking—no You remain the same—it is how much wider our understanding can be; our ability to appeal to You in so many ways; to relate to You differently at different times and in different places.

I believe You want me to write about these new revelations so that more men and women will learn these new ideas. Help me do that. Please help me do that. May I be so much in Your Spirit that what I write will be Your words and Your message.

3/23/99

If these prayer times keep shrinking under the press of other things I have to do, my life and my spirit will shrink as well. I am riding on a high of the power of being in Your flow (of trying to be in Your flow) all the hours of the day and the power of Your Presence in my heart when I stop to feel that power. And I am so grateful for that, for Your abundant blessings that flow over and around and through me whenever I accept them. But I can't take it all for granted.

226

5/22/99

Holy Wisdom. I want to write. I want to write so that women can understand their value in Your eyes. I want to write so that all people will know You as Mother as well as Father. I don't know where to start. Are the words on the next page a beginning? I have to sit down and <u>do</u> it, don't I? And right now I want to play the piano or read a book. If I am going to write I have to sit down and <u>do</u> it! Okay.

5/23/99

I didn't do it. I played Free Cell. I am sorry! I can see a little glimpse of what faces a writer. But this is not just any writing. It is something You want me to do. I know it because my heart opens and Your Presence fills me to overflowing when I think about writing or think about "my" book as much as it does when I am praising You.

Guide me, Divine Guide and Companion of my way. I want to quit Bread. I am so tired and I want to be free of all the work I need to do. I am ready to retire, aren't I! Not to sit still or travel or do nothing but to move into the next phase of my life. The next phase where You will continue to grow me.

Since I was planning to write a book, I bought and read several books by writers about writing. Over and over again these people reported what an exercise in avoidance writing is. Any little thing can keep a writer from sitting down to write. But once she settles down to do it all else fades away.

Writing became an extension of my morning prayer time. Maybe it seems strange to say it this way, but God became and remains my muse, my Author Within. I can stay at my desk and write for hours under the influence of prayer.

As I have been working on this book, *From Heaven to My Heart*, I discovered that going away from home and all the distractions that exist here enables me to write for longer periods of time. I discovered a McDonald's that is light and open-spaced and where they make good iced coffee. Sometimes there is a lot of noise and children running around, but nothing is my responsibility. Only the writing is mine to do. Norm dubbed it the McStudy.

7/6/99

O Lord, I have the sense that the work of writing "my book" is going to merge into my prayer time, my prayer time is going to overflow into writing time. How wonderful that will be. If I am right it could easily be the "great thing" that I felt during Communion on Sunday. It was as if You were making a promise to me that retirement holds a great, important new thing for me. I can't remember the words so possibly it was a feeling only, but I know it came from You. And I praise You and thank You for it.

10/20/99

What a joy retirement is going to be! Can You believe I am saying that! Having time to read and write and think will be so great. And whether what I read and think and write is ever published and read, it will be of value in my journey with You. My prayer as always will be that you will use me to bring glory to Your holy name and witness to whomever You bring into my life.

11/7/99

One of my last duties for Bread for the World before I retired on December 31, 1999 was to have a display at the Call to Action conference in Milwaukee. I have already written about how great the conferences of these radical Catholics were. Even though I was responsible for the BFW display and talking to people there, I was free to attend parts of the conference when the display room was closed. On Sunday morning, instead of going to Mass, I went to Woman Church.

Thank You that I went to Woman Church yesterday. The incense would keep me from going again. It makes my throat sore. My best thought about it was that if that kind of service puts people in touch with You, then it is all right. How people worship is not the point. The point is first that they worship and second what kind of person their worship makes them. I don't know what calling the spirits from the compass points means. Who are they? Is that what Native Americans do?

But calling the spirits of women of the past did mean something to me, but what? It was a remembering and a blessing of them and of us.

And about writing. I felt so intimidated and unfit to write books as I browsed through the book store. There are so many women writing books and they come from such learned and "important" backgrounds. My only hope is that You are truly calling me to write, that You will give me the message.

12/28/99

Received my first pension check yesterday. Only today and tomorrow and I will be retired! I have already felt it in not planning for 2000 organizing! And in disconnecting from folks. I know it is going to be good! That the freedom to do what I want when I want will be most welcome and enjoyable! The change will be exciting!

Just don't let me let go of this most precious of all my hours—my time with You. If it changes I pray that it will only be in the direction of expansion and deepening.

1/1/2000

The very air was full of doom and gloom as the end of the twentieth century and the beginning of the twenty-first approached.

Dear Lord our God and Precious Mother, Ruler of the whole universe! You are so great! How great You are and Your greatness is unsearchable!

The planet is still here! The sun rose again this morning! All of the dire predictions and worries about Y2K did not happen. What do You think when Your children make such a fuss about nothing and don't even give a thought to the needs of so many people, children especially!?

People who call You theirs alone—what are they feeling this a.m. and You have not destroyed the world? How do they feel You? Do they feel You in their hearts? How do they hear your voice, Your truth? What will the people who bought food and guns to protect it do with that food and those guns?

As I watched some of the around the world coming of 2000 yesterday on TV I felt two emotions—wonder and awe at the beauty of the earth itself and of her peoples. And a confidence that You are not going to be the one who destroys this planet or its creatures.

Chapter Ten

1/10/2000

Moving to Arizona was hard, even though we were excited about it and eager to do it.

These transitions are like walking through a dark tunnel into the light; like a sliding scale from sadness to joy. I have had to die to my love and enthusiasm for working with Bread to enjoying and looking forward to retirement. I am having to die to my pleasure in being near Nancy to excitement about having our own home, near Jim in such a different culture. I will have to die to loving the trees and the fields so that I can love the desert. Is it using resurrection too lightly to say that life is a series of deaths and resurrections? It certainly is a series—I have called it phases sometimes—that do not necessarily follow one after the other but that overlay each other. Crescendos, diminuendos.

1/31/00

Heart of Mercy,
my mistakes and failings keep me humble.
They chide me with their blaming voices
and pester me with their mocking comments,
of disgrace and condemnation.
 They hound me with blame and guilt

and a thousand other recriminations.

Walk with me through my mistakes and failings.
Let me hear your understanding and merciful voice.
We both know that I am not a perfect person.
Assure me that I am not a bad person either.
Keep teaching me about myself, about life, about you,
through these characteristics I would much rather not have.
Remind me that they are my friends, not enemies,
That they are my teachers, not my wardens.

May I befriend the unwanted parts of myself
and continually learn wisdom from them.
Thank you for lovingly embracing me as I am
while the murky layers of my many shortcomings
are slowly transformed into love."[1]

This is such a great prayer book! I bought it in January of 2000 and am using it daily for the third time. She uses a wide variety of names for God, which, as I have said, is so freeing. The prayers seem like they were written from my heart. I would recommend it for your prayer time.

4/20/00

On the ninety-fifth floor, the very top, of the John Hancock Center on Michigan Avenue in Chicago is a classy restaurant named the Signature Room. Never in my life did I ever dream that I would be honored at a $200 a plate banquet anywhere, let alone there. It happened because the Illinois Hunger Coalition chose Congresswoman Jan Schakowski and me to receive the Paul Simon Public Service Award.

It seemed contrary to advocacy for hungry people to have a banquet in such a place at such a price, but most of the people who came to it would not have come to a potluck dinner in a church basement. And besides the Signature Room donated the use of the room, the servers and all the fine food. The purpose of the event was to raise funds for the work of the Coalition. My husband and four of my friends, including

---

1   Joyce Rupp, *Prayers to Sophia; A Companion to Star in My Heart,* (Philadelphia, Innisfree Press, 2000) 46.

my boss from Washington, D.C. were able to be there because I was given the table free.

The outer walls of the Signature Room are all glass and the view of Chicago from there is spectacular. The staff had arranged the room so the podium from which the awards ceremony would be conducted was in a corner so people could see out in two directions. The only problem was that fog that encased the top floors of the building. All that could be seen was gray thickness.

As the ceremony was ending and Congresswoman Schakowski and I had given our thank-you speeches, the sun broke through, and we could see the beauty of the city spread out before us.

Thank You for my table of friends. Thank You that I was able to speak so calmly and, I think, fairly clearly. Although I do think back on it and wish I had said a little more and said it more clearly. Norm said I did a good job and Vi said I looked happy and stress-free.

I just read somewhere about women needing to find their voice. How long have You been teaching me to do that?! I certainly found my speaking voice over the past nine years on political and religious topics, but for something like yesterday I tend to be too brief. I see that as being one of the problems I will experience with writing. I will have to learn how to say more. It was said in front of two hundred people yesterday that I am going to write books. I do believe that is what You want me to do. Please help me do it.

6/5/00

When Norm retired five months after I did, we moved to Arizona. We rented a fourteen-foot U-Haul truck and a tow bar for my car. Our son and our son-in-law took turns driving it from Kouts, Indiana, to Mesa, Arizona while Norm and Nancy took turns driving the car. At the end of the four-day trip, we arrived at the apartment we had rented to live in while we looked for a house to buy. It was too hot, and we were too tired to do any unloading so we stayed in a motel for a couple of nights.

I am sitting on the patio in the garden here at the motel. And I can see that the season has changed. The bougainvillea is still blooming but fading, and all the other plants are drying up. It was absolutely lush when we were here in May.

I felt so groundless yesterday. Like standing on shifting sand. (My first desert analogy not chosen intentionally.) You are my rock and my salvation. You are my life and my breath and my strength. You are my reason for being.

10/9/00

As God has journeyed with me from heaven to my heart, some of the tools of her travel have been books. In 1998, I read a book titled, *The Re-Enchantment of Everyday Life,* by Thomas Moore. I was going to write that I don't know what prompted me to read it again at this time of our getting settled in our new home. But I know with certainty that it was God who prompted me. Much of what I read in this book touched me right where I needed to be touched. For instance, Moore quotes a French philosopher Gaston Bachelard saying, "An entire past comes to dwell in a new house."[2] Moore himself wrote:

> Like turtles we carry our homes with us as we move from place to place, all homes mobile, because home is ultimately located in a deep recess of the soul, a cornucopia that pours forth endless gifts.[3]

11/3/00

I am working on the book. Thank You for Julia Cameron's book, The Right to Write. She says first of all you have to lay track. That is certainly a lively metaphor/simile in my mind. I have pushed through three chapters roughly in the direction I want to go. Just now I looked at the epigraphs for chapter four and I have nothing in mind. It is as though my track laying has come to the edge of a dense jungle after crossing an open plain. Only You can do this, Lord. Help me.

---

2 Thomas Moore, *The Re-Enchantment of Everyday Life,*, 84.
3 Ibid., 84.

11/15/00

I am so unworthy to have Your Presence fill me so quickly and strongly when I call upon you. It is obvious that the gift of Your Presence is not based on merit but on love. You are so loving! How loving You are and Your love is beyond understanding.

11/18/00

"I am Beverly Phillips and I am . . . ." It seemed like many minutes passed before I finished my sentence. I was attending a gathering of hunger activists. The leader asked us to go around the circle and give our names and what we do. For twenty years I had been a hunger activist, but now I was retired. I couldn't define myself in this group setting. Lamely, I finished the sentence with "…a retired Presbyterian minister." Someone in the group knew me by reputation so she told the group who I had been. It was a moment that brought together what I had been and what I was becoming. I was changing from a hunger activist to a Christian feminist theologian writer.

Thank You for the affirmation that I received through yesterday's FaithWorks conference that I am on the right track with studying and writing feminist theology. When one of the speakers called you She everyone laughed, I knew again that I have to do something about God-talk.

I am sorry that You have to keep affirming this for me because in my heart I know it is what You want me to do. It just seems arrogant that I think I can do it. And I am so new at it.

Quite often someone writes a book learning as they go. Help me do it. May it be to Your glory! And for the sake of women and children and men everywhere.

11/23/00

Thank you for all the blessings you have bestowed on Norm and me. Through most of our lives together, we thought we would work until seventy and then retire with no "extras." Here we are retired at sixty-four and sixty-five with money to buy a nice house with a pool and to do some of the things we want to do. Take us and use us. May Your great, abundant blessing to us be a great abundant blessing to others.

Later: We were talking about our finances and our life here with Nancy last night and she said, "You are poster children for retirement." And she is right. You have always been and continue to be our caretaker and provider, meeting all our needs just when they need to be met. You meet our needs more abundantly that we can ask or think.

11/26/00

Continue to work in our whole election process. Give Gore and Bush wisdom and patience and a sense of what is good for the country before themselves. What a time this has been! Half of the eligible voters voted, and they were divided almost in half. May it mean that more people will know how important their votes are and that they will vote in the next election.

11/28/00

There are no thoughts or words to express the depth of my gratitude and praise to You for the great gifts You have bestowed on us all of our lives, but most especially now at our retirement with our house! Yesterday after we signed the papers and paid the money we went to 5 & Diner for lunch. As we talked about it, I cried tears of gratitude and amazement.

> *O Lord, You aren't just "pretend" in my life. You are my life. All that I am and all that I have are gifts from You. Thank You and praise be to You for the way You have grown me and are growing me.*

12/21/00

Over the past couple of years, I have thought about authors who have seaside or mountain retreats where they can write and wondered where I could go to do it. You have given me a place. I have a study in a desert place! You satisfy my every need! Thank You and praise be to You for all of Your good gifts to us!

12/22/00

This is different! I don't feel moved to write anything, but just to concentrate on Your Presence in my heart. I am still so full of gratitude that the best way to express it is by the feelings in my heart. Thoughts and words can't do it anywhere near adequately enough. Actually, neither can my feelings because it is beyond human experience. So I give You my life and my being and all that I am all over again. Each day my prayer remains: take me and use me always to Your glory!

12/28/00

The greatest gift of all is Your Presence with me growing me and using me. And that can continue if I stay open to You. So much has ended, but great possibilities lie ahead if I dwell in Your Presence, if I abide with You. Help me do that. It just occurred to me that I may have as many years left as I spent working for You for poor and hungry people.

Can I grant that my strength and stamina are less and still be of service to You? Still answer Your call to work with You? I want to! Oh, how I want to! Please take me and use me. Keep my brain thinking. Sometimes I do worry that there is something wrong up there, but maybe it is just slowing down too, not going out of commission altogether.

1/8/01

I felt so sad and empty at church yesterday. Nobody knows me and what is worse or maybe what is part of that is that I don't know who I am! …I just felt invisible—I smiled and said "hi" to five or six people who didn't even acknowledge me. Granted I got hugs from some others. During church I wanted to cry because I don't know who I am but it came to me that even if I don't know, You do! You know who I am and who You created me to be. You know what my purpose in life is. I want to surrender to that. I want to rest in Your everlasting arms knowing that You know what the future holds for me. That You know of what service I can be.

1/30/01

Thank you for the work I got done on the book yesterday—it would be nice to have a title for it. It is going to be hard work. I know you have called me to do this. Help me give it the time it needs, help me persevere. Help me be open to what you want me to write.

3/5/01

Forgive us all when we think we can neatly define and describe You! When we think that what we have been taught to believe about You is all there is!

4/23/01

Dear Lord our God and Precious Mother, Christ-Sophia, Holy Spirit, You are so great! How great You are and Your greatness is unsearchable. Thank You and praise be to You for this gift of Your Presence. Even when my thoughts wander far afield, You continue to fill my heart to overflowing! I have to yawn for comfort. Maybe sometime I won't yawn and see what happens.

In worship yesterday, I got to thinking about the things I have accomplished in the past. It was Earth Day. Craig preached a lively, poetic sermon about his relationship with nature. Two children, brother and sister, read the opening prayer as a litany with the congregation. Linda read some of what we on the Eco-Justice Task Force of General Assembly had written about twelve years ago. And the Restoring Creation Enabler had a table on the patio. I am proud of what we started, even though I had such a small part in it.

It makes me want to do more, to be a person, a woman, who makes a difference, even though I am retired. Throughout my pre-retirement I did do some significant things, not because that was my ambition, but because they were things I was interested in and cared about. The talents and the interests and the ability and the efficiency were/are gifts from You. You led me and used me (as was always my prayer) into the paths where I could serve You. Why would You stop doing that just because I am retired and sixty-five?

"I would only stop if you didn't want me to use you anymore. Only if you get self-centered with your time and your talents. Be patient. We are building. We are preparing."--God

Thank You, Lord. You know I want to co-create with You. I know all that I have done in the past that is good has been co-creating with You. Help me be patient and do my homework. I really, truly believe that the book is what You are calling me to do now. And I know I need to read more and think more and speak more about Your Name and who You are. Thank You and praise be to You for this affirmation.

I wish there was more to say than "Thank You and praise be to You" but maybe my tears and my faithfulness add to the depth and sincerity of those simple words

5/7/01

I found myself without a book to read at a retreat of Presbyterian Women in Cottonwood, Arizona. I never go without a book, and there were beautiful places to sit and read at this campground. So I borrowed a book from the very small library they had in the campground center.

Thank You for Thomas R. Kelly's book, A Testament of Devotion. I am sure that You led me to read as much of it as I did and I will buy my own copy. He writes about just what I pray for—that I will be able to feel the power of Your Presence in every minute of all my days just as I feel You in these times of prayer.

Thomas Kelly wrote something about touching a person with the Inner Presence is like touching You. I want to be the person who, when I am touched, the toucher is touching You. I don't need to know every time it happens. In fact, it is probably best if I don't know. But may it be so. Always for Your glory.

5/13/01

Thank you and praise be to You that Craig asked me to help him officiate at Communion this morning. He asked me because it is Mother's Day and he thought it would be good for the people to see a woman minister at the

Table. I am sure You inspired that thought in him and he lived up to what You asked. May I live up to it as well. May the people, especially the women, no not especially the women, may all the people see You in me. May they not see just a competent, smart woman there. May they see You and know Your Spirit!

5/15/01

I have such a wonderful sense of peace and well-being this morning. A peace that You have long given me in these early morning hours before the regular day starts. You are the Great Gift Giver!

At the same time, little sniggling, negative thoughts try to work their way into this peace. This morning, they are about what is causing the dampness on the side of the house.

Back to my peace. At least part of it was seeing the cereous bloom yesterday. Well, it blooms at night. So I fell asleep wondering what kind of flying creatures would be visiting it in the night. It is so lovely. I think it only blooms one night.

Having lived all but four years of my life in the Midwest, the plants of the desert Southwest were and still are a mystery to me. I knew about Saguaro cactuses because they are an emblem of Arizona. They only grow here and are treasured so much that they are protected by law.

One of the plants I had never heard of grows in our front yard. It is the Desert Night-blooming Cereus. It is aptly named because it only blooms at night during a period of six to eight weeks. The buds open, two or three, or sometimes more, a night, as soon as the sun sets. The flowers are very large, about four and a half inches wide and some as deep as eight and a half inches. The blossoms on the plant in our yard are white in the center with the outer petals being a luminous pink. During the night moths and fruit bats pollinate the blossoms. As soon as the morning sun touches them they close and dry up. Where each flower bloomed, a round seed pod appears. As it ripens, it turns orange and then bursts open. Inside are hundreds of tiny black seeds. When they split open the seed pods look like bowls and provide a feast for the birds who come to eat from them.

When I wrote this prayer, the Cereus was about three feet tall. Now nine years later it is close to ten feet tall and, with its spines, threatens anyone who walks up the sidewalk to our front door.

Desert Night-blooming Cereus Cactus

5/17/01

This prayer was written on the first of many cross-country drives we made to visit our daughter and son-in-law in Missouri. Every time we made the trip, I experienced the beauty of western New Mexico in a spiritual way.

Oh, what beauty we saw yesterday! The colors and shapes and trees and plants changed as the miles passed. Oh, I'm not a writer now! I am a prayer. All I want to say is how absolutely beautiful and, at times, breathtaking the scenery was that we saw yesterday.

The feeling of great space that I used to feel when we were in this part of the West was real. And as I was driving the miles between Springerville, Arizona, and Red Hill, New Mexico, the sky was blue with scattered white clouds like it had been so many times when I used to drive to Hastings, Nebraska from Chicago. I felt the power of Your Presence so strongly. Thank You and praise be to You for all of these great and wonderful gifts.

5/28/01

The deck on the home of Nancy and David was a perfect place for me to meditate and write my prayers. Their house was beside a lake in the woods in Missouri. As I sat on the deck for my morning prayer time, I could look out over the lake from the midst of trees. However, not all my time was spent meditating when we visited them. Things we did entered into my meditations.

You love your creation with deepest and never-ending love. You put us here to help You care for it. Forgive us that we are so prone to destroy it instead. Help us know that You are in all of creation and that You want us to protect Your body, the creation.

We went to the "Remember the Veterans" air show yesterday. I had never been to an air show before. This one was purposely all military. As we walked through the gates at the tarmac, I wanted to cry. There was a big sob in my chest, in my heart when I saw those big, ugly air planes. I respect that they are absolutely beautiful and are a marvel to people who see them differently than I do. The idea of what those planes helped ordinary, loving men do brought such sorrow.

Then when the planes did the demonstrations of how they bombed and napalmed I could only think of Your human and nonhuman creatures on the ground who would be destroyed in horrible ways. It was so hot and the smoke so black. Of course it was pyrotechnics that they lit on the ground, but it felt real. Comments from other folks around us were, "Neat!" "So cool!"

There was a precision drill team from the Air Force that was absolutely perfect in the drills they did with their guns. A father standing next to me had his older son (maybe five years old) on his shoulders and his younger son (maybe four) in his arms. He was extolling the virtues of the teamwork and cooperation and hard work of these men and how they needed to depend on each other. The younger son asked, "Why are they doing that?" In a very surprised voice after a pause the father said, "Because." After another long pause the older son assured his brother, "They are doing tricks with their guns." Another child on the other side of me asked in a frightened voice if they were going to shoot their guns.

Isn't there some other way with some other tools that men could demonstrate just what the father was talking about: teamwork, cooperation, hard work?

5/30/01

On one of our trips to the Midwest we stayed in a cheap motel in a rundown neighborhood in a small town in Oklahoma.

So many of your precious, beloved human creatures live in this kind of ugliness and WORSE every day of their lives. We stay here only because it is only $20 a night. I am sorry for complaining and for feeling ill at ease here. It is clean and quiet and safe.

Hundreds of thousands, probably hundreds of millions of people, children too, wake up to and face this kind of ugliness every day. Inside what makes it ugly is a door that is battered at the bottom and cheap chairs whose seats are water stained. Is that too bad?!

Forgive me. I have spent most of my life trying to make things better for such people. Keep me at it. Give me things to do to make a difference. You so graciously and patiently forgive me. Fill me with Your grace and patience and love so that I may make Your Presence real wherever I go and whatever I do.

6/3/01

Dear Lord our God and Precious Mother, Christ-Sophia, Holy Spirit, You are so great! How great You are and Your greatness is unsearchable! I read in the National Geographic last night about a fish that lives at 2,000 feet deep in the ocean off the coast of northwest Africa. It has headlights! There are three hundred kinds of cacti in the Sonoran Desert and five hundred species of birds can be found here. And that is a miniscule part of all You have created. …How did You do that? Thank You! Praise be to You that You did.

…For so many reasons You are worthy to receive all honor and glory and blessing and worship and adoration! With all of that You are still my life and my breath and my strength. You are my reason for being.

6/19/01

Desmond Tutu writes of an old African farmer who used to sit in church for long periods of silence. When asked about this practice, he said of our Lord, "I look at him and he looks at me and that is enough." What good words for me to hear on these mornings when You fill my heart to bursting and I don't have much to write. I look at You and You look at me and it is enough.

6/23/01

National Gatherings of Bread for the World were mountain top experiences for me before, during and once after I retired. They were like the church at worship and at work. Art Simon, one of the founders of the organization, built into the basics of the mission of BFW prayer, study and action. At the gatherings attendees worshipped, studied in workshops and then took action by visiting members of Congress to talk about the hunger legislation BFW was introducing at the time.

Your power and Your Presence were so fully upon us last night at the opening service. Thank You and praise be to You for Bishop Charles Palmer-Buckle, Diocese of Kaforidua, Ghana. I looked into his beautiful black, white-bearded face and I could see all Africans and feel all the love

243

for that continent that You have placed in my heart. Praise be to You for the powerful speech he gave! Bless him in all he does. Bless his ministry and his people. Bless Ghana and bless Africa. Thank You and praise be to You for that. I wondered if I will ever be able to go there. Thy will be done.

To go to Africa was a childhood dream that accompanied me into adulthood. As a child and as a teenager I read all the books about Africa and African people I could find. Much of the work I did as a Hunger Action Enabler was geared toward Africa. That focus continued in my work for Bread for the World because in alternating years the federal legislation we wrote centered on the needs of people and nations in poverty in Africa. Through all those years I wanted to visit Africa, any of the forty-three countries would have been fine. I just wanted to go there!

6/25/01

Your wonders never cease! When I was listening to Bishop Palmer-Buckle I really, truly felt that I would never get to Africa. Yesterday morning after the plenary I was standing alone searching the crowd for Jenna. A lady I had never met before came over to me and said something about my standing there all alone and we started talking. It was her first time at a Bread gathering and she was here to learn all she could about Africa. She is the person who will lead the next Global Exchange for Presbyterian Women. She thought they would have her lead a group to a place she was somewhat familiar with, but they chose Africa for October of 2002.

I just wanted to cry. She told me how to go about applying and when I told her my background—including that I had read about Africa when I was a little girl—she said I would be a perfect candidate. It would cost $3,500.00, but they want you to raise as much of the money as possible from Presbyterian Women and the churches in your area.

Another thing, as I have been at this meeting and awhile prior I was beginning to realize that You are calling me more to women's work. This would be so perfect. They expect you to be available for two years to speak throughout your presbytery and synod.

I am sure that this is a call from You. An opportunity that I was thinking I would never get and here You have put the possibility before me.

And if I am right, I know, I trust that You will prepare Norm's heart and mind for this as well.

7/11/01

I get so self-centered. Please forgive me. You do cleanse me and improve me and have for all these years. Thank You for Your grace and for Your never-ending patience with me. Please never leave me or let me fall away.

Thank You that Norm is so supportive of my going on the Global Exchange trip to Africa in 2002! I hadn't said a word about it to anyone and then yesterday at breakfast at Denny's in Albuquerque we were talking about how tired we were from the trip. I had been waiting for the right time to bring it up and that seemed right because I have wondered if I could take a sixteen day trip anywhere let alone to Africa. I just said I had been invited to go and that I worried about tiredness. He didn't even respond to the tiredness part just immediately said that I should go.

I really want to get down to work on our book (Learning a New Language) now. Especially if I get to go to Africa in fifteen months. Hopefully, after that I will have some speaking engagements etc. Currently, I am hung up on Jesus-Sophia. I am thinking that maybe it is because I wasn't thorough enough on Spirit-Sophia. Please help me think this through and write it down.

7/22/01

Deep within us there is an amazing inner sanctuary of the soul, a holy place, a Divine Center, a speaking Voice, to which we may continuously return. ...Here is the Slumbering Christ, stirring to be awakened, to become the soul we clothe in earthly form and action. And He is within us all.[4]

"The secret places of the heart cease to be our noisy workshop."[5] Mine is a noisy workshop of self-centeredness. Of feeling slighted or ignored by those I love. A noisy workshop where I sometimes build my own righteousness

---

4   Thomas R. Kelly, *A Testament of Devotion*, (HarperSanFrancisco, 1941), 3.
5   Ibid., 4.

after the pattern I choose. Please forgive me and make my heart and my mind cleaner places.

7/24/01

Thank You and praise be to You that the UN has gone ahead on the Kyoto Treaty without the U.S. May their actions together work together to stop the global warming that we are causing. May it help stop the destruction of this wonderful creation You have given us. May the U.S. sometime in the future join the other nations of the world in efforts that are good for all the earth's people and for the whole earth itself.

7/26/01

Thank You and praise be to You for Matthew Fox and all that he has passed on to us through his writing. Especially now One River Many Wells. As I was reading it last night (the pages about You being Mother God) I felt like I am just on the verge of a new and deeper knowledge of who You are, like there is a thin film between me and that new understanding. It feels like the Jesus-Sophia idea only I am closer to it.

If You reveal Yourself to me as Mother in the ways Matthew Fox writes about, my experience of You will be so different from that of most of the people who worship You. If that happens and even if it doesn't please use me in whatever ways You can. Thank You and praise be to You for using me and help me be patient and open to Your leading in all these coming days and years.

7/30/01

Matthew Fox writes that the Upanishads teach that there is in the center of our body a small shrine in the form of a lotus flower "and within can be found a small space. We should find who dwells there, and we should want to know him."

And that Black Elk says, "The heart is a sanctuary at the center of which there is a little space, wherein the Great Spirit dwells, and this is the Eye. This is the Eye of the Great Spirit by which he sees all things, and through which we see him."⁶

I have known You in my heart for many years. I know without a doubt that You dwell there. And these of other faiths know it too. How wonderful and amazing! And what a beautiful way to say it—that there is a lotus flower there.

8/3/01

Yesterday a woman from Presbyterian Women in the Grand Canyon sent me the application papers for the Global Exchange trip to Africa. I want to go so much that I get a lump in my throat thinking about it. I am also concerned whether I can last physically a two week trip. I just need to keep swimming and when it gets to be winter to walk. If You want me to go on this trip I know You will make me able. Thank you and praise be to You that Norm understands how much I want to do this and is so supportive.

Jim and Nancy were supportive too. They both said to me on separate occasions, "I'm not surprised." They both knew I would go to Africa some day. They hadn't given up on the idea like I had. Jim said he just thought it would be before I retired.

8/19/01

We were driving to a friend's cabin in the mountains to a gathering of people from our church. My new acquaintance (soon to be my good friend) and I were sitting in the back seat with her husband driving and mine sitting in the front with him. She asked what I was doing in my retirement. Instead of giving her a quick answer like I would have given to someone I thought was not really interested, I told her about my writing a book about feminine language for God. The idea was all new to her. She wanted to know more and said she had several friends whom she thought would also be interested.

---

6   Matthew Fox, *One River, Many Wells* (New York, Jeremy P. Tarcher/Putnam, 2000), 155.

Thank You for Susie and how we shared a conversation. Thank You that she was so interested in She Who Is and for her idea for starting a luncheon group to discuss Your feminine names. May she follow through if it is Your will.

She followed through. Six of us met monthly for the next year to discuss the drafts of each chapter of the book. These women, their thoughts and support were essential to me as I labored on the book which became *Learning a New Language, Speech About Women and God.*

9/1/01

You are working a new thing in me and I love You and praise You, worship You and adore You, bless You and honor You, and want always to be in Your flow in all things, in all ways.

I know the book is what You want me to do, without a doubt I know that and for that reason I know it will be published. You have given me the thoughts and the words for it all along. Now what You are growing me to understand is that I need to know You and love You and worship You in the new way and with the new words of Sophia language. By Your love and grace I will do that.

9/12/01

The Day After the Attack.

Dear Lord our God and Precious Mother-Sophia, Christ-Sophia, Spirit-Sophia, You are so great! How great You are and Your greatness is unsearchable!

What a travesty against You, against who You are, this terrible terrorist attack has been. The men who did it, who are now dead, and the men who planned it may think they died doing Your will and that they have earned glory, but most certainly they have not. Neither they nor any one of any race or creed or nationality who has bombed and killed others can feel that they have pleased You, Giver of Life, Lover of Life.

By Your grace and mercy may they be found and punished without the U.S. bombing and killing hosts of people elsewhere in the world.

I can see this morning that it does mean war and war means more death and destruction. Forgive us for our warring ways. This whole thing is too massive, too complex to understand it whole. Only little pieces sink in at a time.

Protect all Arab people who live here in the United States. There will be people here who are almost as demented as the perpetrators of this tragedy who will attack and harass them.

Be with the rescuers and with those who are still alive in the wreckage. Abide with them, strengthen them, save them.

9/13/01

Dear Lord our God and Precious Mother-Sophia, Christ-Sophia, Spirit-Sophia, You are so great! How great You are and Your greatness is unsearchable. You have created such a magnificent, beautiful, mysterious world filled with all kinds of creatures who are also magnificent, beautiful and mysterious. Among them all Your human creatures are the finest and most gifted with the potential for such goodness and love and beauty and ability to love and protect and enjoy the rest of Your creation. But in spite of that potential we hate and destroy each other and all of creation.

Sophia, Mother God, Bearer of Life, Nurturer, would terrible things like this have happened if down through the generations we had known and believed that You are God. I believe so much would have been so different. People down through the ages would have made different choices. Children would have been taught differently. Human beings would still have sinned against You and against each other, but maybe they would not have been so cruel to each other, so judgmental of each other. Maybe creation would be spared from all the havoc human beings have wrought upon it.

I want to make a difference in all of this. In how we name You and how we let You work in our lives. Is that presumptuous or what! Just take me and use me in whatever ways You can in bringing Your life of peace and love to the human race.

Be with all the people whose loved ones have been killed. Give wisdom to our leaders and the leaders of the world. I agree this was an act of war by really cowardly people. May they be treated in accordance with Your will, with Your love for the life of every human being. May the Taliban care about their people enough that they will hand over Bin Laden.

9/14/01

President Bush has called for this to be a day of remembrance. The estimate now is that 4,700 are dead. The search is on for anyone connected to the hijackers whose names they now know—eighteen of them—and they have found the place where they lived. Indonesia's president says she will still come here next week—Indonesia is a Muslim nation.

Is our sin that we have turned away from You to worship a god of our own making, a god who is powerful and vengeful?

Norm and I both struggle with mixed feelings. Obvious horror at the enormity of this savage act along with a prayer for forgiveness and a knowledge of how guilty our country is of atrocities usually of a more subtle nature.

Oh, God of Justice and Love and Peace, Your will be done with the regards to the people responsible. May we not "HAVE" to kill innocent people in order to punish the guilty.

9/15/01

CNN instead of calling their program "Attack on America" like they have been since Tuesday are now calling it "America's New War." That is a phrase Bush used and now it is becoming a mantra. Guide him and all other decision makers as they carry out the justice that is called for. Help them know what justice is. Help them know what shape it should take.

9/17/01

President Bush is like a cheerleader for war. He and others are trying to keep us riled up with all kinds of emotion-laden statements about going to war. And for some people it is working to the point where they are now running a banner on CNN with the number of a hot line for hate crimes. A man from India was shot and killed in Mesa, Arizona, because he looked Middle Eastern. The murderer tried to kill two other people. The victim was a gas station/convenience store owner and was loved by his neighbors and customers. This hatred is as terrible a thing as the death of all the people on the airplanes.

What the leader of a nation thinks and believes so easily becomes the thoughts and beliefs of the people of that nation. The peddling of ideas that Muslims are to be feared and hated was the stock in trade of the administration and even by groups on the "Christian Right." Thus the increase in hate crimes in the days and months following 9/11.

During the years of the Cold War we were led to believe the Communists, one behind every bush, were out to get us. At that time it seemed to me that the Communists could do more to hurt us just by making us believe they were an imminent threat. That fear caused changes in our respect for our own laws and traditions. Fear cast a shadow over the necessity of free speech and free expression of ideas.

In the aftermath of 9/11, I think "terrorists" only have to make us believe they are after us and we will weaken, if not destroy, our democracy and the freedoms that we cherish. In order to make us react in fear they will only have to say, "Boo!"

9/24/01

Help me with my thinking and writing about women. I want to be good and to tell the truth, but I don't want to be bitter and ugly. I want to help people see things in new ways. In ways that could be of some help in making this world a more peaceful, loving place for all people everywhere and for every part of creation. …Take me and use me, dear Sophia-Jesus.

10/5/01

Sometimes people from the Midwest tell me they couldn't live in the desert Southwest because they love the change of seasons which happens in their part of the country. What they can't believe is that seasons change in the desert as well.

Dear Sophia-God and Precious Mother, Christ-Sophia, Spirit-Sophia, You are so great! How great You are and Your greatness is unsearchable! What a wonderful thing it is to feel the changes of seasons. Every morning now I open the study window and the patio door in addition to our open bedroom windows. The air is so cool and so fresh. What a great and awesome mystery is the care with which You created all things in the universe so that they work together in perfect harmony.

Forgive us humans for disrupting that harmony with all of our destruction and misuse of what you have given us. Help us worship You in spirit and in truth and thereby honor Your creation!

10/7/01

The United States began bombing Afghanistan today!

Dear Sophia-God and Precious Mother, Christ-Sophia, Spirit-Sophia, You are so present with us! What a difference it would make in all the happenings of the world if all people knew that You are so close! I think we would not be shouting praise to Allah or Almighty God and then hurting and killing each other if we knew how You are the Spirit of Life within us.

10/10/01

I look at the faces on the TV—world leaders, soldiers, terrorists and they are men! Men! Men! Men! I have been taught and always believed that sin was turning away from You. But maybe our sin is turning you into a man.

I believe that if women were treated as of equal value, if women had been of equal value through all these centuries, if You were seen equally as male and female, all creatures would be treated better. I think there would be justice for all. Not because women are better than men but because we would be free of the belief that some are better than others and deserve more than others.

God of peace and love and justice, forgive us and help us. Ridding the world of terrorists by bombing will only create more terrorists. Sharing the world's wealth equitably is what will rid the world of terrorists. That's a Sophia idea.

A conservative senator says now we need to mount "a humanitarian response to terrorism." He says massive U.S. investment in health, education, agriculture and other areas that will change the environment that "breeds terrorism." He is a very conservative Christian. Oh, Everywhere Present Sophia, may he mean it and may more and more people like him see this truth.

10/11/01

Norm just heard on TV that there are rumors that Bin Laden has been captured. Please may it be so. And may this be the beginning of the end of terrorism. May this be the beginning of a new era in which the U.S. and other nations will have as their top priority the health and well-being of all people everywhere. May the world's top priority be the care of people and of creation. Guide us all and give us wisdom.

10/12/01

Forgive us human creatures that we hurt each other so much and thereby hurt You so much. May this terrible attack and now the multiple attacks on Afghanistan help us realize that this is not the way to settle things.

Forgive those men who shout "Allah be praised!" and then wish for death and bring about death for others. Even though they use the beautiful name, "Allah" for You, they have redefined it to describe a vengeful, hateful, brutal being who doesn't come close to being You.

The world's problems are truly theological problems, aren't they? All the masses of people who are gathering at memorial services to honor the fallen, our political figures are calling on You, are using Your name times without number. May large measures of this piety remain in all people as time goes on.

With very few exceptions the people we see in the crowds from the Middle East and particularly from Afghanistan are men. What have they done to the women? It seems that they have completely paralyzed that part of themselves, of You.

10/17/01

I am so thankful for how good my life is and at the same time pray for all of those whose lives are so bad. Especially I pray for the people in Afghanistan who have known nothing but war for so long. Help us do what we need to do to rid the world of the evil that is terrorism, and forgive us for all the harm and injury we cause others as we do that.

May the anthrax scare be short-lived. Protect all people who come in contact with it. Stop the people who are spreading it. Forgive us for our greed and selfishness as a nation that has led us to this place where there are people who hate us so much.

Why do You put up with all of this? How do You put up with it?

"It is who I am." --God

If You washed your hands of all of this would You be ending Yourself? If You ended humanity would the rest of Your beloved world be enough for You?

All these questions and yet I know beyond a shadow of a doubt that You can bring good out of evil. Please forgive us human creatures who cause the evil. Use us for good for You, for each other and for creation.

"...would You be ending Yourself?" What kind of a question is that! Of course wiping out humanity would not end God. God is above and beyond and around human beings and could easily and quickly wipe us all out and not be changed in anyway. Or could He? Maybe it is a good question after all. It is the persisting question of how God is related to His creation. One of the answers is that God can and will someday wipe out at least the nonbelievers and not be changed one little bit Himself. But there is another answer that suits me better. It is that God is involved in creation in a bodily way, that God's presence is the life and energy of all that is. In such a view of God, He could not end humanity and still exist himself.

11/2/01

Help us Americans deal with our fears. The governor of California announced that there was a good chance of a terrorist "event" of blowing up bridges in California this week! City halls are beefing up security. It seems like it is rising to panic proportions. Give our leaders good sense as they consider stopping the bombing during Ramadan. Guide them to do what is best.

11/4/01

Thank You that the U.S. has the resources to combat anthrax. May we be generous enough to share with any other peoples who might be affected by this terrorist act. Give our leaders and the leaders of other countries wisdom and patience as they deal with this whole terrorist thing.

12/1/01

This morning the Presbyterian Women of the Presbytery Coordinating Team is meeting at University Church and one of the items on their agenda is how to pay for my trip to Africa. I know I am going on this trip because You want me to. It was all more than coincidence how it came about. Help me know how to work with them to raise the $3,500.00 I need. Inspire us all so that this trip will bring glory to Your Holy Name and new understanding and love between the women of our three countries, Ghana, Kenya and the United States. May I be a blessing as You have blessed me.

I am at a tough spot—another one—in the book. Help me think through what Sophia means in the New Testament so that I can put it in Your words.

12/23/01

When I get really old and can't do much but sit will You flood my heart all the time like You do now in these prayer times? It is such a gift and an honor!

1/1/02

I get so discouraged about the book. When I read about the use of quotes in the book, I am afraid a publisher will not want to publish it because so much of it is Elizabeth A. Johnson's material. I still know that this is Your project and that if I am faithful to You, You will see it through. So help me be faithful! Help me listen to Your words to me.

1/5/02

How dare I think any bad or unloving or critical thoughts when I know that my heart is Your dwelling place!

1/12/01

These words of Thomas Kelly express what I was learning about where God lives.

> It seems to me. . .that the Everlasting is the singer, and not we ourselves, that the joy we know in the Presence is not our little private subjective joy, pocketed away from other men [sic], a private gift from a benevolent and gracious God. It is the joy and peace and serenity which is in the Divine Life itself, and we are given to share in that joy which is eternally within all Nows. The song is put into our mouths, for the Singer of all songs is singing within us. It is not that we sing; it is the Eternal Song of the Other, who sings in us, who sings unto us, and through us into the world.[7]

2/14/02

Thank You for the power of Your Presence with me last night at Ash Wednesday Communion. I wasn't even sure I wanted to go—and then during the bread I began to think of Christ's body broken as the bodies of all broken and abused women forever. And then when I held the cup in my hand the words "the blood of God" came to me and I felt all the blood spilled by hatred and violence as Your blood spilled.

Your power and Your might is overwhelming, but so is Your compassion and Your unity with us!

3/20/02

We went to the Grand Canyon yesterday. That awesome creation of Yours must bring You much joy! And the San Francisco Peaks—they were snow-covered and as we were driving home at sunset the snow was a rosy color! And last night the sky was black and the stars brighter than I have ever seen them. We could even see the Milky Way. Thank You

---

7   Kelly, 73.

and praise be to You. You are worthy to receive all praise and adoration and awe and worship and blessing and honor and glory.

4/5/02

Thank You for leading me to read Mary Daly's book, Outercourse. At first I thought I wasn't going to like it, because she makes up so many words. But she is funny and thought-provoking e.g. foreground for patriarchal society and background for the depth of the feminine that has been hidden so long. There have been several places already where her experience resonates with mine even though she has three or four doctorates and I have none.

It turned out that the excitement I felt about reading her book was generated by the words she makes up and the words she re-forms. Spelling "reform" the way I just did is typical of the way she spells words in order to make her thoughts startling to her readers and to plumb the depths of the meaning of the word. Her way of re-forming words is illustrated by the use of re-membering (putting memories together) and dis-covering which describes the process of taking the cover off something to reveal what lies hidden there. Her use of Be-Dazzle instead of bedazzle almost causes the reader to see and feel the dazzle.

Her expression of her philosophy became so full of made up and reformed words that she wrote a book with Jane Caputi, *Webster's First New Intergalactic Wickedary of the English Language*, a dictionary of words she has invented. For instance, one of her made-up words is "maledom" which she sometimes uses in place of patriarchy. Another word she uses to describe patriarchy is "phallocracy."

She uses the word foreground to describe the male-centered domination of society. The word background is the "Homeland of women's Selves and of all the others; the Time/Space where auras of plants, planets, stars, animals, and all other animate beings connect."[8]

4/6/02

Thank You for Mary Daly and her book, Outercourse. She is so, so radical and yet there are many parts of her journey that I can feel because they are

---

8   Mary Daly, *Outercourse, The Be-Dazzling Voyage* (NY, HarperCollins, 1992) 1.

mine as well. She is also helping me identify and name some things. She calls herself a "Radical Feminist Philosopher."

4/9/02

I have been thanking You for Mary Daly and I am still glad I am reading her book. But I want to be done with it. She is getting more and more hateful. She talks about all the laughing, happy experiences, beautiful visions that she and her sisters are having, but the only emotions she expresses about men is the disgust and hatred that she feels towards "phallocracy," her word for patriarchy. It seems that the only men in her life are the ones who are persecuting her and they truly are persecuting her. Her feelings of hatred and deep animosity toward them prevail.

The sex discrimination against her was pervasive and devastating. It began when she was a young woman who wanted to study philosophy. Since philosophy was a "man's" field, she was thwarted and denied at every stage of her studies and career. In the woman's college she attended, all the philosophy and religion courses were taught by priests who expressed only contempt for women's intellect. They would not allow a woman to earn a degree in philosophy or religion. So she graduated with an M.A. degree in English, which was not at all what she wanted.

At St. Mary's College Notre Dame in Indiana she earned the degree of Doctor of Theology, but she was still in search of a doctorate in philosophy. The University of Notre Dame, which is right across the street from St. Mary's, would not accept her as a candidate for a doctorate in philosophy because she was a woman. After teaching in a Catholic college for two years she applied to Catholic University in Washington D.C. to study for a doctorate in philosophy, but they said no because she was a woman.

After that she went to Fribourg, Sweden where she studied religion. For awhile it looked like she would be denied a degree there because every doctoral student was required to take an oath against modernity. She would not take the oath because she believed it an effort to control thought. However, a real twist in logic came to her aid. The rules of the university would not allow a woman to take the oath, but they couldn't deny her the degree she had earned so she received the degree of Doctor in Sacred Theology.

After seven years and with two doctoral degrees she returned to the United States where she accepted a professorship at Boston College. In a gathering of professors in which she was the only woman, all the men were introduced as "Dr." She was introduced as Miss Daly.

In 1969 Boston College fired her because of her latest book, *The Church and the Second Sex*. After a long and bitter fight, she was rehired, granted a promotion and tenure.

It really is no wonder that bitterness and disdain became part of her journey. Those same emotions and experiences were her inspiration for her writing which has led to great insights and produced new found freedom for thousands and thousands of women the world over.

4/11/02

Mary Daly gave up completely on Christianity but all through the book she gives credit to the Great Wind as being her guide and muse. She tells the story of her life in four stages, which she titles, with her great creativity and imagination, Galaxies.

I certainly don't agree with where Mary Daly ended up, but I see truth and wisdom on her way there. And the presence of the Holy Spirit-Sophia. Wherever she is, whatever she is doing, may she be in Your flow.

4/12/02

While visiting Norm's brother and sister-in-law, Ken and Donna, in Houston we went to a nature preserve where alligators were the main attraction.

What a wonderful Creator You are! Yesterday we saw eight alligators, beautiful trees and grasses and fantastic birds! You created this world and decorated it so wonderfully! And so intricately, each part deriving its life from another, all intertwined!

4/20/02

Thank You for the group of women who are discussing "our" book. They say they are learning a lot and enjoying the new ideas. May others who read it find new thoughts and new light for their paths.

I am getting shots toady: yellow fever, hepatitis A and B, tetanus, diphtheria and maybe rabies. I am a little concerned about a reaction to them, but people say they will be easy. One friend told me to take Tylenol before I go because I will get a little fever as my immune system fights to overcome the germs of the diseases. I know this trip is Your will so I know everything will be all right.

4/24/02

Are You Thought Woman (Keres) and Hard Bump Woman (Hopi) and Sky Woman (Seneca)? I believe You are! I am reading The Sacred Hoop by Paula Gunn Allen. She writes about how Indian culture was gynocentric, gynocratic, and that was what irritated the Whites. One man even said some Indians were ruled by a petticoat government. This is all new to me! I want to learn more and more about this and about who You are. And I want to pass it on to other people. Words can change the way things are. I want to be a part of that change in language about You! Take me and use me however You can.

5/4/02

The women in the group reading Learning a New Language really liked the "Spirit Sophia" chapter. They said it was one of the easiest chapters to understand and they confirmed the thesis that we are not taught enough about the Holy Spirit. How blessed I am that you have called me to write this book.

5/21/02

Thank You for the book on African spirituality that is required reading for the Global Exchange. Thank You for Malidoma Some's explanation of how

Africans, at least the Dagaba tribe from Ghana and Burkina Faso think spiritually. He said in essence that nature—trees and plants and water and mountains—don't need language, don't need to speak because their very presence is Spirit, the birds and animals make sounds but they don't need words either. But human beings need words to search for the Spirit from whom they are removed.

These are his actual words:

> So to the Dagara, there is an understood hierarchy of consciousness. The elements of nature, especially the trees and plants, are the most intelligent beings because they do not need words to communicate. They live closer to the meaning behind language. The next most intelligent species are the animals, because they use only a minimum of uttered communication, so their language is closer to the Source, the world of intrinsic meaning. Wise men and women in the indigenous world argue that humans are cursed by the language they possess, or that possesses them. Language, they insist, is an instrument of distance from meaning, an unfortunate necessity that we can't live without but that is so hard to live with."[9]

5/24/02

You are like a gently flowing river that invites me in and when I accept and put myself in Your flow, You carry me smoothly and effortlessly where You want me to be. Praise be to You!

You are like a beautiful symphony. I am an instrument and when I play Your composition I am part of perfection. Praise be to You!

---

9   Malidoma Patrice Some, *The Healing Wisdom of Africa, Finding Life Purpose Through Nature, Ritual, and Community* (NY, Jeremy P. Tarcher/Putnam, 1998) 50.

6/7/02

My preaching on Father's Day is such an opportunity to speak about what You have been teaching me about Yourself. But to do so is scary! I want it to be a feminist sermon without raising any hackles. And I have to think harder about it and probably write it out so that I can say it clearly and strongly. Guide me with Your thoughts and words and then give me courage. Well, I need courage even to write it down. I will look at the book, Real Boys, in a little bit. That might help me be more inclusive.

Later: You know how I am feeling about this sermon—it seems so jumbled and I think it is because of the lectionary passages and what I ended up saying. But I believe You gave me both so it must be good. Did I pray fervently and listen closely? It is always, only by Your grace and Your goodness that I speak or preach well. By Your great goodness fill me with Your grace as I preach this morning.

6/12/02

I was ready to send the manuscript of *Learning a New Language* to an editor at a traditional publishing company. It turned out that he was a good friend of one of my favorite professors in seminary. They had been working together on a book for three years. So I knew something about who he was even though we had never met and had only spoken a couple of times on the phone.

It makes me feel sheepish and inadequate to have such a man reading my manuscript because I may have said some inaccurate things theologically and historically. Then it comes over me, I am reminded, that You and I did this book together. You were continually motivating me to keep working, giving me the ideas and thoughts and words. So I have confidence that it is going to be published. I will get it mailed today. May Your will be done.

6/17/02

The people at the church where I preached the sermon on Father's Day that was causing me so much consternation were friendly and welcoming to me.

Thank You that the service went so well yesterday. Thank You for the sermon and for the courage You gave me to preach it. As far as I could tell it didn't stir up anything. One person said I gave them a lot to think about Moms more than Dads. I suspect that comment would be representative of what most of the men and maybe even some of the women thought.

Maybe what I learned yesterday is that ideas about Your name are so new that people don't know how to respond or even how to think about it. Look how long it has taken me to learn to think about it. And sermons are probably not the place where it is going to get done, but rather in classes or study groups.

It was a let down, but they do want me to come back to preach in July.

They said they wanted me to come back to preach in July, but they have never invited me back—except to do a program for the women. There could be many reasons for that.

7/17/02

You have given me so much time. May I use it wisely and well and always for Your glory. It is still hard to realize how much of it there is. And thank You for showing me that I need to do some "house work" every day. Yesterday I vacuumed and scrubbed floors. It does make me feel better, more grounded.

8/10/02

I didn't hear from the editor at the publishing company. He said he would call me last Monday. The first editor told me sometimes it takes a year, maybe he meant that it can take them that long to decide yes or no. I thought he meant to get the manuscript ready to print. They have had it for almost six months. It really, truly is Your book and You are in charge of the time table, of them and of me. Praise be to You for that and for the good things You have given me to do in the meantime.

8/11/02

I love those little hummingbirds! I am at the dining room table where I can see the feeder and one was just there! They are such a sign of the wonder and the intricacy of Your imagination and inventiveness! They are such a witness to Your existence! Praise and adoration and worship and honor and reverence and blessing and honor be to Your name forever and ever and ever!

8/18/02

Our pastor asked me to help with prayers for healing this morning at worship which is going to be like a Taize service. Please fill my heart for each person who comes to me. Give me the right words to say. I wish I could say when anointing them with oil, "In the name of the Mother or Parent, the Son and the Holy Spirit." Or better yet, "In the name of the Holy Spirit, the Son and the Mother." But that is not a time for teaching.

9/9/02

There are forty-four women signed up for the retreat. May I be Your person that day and always. My Mother Teresa calendar said yesterday,

> Christ must be the light that shines through you, and the people looking at you must see only Jesus. You have a challenge from Jesus to meet: he has shed the light, and you will take his light and lighten every heart you meet.

I want to be that and do that!

9/16/02

One lady at the retreat told me that she loves our male pastors and always gets something out of their messages, but that my words touch her in a deeper way, like we share experiences. That is what being able to call You by feminine names means, isn't it. Keep me on Your track of learning and teaching about names for You.

Chapter Eleven

9/17/02

The itinerary for my Africa trip arrived yesterday. Norm and I looked up the places on the map and I cried and cried! I am going to Ghana and Kenya! Most of the time in Kenya! Why have You bestowed this wonderful gift on me! If I am not careful I will cry again. Your Presence so fills me!

This is a strange way to put it but: May Your investment in me pay off for You and for all whom I meet. May I (we, all of us on the Global Exchange trip) fulfill Your call to us.

9/24/02

My tickets and my visas are here as is the itinerary. Thank You and praise be to You that I am going to Africa! To Africa! Africa! What a sound that has to it! What a call! A sound heard in my inner most self since I was a child. I know it is Your doing and it shows how good and faithful and true You are. How You know each of us from our conception and have a plan for who we will be. Thank You and praise be to You for keeping me in touch with You!

10/1/02

Please dwell with Congress and help them be on the side of peace. Don't let us bomb Iraq! Whatever Hussein is doing, don't let us bomb his country. We call warlike men in Africa "warlords." Why can't we see that name applies to some of our leaders as well.

10/6/02

Today was World Wide Communion Sunday and I was served Communion at Emmanuel Presbyterian Church in Dansoman, Ghana. After all these years of praying for Africans on this special day!! The service lasted over three hours (we were there two and half) and was done in Twi, Ga, and English. It was so good! You were so present! You are worthy to receive all honor and glory and power and praise and love and adoration and reverence now and forever more!

In my diary of the trip I wrote,

It was World Communion Sunday! What a thrill to be in Africa that day! The pastor invited the three of us who are clergy to receive the elements with the pastors of the congregation standing behind the Communion Table. The elders from among us were invited to stand with the elders of the church to receive the elements.

The men's fellowship, about thirty men, sang a song. They were dressed in colorful traditional garb. The choir sat in the balcony on white plastic chairs like Wal Mart sells. The women wore white robes and the men wore black robes. They all wore mortar boards like college graduates wear on graduation night.

For the offering the 'helpers' brought out pedestals on which they placed large plastic pans and large wooden bowls. Then to African music the people shuffled-danced past and put their offerings in. One was for the building fund.

They were in the process of building their church which was very unfinished because they only build when they have the money to do so. They work on part of it and then wait until more money comes. The sanctuary was pretty much finished but the rest of the building had a long way to go. There were second story doors that had no steps going down. And rooms that had no flooring. Their first big building effort had been to erect a two story school house on the grounds because the education of their children was more important than their having a beautiful church building.

We were strangers there, but they made us feel at home. When we got to Kenya a couple of days later, we went to the All Africa Council of Churches' headquarters. Their interim general secretary welcomed us by saying, "You have left home to come home." That is the kind of hospitality we received wherever we went.

We arrived in Accra, Ghana, at night, but our flight to Nairobi arrived in the morning. Looking out the window of the Kenya Airlines plane and seeing Kenya for the first time was like looking at a familiar place—like I had been there before—the plains and the Acacia trees looked just like pictures in the National Geographic.

10/8/02

I expected to weep for the suffering of the Africans when we were at Elmina Castle which is a place where Africans were kept until the slave boats came to take them away. Instead of grief I felt only anger at the church, not the real church, the earthly one. The first building is the Portuguese Chapel. Next you see the female slave quarters on the first floor. On the second floor was a Catholic Chapel which later became a Methodist church, overlooking the courtyard where the African women were paraded naked so the governor could choose one to rape whenever he felt like it! What a travesty! What an abomination! That the Body of Christ should be named in that place!

10/9/02

I am in Africa! It is so wonderful and still hard to believe. It is amazing that nothing so far seems new to me. It is like I have been here before, and I know it is because of Your making a place in my heart for this place. Thank You and praise be to You!

10/14/02

In Nairobi we stayed in the Methodist Guest House, a comfortable hotel provided by the Methodist church for conferences and for a place for rest and relaxation of the people who serve the church's mission in Africa. It was in a nice area of Nairobi.

We walked to the restaurant tonight—single file along the side of the road, Kenyan style. A breeze was blowing and the temperature was so pleasant. I had a steak similar to a filet mignon, lots of fried potatoes and spinach and veggies (which I didn't eat.) I had feelings of guilt from eating too much food in a such nice restaurant. It is so unfair that even here we eat too much—we, privileged people—and so many have little or nothing. Forgive us, Lord!

10/16/02

I am needing "alone" time and I have a few minutes right now while my roommate mails some post cards. Every morning the birds' songs really FILL the air. Thank You and praise be to You for all Your bountiful gifts! Thank you and praise be to You for the warmth and hospitality of these Kenyan people.

10/26/02

Senator Paul Wellstone from MN and his wife and daughter and five others were killed in a plane crash yesterday. Oh, Lord, he was one of the really, really good guys in all of Congress. Thank You for his life and his witness to justice for all people. Comfort the rest of his family and the families of the other people who died.

Help the citizens of our country elect good men and women in November. The whole world needs them so much!

11/10/02

My manuscript for *Learning a New Language* was rejected on the basis that they had changed their marketing strategy and there was no room in the new strategy for such a book as mine. The editor who rejected it made two suggestions. One was that I rewrite it as a study guide to Dr. Johnson's book, *She Who Is.* That was not even a possibility in my mind after all the work I had done on "our" book. Although, I did subsequently write a study guide that the publisher said would be put on an online site. His other suggestion was that I have it published by iUniverse.com and distribute it myself.

As "we" (God and I) were writing the book I said I would not self-publish, but if it was rejected I would find a way to make copies and get them out through retreats, etc. That is exactly what is being offered to me, suggested to me. My out-dated idea was to make copies at Kinko's and staple them together. This idea is to use modern technology.

Help me know what Your plan is for this work that we have done together. I think maybe You are saying that I should submit it to Westminster Press or Geneva Press before I go to any of the other options. And that would be a good thing to do since it will be a couple of weeks before I can really settle down to any kind of a rewrite.

11/21/02

For two years the trip to Africa occupied much of my thought and activity. Groups of Presbyterian Women from Arizona and New Mexico, the women who had subsidized my trip wanted to hear all about it. In that period of time I visited thirty churches to give reports on the trip. It was a joy and delight to share the inspiration and knowledge I had gained from the trip. God journeyed with me wherever I went. One morning in a motel in Williams, Arizona I wrote:

All night my heart has been full of the power of Your Presence! As I fell asleep I thought of the beauty of the people in the Kingman church, the beauty of the African people, the beauty of the San Francisco Peaks—snow covered with the pink glow of sunset, and the bright beauty of the moon in this crisp, clean air! I awakened a couple of times in the night—I would like to remember that it was many times because it was so sweet—and each time I felt possessed, filled almost overcome by Your Spirit. And I awoke this morning with the same blessed feeling!

Please accept the openness of my heart as praise and thanks because there are no words to say it! O Sophia God, You are so good and so loving. You are such a caregiver! A lover!

11/29/02

You are so loving and so kind and gentle and forgiving and we show ourselves, Your people, to be the opposite. Yesterday a suicide bomber killed thirteen people in a resort hotel in Kikambala, Kenya, near Mombasa. They also fired a missile at an Israeli plane that was taking off from Mombasa International Airport. Three killed were Israelis (two teenagers and a sixty-year-old man), ten were Kenyans (hotel workers.)

Now the defense minister of Israel says: "If anyone doubted that the citizens of Israel cannot stand up to the killers of children, this doubt will be resolved." And Bush says: "Today's attacks underscore the continuing willingness of those opposed to peace to commit horrible crimes. Those who seek peace must do everything in their power to dismantle the infrastructure of terror that makes such actions possible."

Oh, Prince of Peace, forgive our warlike ways and help us be better. Act better.

1/1/03

The beginning of another year! A friend wrote an email: We are still here and are pleased to know that you are too." We laughed and laughed, but it is a good statement! Thank You that all my loved ones are here to enter another year.

1/21/03

You are our God of love and peace! And yet, many who worship You and call You their Father are sending troops to the region of Iraq preparing to attack innocent people. So it has always been, I guess, but must it always be so? There are also hundreds of thousands of people of all faiths all around the world who are demonstrating for peace. May Your love and peace prevail!

1/31/03

One of the religious publishers rejected our book! It was a purely form letter with no help or ideas in it. I am sure now that I need to explore self-publishing. I know, help me know that this book was and is Your idea. I felt Your Presence so strongly during the study and writing of it.

I am glad in a way to have it back to work on some more and to get back into the flow of ideas. It amazes me that I am not bummed out and crying about this second rejection. That is pretty amazing self-confidence for one like me. But it is really not self-confidence. It is confidence in You. Faith and trust that this work is not "mine" but "ours."

2/10/03

O God our heavenly Mother, You who love beyond measure and desire shalom for all Your creation, hear the cries of the people who hate war and desire peace! Hear our cries above the sound of the war drums. May we, Your human creatures, raise up our voices to You and to the world in a great chorus calling for the war mongering to stop!

2/15/03

People who live in fear imprison themselves in their fears. Obviously, there are many things in the world to be afraid of both individually and as nations. And appropriate precautions should be taken, but people who fan our fears into flames that disable us should be avoided. Or not re-elected.

Please may no terrorist acts happen this weekend as they are so afraid they will. I may very well not be taking all of this seriously enough. I think it is all or almost all about a campaign of disinformation. Even it if is that it is just as dangerous as if every word of it were true.

2/16/03

The church we attend in Tempe, Arizona, dedicates the month of February every year to mission. Fittingly, it is called Mission Month and is celebrated with speakers, classes and potluck dinners. All of these events as well as others are focused on the topic chosen for the month. The topics cover a wide range and have included Africa, our neighborhood, spiritual practices, Christianity and art. In February of 2004 the topic was From Desert to Desert, in an effort to help people understand the region in which we had become involved in war for the second time. Each year Mission Month helped me grow in many ways. In 2003 the topic was Science and Religion. It had a powerful impact on my thoughts and beliefs.

Father George Coyne spoke last night. He is the Pope's astrophysicist who spends part of each year at the Vatican Observatory near Tucson, Arizona. He gives new meaning and depth to my invocation about Your greatness…How can I (we) have ignored astronomy all these years? … We have indeed kept You too small. We want to make You manageable! These new discoveries give whole new meaning to the word and concepts of transcendental and immanent.

2/17/03

Father George Coyne has been this week's speaker at UPC and, oh, the wonders he has shown us! I was going to ask, "Why do we think we are so important in this universe that is beyond vast?" I think the answer is that if we are the only "intelligent" life in it then we are very important and must be very special to You! Since You are the God of billions of years and 100 billion galaxies holding 100 billion stars that has all been in existence for 137 billion years how can You be concerned about us!

"Because you are in my image." --God

2/18/03

I want to study more about astronomy, but I fear it will disrupt my faith, my relationship to You. Father Coyne says such study deepens and enriches faith. As I was showering this morning I was thinking about how what I may learn further about the universe will affect my knowledge of You residing in my heart and the phrase, "God is the essence of everything," came to my mind. Is that a good way to say it?

Essence means more than that You live in my heart. It means You are the core of my being, of me. Are You the Essence of all that is? Even nonhuman creatures and inanimate creation. This makes sense to me—as little as I understand—but I surely do need to think about it more.

3/17/03

Even though I wasn't well enough to go to worship yesterday a.m. You blessed me so richly by guiding me to read all of Jay McDaniels' book, Living from the Center. Much of it was stuff I already knew, but what was new to me was powerful!

It is at least part, maybe all (no, never all), of the answers to my questions that have arisen since Science and Faith month. Thank You and praise be to You for guiding me to read it and to fill my needs the way it did. I want to spend more time with it, but it will probably be awhile.

"Yes, daughter. Like the rest of your life. Don't rush." --God

O my Always Loving, Always Creating Companion and Savior, never let me fall away from You. My "new" thoughts tell me I can't fall away from You because there is nowhere but You to fall. So my prayer should be: never, never let me close myself to You. You are my life and my breath and my strength! You are my reason for being.

3/18/03

I am beginning to think about You and experience You in a new way(s) that is awesome and scary and very inviting.

This a.m. about two, I heard noises outside and went out in the back to look. It was a full moon, clouded over, but still almost as bright as day. When I got back in bed I lay there and thought about the idea that all of this and me are inside You! I can't imagine such a thing in terms of just the planet, but it feels true when I think of it in terms of the whole universe being inside You.

…President Bush last night announced that unless Saddam Hussein leaves Iraq we and our allies (Great Britain and Spain) will start bombing in forty-eight hours. That means tomorrow sometime. "My" new theology makes even more real the suffering that will be caused to You! This You, Your body, Your being that is about to be assaulted viciously!

3/19/03

At the same time Your creation is singing Your glory, some of Your human creatures have intentions to destroy it by bombing another wonderful part of it. Headlines say 300,000 troops are ready to move into Iraq. And the front page above the fold color picture shows the roads out of Baghdad jammed with fleeing people. Doesn't even show those who have to flee on foot with their children and their elderly.

Dear Heart of the World, Heart of all that is forgive us and help us! We get ourselves into such awful messes.

Would lifting the sanctions and flooding the people with what they need have been a better way to topple such a man as Hussein?

3/21/03

The war on Iraq started.

3/24/03

O Lord, they are killing and capturing people. The TV says when the "coalition" captures people they let them go, but when Iraq captures people they take their pictures in demeaning poses and situations. My heart breaks and I can barely think about it. Oh, dear loving Creator of us all, how much more must this grieve Your loving heart! And over the ages how much of this You have seen and felt. I pray for comfort for You! That the love and lives of most of us human creatures may be a balm to Your bleeding heart.

Help us seek, diligently seek, the truth in every matter and then have the courage to follow it and live by it.

As you can see from the date of this prayer it was written three years before photos of American torture of war prisoners were made public. Early in 2003 there were already rumors of torture done by the Coalition forces.

3/25/03

Please, please bring good out of this great evil. Be with the soldiers and their families—all of the soldiers and their families whether American, Iraqi or British. Comfort them and hold them close to You.

4/10/03

Thank You that Baghdad "fell" yesterday. May they find out without a doubt what has become of Hussein. May this all be for the good of the Iraqi people.

Forgive us for the great harm and suffering we have caused so many people. We saw pictures of a twelve-year-old who lost both arms and has third degree burns over sixty percent of his body. His mother was killed. Our corpsmen are seeing horrific things.

4/27/03

I read these words in an essay written by Annie Dillard.

> We can live any way we want. People take vows of poverty, chastity and obedience—even of silence—by choice. The thing is to stalk your calling in a certain skilled and supple way, to locate the most tender and live spot and play into that pulse. This is yielding, not fighting. A weasel doesn't "attack" anything; a weasel lives as he is meant to, yielding at every moment to the perfect freedom of single necessity.[1]

You spoke to me in that one sentence about enjoying my life moment by moment and not filling each moment with thoughts and plans about what I am going to do next or what is going to happen next. I took it to mean that there is perfect freedom (and thus joy and contentment, relaxation and enjoyment) in each thing I am doing. I spend a lot of time thinking about and planning and, yes, even worrying about what is going to happen next and how I can facilitate it.

---

1   Lorraine Anderson, *Sisters of the Earth* (NY, Vintage, 1991), p.110.

Dillard goes on to widen the meaning of "single necessity" by writing, " I think it would be well, and proper, and obedient, and pure, to grasp your one necessity and not let it go, to dangle from it limp wherever it takes you."² This says to me that I should "grasp the one necessity" of writing and do it. I have been thinking a lot lately: you don't write just by thinking about it or wanting to do it. You write by sitting down and doing it.

I know my single necessity for the past months has been speaking about Africa. Help me now turn to "our" book or whatever it is that You want me to write and make it my single necessity at least for the summer.

5/14/03

Grants, NM. I wonder if the last person to stay in this room was a holy person and some of her holiness remains. If so may I be continuing the power. This is what prayer is about—abiding in Your presence.

I want to be me for all of eternity. You are creating a good thing in me, of me and I want to enjoy You forever as me. What made me think of this was connecting my spirit to Yours which is the Spirit of the whole universe and then wondering whether I would be swallowed up in Your immensity or whether I would enjoy You as me forever and ever. Not only me but all my loved ones.

…Another question which is probably pretty elementary. Can I be a conduit to others of Your presence and power? I think that must be what putting your candle on a hill instead of under a bushel means. Does this Presence of You in me show to other people?

I have been feeling Your Presence powerfully for almost forty-five minutes. (I am timing me not You ☺) even with my mind wandering. I think You would stay all day if I would. You are my life and my breath and my strength. You are my reason for being! You are worthy to receive power and glory and blessing and honor and praise and adoration and worship now and forever.

6/4/03

Even though I had submitted the manuscript to a couple of publishers, I was still rethinking and rewriting parts of it.

---

2   Ibid., 111.

As I work and reread She Who Is, I think, "What is the purpose of my doing this? How will I use it?"

"Just do it." God

You keep telling me, "Just do it."

> *"The time for doing this is now. The future will unfold for you in my good time. This is not the end. It is part of your journey and needs to be attended to faithfully and with care and attention and with patience to change things." --God*

Help me know what needs to be changed and to do it. Always for Your glory.

6/9/03

It really is quite like me that I do things to get them done and when they are done (no matter how well or how poorly) I am ready to move on to the next thing. Help me stay the course with You on the book.

6/18/03

"The moment a woman becomes conscious of the way her world goes together, she is obligated to say her truth for the sake of all women yet unborn."[3] *This statement reinforces my wanting to get the book published and to teach it. Praise be to You, my Great Teacher! Give me courage and wisdom to do this. "Unless we take risks in our time, the time to come will be no better for the women who depend on us to make the path."*[4]

6/21/03

It is an understatement to say that one of the best places to learn how to pray is the Psalms. Written centuries ago, these prayers still and always will, express the deepest desire that humans have for God. Praise, joy, grief, anger, revenge, jealousy—all these human emotions surface in these prayers. You can create your own prayer book by reading through

---

3   Joan D. Chittister, *The Story of Ruth, Twelve Moments in Every Woman's Life* (Grand Rapids, MI, William B. Eerdmans, 2000), 67.

4   Ibid., 69.

the Book of Psalms from beginning to end and marking the ones that move your spirit. Then you can go back to them time and time again to find what you need to strengthen you whatever your situation. From time to time read them all again and mark the ones you haven't already marked. These prayers will connect you to God in marvelous ways.[5]

I love you, O LORD, my strength.
The LORD is my rock, my fortress, and my deliverer,
my God, my rock in whom I take refuge,
my shield, and the horn of my salvation, my stronghold.
I call upon the LORD, who is worthy to be praised,
so I shall be saved from my enemies.
(Ps 18:13)

Sometimes a Psalm will sing itself to you as you read it.

The LORD lives! Blessed be my rock,
and exalted be the God of my salvation. (Ps 18:46)
Make me to know Your ways, O Lord;
teach me your paths.
Lead me in your truth and teach me,
for you are the God of my salvation;
for you I wait all day long. (Ps 25:4,5)

6/24/03

Ascribe to the LORD, O heavenly beings,
ascribe to the LORD glory and strength.
Ascribe to the LORD the glory of his name;
worship the LORD in holy splendor. (Ps 29:1,2)

Ascribe to the Lord the glory of His name. That is what "our" book is about: the glory of Your name. Help me understand in the depths of my being what that means and help me be able to speak it as well as write it.

7/2/03

My soul is satisfied as with a rich feast,
and my mouth praises you with joyful lips

---

5   Other Psalms that I noted in my prayers are: *Ps. 36:9; 38:18; 43:3; . 51:6, 15; . 52: 8,9; . 54:2; .57:5, 7-11; 62:1,2.*

when I think of you on my bed, and meditate on you in the
watches of the night;
for you have been my help, and in the shadow of your
wings I sing for joy. (Ps 63:5-7)

I do meditate upon You in the watches of the night. I seldom thank You
for that grace when I write these morning prayers, but feeling Your Presence
in my heart as I am falling asleep and if I awaken in the night is a blessing
beyond blessings. Thank You and praise be to You!

7/3/03

You crown the year with your bounty;
your wagon tracks overflow with richness. (Ps 65:11)

So beautiful and like I had never read it before. Your wagon tracks
in my life certainly overflow with riches! Thank You and praise be to You
forever and ever.

I looked for this passage in commentaries so that I could understand
what the psalmist meant by wagon tracks, but I couldn't find anything.
Then I remembered how we used to glean corn fields when we lived in
northeastern Nebraska. Every fall we would take the youth from our
church into the corn fields that had been picked by machine and we
would pick up the ears that had fallen from the pickers or from the
trucks. The yield was so bountiful that bushels and bushels of corn were
left on the ground. The tracks overflowed with richness.

Norm and I even went so far as to stop and pick up ears of corn
along the road that we drove between Norm's two country churches. We
would throw them in the trunk of our car and add them to the bushels
that the kids gleaned. After the gleaning, one of the farmers from the
congregation would add what we had to his truck load of corn to be
taken to the grain elevator. An estimate of what we had harvested was
made and the youth group was paid for the corn.

Indeed, God's wagon tracks overflow with richness in my life.

7/5/03

I have mentioned before the power in changing the pronouns in a
passage of Scripture. Meditating on God as "she" in these powerful

verses helps me visualize God in all her glory and gives power to the concept that it is appropriate to call God "She."

Sing to God, sing praises to her name;
  lift up a song to her who rides upon the clouds—
her name is the LORD—
  be exultant before her. (Ps 68:4)

Awesome is God in her sanctuary, the God of Israel,
  she gives power and strength to
  her people.
Blessed be God! (Ps 68:35)

Let heaven and earth praise her; the seas and everything that moves in them. (Ps 69:34)[6]

7/26/03

The LORD is king, he is robed in majesty,
  the Lord is robed, he is girded with strength. (Psalm 93:1)
As I read that You gave me the insight that it is all right to call You king, but not that name alone. I have been writing this in the book for almost four years now and it just now connected for real for me. Maybe it is partly because of the way Shelley dealt with Mary and Barb's comments about calling You Father. She said in essence: if that is the noun that suits you use it.

No, it's not that simple. The first part is right. I needed to make that connection in my thinking. Using only one name or sex for You is too limiting. She can survive and have a deep faith but she is missing a lot. And as far as peace and justice are concerned using more names for You is essential.

Got the title for the book!

Thinking of titles for sermons and articles has always been a stumbling block for me. I think it started in my preaching class in seminary when my professor, whom I admired greatly, thought the

---

6   More Psalms that I recorded in my prayer journal: 86:11,12,13; 89:1, 11, 14-17; 90:12,17; 92:1-5; 93:4; 95; 96; 103:1- 5, 10; 108:1-5.

title of the sermon I preached for the class was too cute. It was "Danger in the Manger," a Christmas sermon. Anyway, I had been writing my book for four years and didn't have a title. Then one day, this day, I got it: *Learning a New Language, Speech About Women and God.*

7/29/03

We went to hear a speaker from the American Friends' Service Committee speak last night about U.S. foreign policy. It was very disheartening and sad. He said, and cited policies, that we have always been an empire building nation.

He said people in Europe and other places are starting to see in us the same patterns they saw in the rise of Nazi Germany. Our military bases in so many countries, always putting our interests first. And now the taking away of our civil rights.

Oh, Lord, help Your will be done in this country. May we come to see that we are not Your nation in so much of what we do. Remove or mute the people who are causing us to move in these directions.

I believe that She Who Is could change all of this but what chance does She have when all the power is in the hands of people—good ones and bad ones—who won't even listen to such talk.

What difference would it make if the U.S. went down like other empires have? We are talking the course of history here.

7/30/03

Rain takes on a whole new significance when you live in the desert. I grew up in Nebraska where from time to time there were droughts that made the land dry. My maternal grandfather was a farmer in central Nebraska where rain was usually sufficient and the soil was rich. My paternal grandfather was a farmer whose land was on the edge of the Sand Hills and whose soil was largely clay. His fields were usually thirsty for rain until the days of irrigation dawned. However, those dry times and places were wet compared to the desert. In the desert rain is measured and reported when it is less than half an inch.

After one hundred and four days without rain, a monsoon hit last night. I think we got half an inch. We turned off the TV because of lightning and it was such a good feeling to listen to the rain. Everything looks refreshed this morning.

Dear Lord our God-Sophia and Precious Mother, Christ-Sophia, Spirit-Sophia, You are so great! How great You are and Your greatness is unsearchable. This desert part of Your creation is singing Your praises this morning. Some plants are windblown and broken but there is a cleanness about things, refreshment. If You are in all of this it must feel good to You too! The good health of Your precious creation pleases You.

8/7/03

As I wrote Learning a New Language, Speech About Women and God, I wanted it to cause great changes, to help change the world and world systems. Deliver me from proud thoughts and vain desires. What is happening is that individuals are being changed by it already. And I give You thanks and praise for that. May I always be a co-creator with You in making this a just and peaceful world. Take me and use me in whatever ways You can.

8/23/03

Yesterday I googled Sophia and found a list of Scriptures where Sophia is referred to and an article by Joyce Rupp on seeking Sophia. She said her spiritual journey deepened and she began to know You as Sophia when she used Sophia passages for her devotions. So I am going to put aside the Psalms and do what she did. Sophia needs to be as real in my heart as You, whom I have always known, are. Sophia, speak to me and help me know You for my spirit's sake and for the sake of my proclaiming You!

…I am not learning to love and worship a different "person." I am enriching my faith, making it possible to be touched by God in different ways. God is God. Our names for her are only partial descriptions. The ancients' understanding of Sophia teaches us that. I understand. Help me understand more.

Chapter Twelve

8/26/03

What I name You doesn't change You or Your response to me in any way, does it? What changes is me and my response to You. And since I want my faith to deepen and be enriched always, many and new names are good, beautiful and helpful.

Presbyterians don't pay much attention to the books called the Apocrypha, but I have found passages there about God, Wisdom/Sophia that have enhanced and expanded my ways of relating to God. The Wisdom of Solomon is one of those books. Especially inspiring is this passage from 7:21 through 8:7. I have copied it in its entirety because few Protestants have Bibles that contain the Apocrypha.

> [21]I learned both what is secret and what is manifest,
> [22]for wisdom, the fashioner of all things, taught me.
> There is in her a spirit that is intelligent, holy,
> unique, manifold, subtle, mobile, clear, unpolluted,
> distinct, invulnerable, loving the good, keen,
> irresistible, [23]beneficent, humane,
> steadfast, sure, free from anxiety,
> all-powerful, overseeing all,
> and penetrating through all spirits
> that are intelligent, pure, and altogether subtle.

²⁴For wisdom is more mobile than any motion;
because of her pureness she pervades and penetrates all things.
²⁵For she is a breath of the power of God,
and a pure emanation of the glory of the Almighty;
therefore nothing defiled gains entrance into her.
²⁶For she is a reflection of eternal light,
a spotless mirror of the working of God,
and an image of his goodness.
²⁷Although she is but one, she can do all things,
and while remaining in herself, she renews all things;
in every generation she passes into holy souls
and makes them friends of God, and prophets;
²⁸for God loves nothing so much as the person who lives with wisdom.
²⁹She is more beautiful than the sun,
and excels every constellation of the stars.
Compared with the light she is found to be superior,
³⁰for it is succeeded by the night,
but against wisdom evil does not prevail.

8She reaches mightily from one end of the earth to the other,
and she orders all things well.
²I loved her and sought her from my youth;
I desired to take her for my bride,
and became enamored of her beauty.
³She glorifies her noble birth by living with God,
and the Lord of all loves her.
⁴For she is an initiate in the knowledge of God,
and an associate in his works.
⁵If riches are a desirable possession in life,
what is richer than wisdom, the active cause of all things?
⁶And if understanding is effective,
who more than she is fashioner of what exists?
⁷And if anyone loves righteousness,
her labors are virtues;
for she teaches self-control and prudence,
justice and courage;
nothing in life is more profitable for mortals than these.

8/27/03

One who rises early to seek her
    will have no difficulty,
for she will be found sitting at the
    gate.
To fix one's thought on her is
    perfect understanding,
and one who is vigilant on her
    account will soon be free
    from care.
because she goes about seeking
    those worthy of her,
and she graciously appears to them
    in their paths,
and meets them in every thought. (Wisd. of Sol. 6:14,16)

Oh, Sophia, I want You to meet me in every thought…Wherever my mind wonders this morning Your Presence is strong in my heart! I love that and I thank and praise You for such a great and wonderful gift!

9/17/03

At the time I wrote this prayer I had been working on my book, *Learning a New Language,* and wrote the introduction based on the idea of God growing me. Joyce Rupp also wrote about Sophia growing her.

> Sophia has given me much hope and courage in my process of growing up. It is her "bread of understanding" and her "water of wisdom" that continue to nourish and to strengthen me as I search for and accept the person I am becoming. I have grown in my trust of her presence. Each time I approach another step in growing up, I realize that it is Sophia's movement in my spirit that leads me to greater understanding and wisdom. I see

Sophia as an ever-present guide who is always ready to help me to continue to grow up.[1]

9/29/03

Thank You and praise be to You for the beauty of the planet that I saw as I flew home from Albuquerque! The changing terrain and the light of the sun going down and changing was so beautiful! The shadows of the mesas and bluffs and mountains turned the mesas, bluffs and mountains into islands floating in a dark sea! Somewhere the sunlight shining on rock ridges turned them white and the land itself red.

10/6/03

Thank You for the thoughts and words You gave me in Sunday School yesterday in our discussion of whether homosexuals are entitled to "marriage" and legal rights. In a nut shell it was that the relationship gives meaning to the word not the other way around.

Parts of our society believe that marriage can only be between a man and a woman. In their minds that defines what marriage is. Gourmet cooks and connoisseurs of good food talk about a marriage of flavors. Interior designers converse about the marriage of color and style. So what does the word marriage mean? It can be whatever unites two different things, two different persons together to make unity and perfection.

A friend told me about her sister and her sister's partner, a woman, and the kind of relationship they had for decades. It was a description of a near perfect marriage—way better than what some marriages between a man and a women are.

Jesus said nothing about people who are homosexual. I am sure that if he were in our midst in human flesh today he would invite himself to their homes or sit down to eat with them wherever he would find them, just as he would with the rest of us. And he would encourage their love and commitment to each other.

---

1   Joyce Rupp, *The Star in My Heart, Experiencing Sophia, Inner Wisdom* (Philadelphia, Innisfree Press, 1990) 26.

10/19/03

What has naming Jesus Sophia done for my faith?

Seeing the feminine in my Lord and Savior not only gives me a true picture of the fullness of God, but it also helps me see and feel that I, a woman, am a worthwhile and acceptable representation of God. I revel in the fact that the man, Jesus, did so much in feminine ways.

12/13/03

It is beautiful the way You work in me! You are continually changing me—I could wear the label: new and improved. Thank You for the sensitivity and insight You give me. Help me always be aware of it and always may it bring glory to Your holy name and be useful to others. Make me useful to others.

12/25/03

Our granddaughter was born on December 2, 2003. We went to stay with our daughter and her husband to help out with this new little person who had come into our lives.

What a miracle she is. O dear Sophia, sometimes as I look at her and the love and comfort with which she is surrounded I grieve for all the babies in the world who are not loved and all those who are loved but whose parents don't have the means to care for them. Please forgive all of us for allowing a system to exist that makes babies poor. Show me what I can do about it now that I am retired.

1/24/04

Today I mailed the manuscript to a publisher.

1/27/04

Marcus Borg uses the words "thin places" to describe times when people are sharply aware of Your Presence. I thank You and praise You that I experience so many of these places! And in giving that thanks I would also ask for more "thin places!" Always for Your glory and my love for You.

Based on the Apostle Paul's words that in God we live and move and have our being, Marcus Borg suggests that God is a non-material layer of reality all around us. He writes that God is "right here" as well as "more than right here."

> "Thin places" are places where these two levels of reality meet or intersect. They are places where the boundary between the two levels becomes very soft, porous, permeable. Thin places are places where the veil momentarily lifts, and we behold God, experience the one in whom we live, all around us and within us.[2]

He goes on to say that people can become thin places. Jesus must have been a thin place as are the saints known and unknown, Christian and non-Christian.

1/28/04

When she received my manuscript, Dr. Johnson emailed: 'Your manuscript arrived. Congratulations! It's a wonderful accomplishment. I look forward to a good read when spring break arrives next month. And if this publisher does not accept it, there are other possibilities. As they say down under, good on you, mate! Cordially, Beth Johnson"

3/2/04

Dear Lord our God Sophia and Precious Mother, Christ Sophia, Spirit Sophia, You are so great! How great You are and Your greatness is unsearchable.

You are Love. You are love shared!
Love connecting!
Love growing!
Love creating!

---

2   Marcus Borg, *The Heart of Christianity, Rediscovering a Life of Faith* (HarperSanFrancisco, 1989), 155.

> *Love amazing!*
> *Love blessing!*
> *Love elating!*
> *Love discovering!*
> *Love unending!*
> *Love abounding!*
> *Love prevailing!*

4/26/04

You are so good! How good You are and Your goodness knows no bounds! You have filled my life with such goodness! Good husband. Good children and granddaughter. Good family. Good friends. Good home. Good church. Good pastors. And such beauty—the beauty of nature around our home and in all of Arizona. The beauty of love and friendship. And most of all the goodness and beauty of friendship with You.

6/19/04

O Lover of all humans and all creation, I read part of the paper before I sat down to pray and it makes me want to cry! How can human beings created in love by Love be so love-less! The deaths of the "illegals" coming across the border, the beheading of Paul Johnson by al Qaeda, the boy taking a shotgun to school in Florida. It just goes on and on. I ask, "How are You there?" You are there as one who suffers with her loved ones, a loving, comforting Mother, as one seeking justice, as one caring for the needs of the injured. The warrior, king, sovereign images of You don't fit.

6/21/04

Thank You and praise be to You for giving our pastor the sermon You gave him for yesterday morning. "The Mothers and the Midwives." All about the women in the first chapter of Exodus. It felt so good to have women as the main characters in a sermon!

7/4/04

Bless America today and because of Your blessing America may we be a blessing to the peoples of the world and, indeed, the world itself. Elizabeth Schussler Fiorenza writes that a democracy needs a vision and a civil imagination. At this time I think my country does not have either. I think the current administration et al have a vision for their own power and riches, but they present it cloaked in a vision for democracy for the world. There is no opportunity for a civil imagination because the vision that prevails is secret and resists, indeed, battles any idea from citizens who are outside this vision. Sophia, help us and help the world and all its inhabitants, human and nonhuman.

7/12/04

We took a bus tour of the Canadian Rockies and saw the most beautiful scenery.

The rainbow on the way from Calgary to Banff! I can't remember ever having seen a complete rainbow, ends touching the ground and so transparent that things behind it showed through. It is no wonder the Hebrew people took that as a sign of special love and promise from You!

The massiveness of the Canadian Rockies. They are so different from the Colorado Rockies. Both are breathtakingly beautiful, but the Canadian Rockies are absolutely massive! And separated by valleys and meadows. And the glaciers are one more tribute to Your greatness! We walked on the Athabasca Glacier in the Columbia Icefield. It is amazing! Absolutely awesome! It has been there for tens of thousands of years! For me this makes You so much more awesome and powerful than believing that You did it all in seven days! Praise be to You forever and ever world without end.

8/22/04

Dear Lord our God Sophia and Precious Mother, Christ Sophia, Spirit Sophia, You are so great! How great You are and Your greatness is unsearchable! You are the Fashioner. You are and always have been fashioning me. Today that fashioning is taking public expression. You have been fashioning me to be a feminist theologian. Today I have to say it out loud in front of the congregation at Celebration of Life Church.

I am preaching on "Naming Toward God" and I am afraid for two reasons. One is that I might offend someone and cause them to be angry with the pastor, the session and the church. …Give me the courage to speak boldly! And clearly!

I am also afraid that I won't be able to express the richness of the experience of naming you. Of speaking to You. This is all truly a new language. The words are familiar but the thoughts they express are new. I have a partial manuscript. Please give me the thoughts and words to make it come alive for me and for the people. Open their hearts and their minds to what You want them to hear and understand and do.

8/26/04

This morning I didn't even ask (I was thinking about the manuscript) and You gave me the topic for Saturday morning's devotions for the PWPCT.[3] Names for You. I had been thinking about using a passage about a woman, but this is better. Elizabeth Kubler Ross, who died just a couple of days ago, was quoted as having called You a "damned procrastinator" for not letting her die sooner after her stroke. (Today she is quoted as having said that after her death she will be "dancing across the galaxies.") Norm had read to me that Garrison Keillor called You the Great Listener. You gave me the idea to use these two illustrations as the "thesis" of devotions about naming You.

You are Holy Wisdom, the Divine Communicator, Teacher, Healer, Helper, Guide and Stay. You are worthy to receive all honor and glory and power and praise and love and adoration and worship.

9/10/04

I am reading Mary Magdalene by Lynn Picknett and she says so many things about You—most of which I believe—and about Jesus—which upset me. I do believe that You came to earth in Jesus and lived a human life. She doesn't. I need to ponder that. What is wrong if I believe it? What

---

3   Presbyterian Women of the Presbytery of the Grand Canyon Coordinating Team.

is wrong if I don't? So much good has been done on earth because of Jesus. And so much evil has been done in His name as well.

Regardless of who Jesus the man was, I have known You in him! And I praise you and thank you and worship You and adore You! Guide me in this thinking about You and keep me always near You. Never let me fall away.

9/11/04

The way You have guided and helped us through the whole process of preparing this women's retreat is witness to the fact of Your immanence and Your faithfulness. Now the day is here! Bestow upon us, the leaders, courage and faith and wisdom. Fill us with Your Holy Spirit that we may touch the hearts of Your beloved women who come and that we may bring glory to Your great and wondrous name.

Fill the women who come with Your Holy Spirit so that they may hear what You have to say to each of their hearts and that they may hear each other's hearts.

Planning and leading this retreat is a sacred trust. You have filled my heart with Your Presence all along the way. And You have given me ideas as well. May that all bear fruit today. It is all in Your hands today. Praise Your Holy Name.

Thank You for the women who are acting out the biblical women for the retreat. One of them is going to be Mary Magdalene and will present herself as the mother of Jesus' child soon to be born as a girl. Help all of us at the retreat deal with that. Our pastor said it should be all right if we do a good debriefing. Help me do that—and a good introduction for her.

9/12/04

Thank You and praise be to You for how beautifully the retreat went! Thank You for the great job the actors did and for how people responded to them! Thank You that as far as I know no one was upset by the actor's suggestion that Jesus and Mary of Magdala were married and had a baby. She did the whole portrayal so realistically and with such feeling.

If anyone was upset, please abide with them and grant them understanding. Thank You for all the positive effects this will have in the lives of the women.

Thank You for giving me the idea of midrash. It was a perfectly comfortable idea in which to couch the stories. Thank You for giving me the skills to be the leader of the day, the skills and the power of Your Presence.

10/27/04

I have been reading a book titled Jambalayla[4] about West African religions. So much of it rings true with my feelings and beliefs about You. But having all the orisha and building altars and making sacrifices is beyond my understanding or accepting. But then I am not a black African with that heritage.

I can see some ancestor worship and summoning in the way I think about my "ancestors" and how frequently. I feel reverence for flowers and plants and mountains and seas. Maybe, quite likely, I don't have to summon their spirits because they are already here. I already experience them, dare I say, as part of You.

After all these years of having the little picture of Mom in the gold frame in my dresser drawer, I got it out and put it beside her Van Briggle lamp on my night stand. Does that make it an altar? Anywhere I put things that bring back memories of loved ones or special places can become, or is, an altar, I think.

This picture of Mom is special because it was taken when she was getting ready to attend my ordination and she was so sick with cancer. It reminds me of her courage and her determination to be at my ordination as well as her love for me.

12/10/04

Thank You for the drug (Ambien) that the doctor gave me yesterday and that it helped me sleep so soundly for ten hours! I am groggy and a little dizzy this morning. The warnings that came with it describe how I am feeling.

---

4   Luisah Teish, *Jambalaya: The Natural Woman's Book of Personal Charms and Practical Rituals* (NY, HarperCollins, 1988)

He also gave me Amitriptyline. I didn't take it last night. It is described as an antidepressant used also to control pain. He left it pretty wide open about when to take it. Clear that I should take it 2 hours before bed time and could take it with Ambien. The Ambien alone worked so well. I think I will only take it. Too many side effects to Amytriptyline.

1/6/05

We went to "truck training" for Humane Borders water ministry last night. I want to do it so much, but I think it will be work that is too heavy for my back. Someone had slashed four of the tires on the water truck as it was parked in our church parking lot. After the training we ate supper at Burger King and I couldn't help crying over the necessity for us to haul water to the desert and the hatred that must be in the hearts of those who slashed the tires and so many others.

Forgive us, Lord. And may we follow people, leaders, who have a real heart for You and Your love.

Humane Borders is an organization in Arizona whose mission is to provide water for the immigrants who are crossing the border illegally from Mexico. Humane Borders, motivated by faith, was founded in June 2000 to create a humane and just border environment. The two hundred core members, more than 1,500 volunteers and one hundred affiliated organizations including congregations, denominational groups, human rights groups, legal assistance organizations and businesses work together to provide humanitarian assistance to those risking their lives and safety crossing the border. Here are their priorities.

Reduce the number of migrants dying in the desert.

Invite public discourse on migration issues.

Change U.S. policy to return migration safely through ports of entry.

Provide legal status to undocumented workers already in the U.S.

Provide legal work opportunities in the U.S. for migrants.

Provide economic relief for U.S. agencies engaged in helping migrants.

Our local congregation supports Humane Borders with volunteers who go to the water stations to refill the barrels of water. The truck is a crew cab pickup (six wheels) that has been refitted with a barrel to carry the water, wheel barrows, five gallon water jugs, tools, a ladder, food, blankets and first aid supplies.

Humane Borders crew filling jugs to carry to a water station.

2/10/05

Our pastor had us "bury the alleluias." That just seemed like nothing to me. I won't bury my alleluias for the next forty days. I want to sing and shout Your praises every day! Always!

I kept wondering: where am I going on this faith journey? It is scary when the old words and the old practices are losing their meaning and their effect on me. I really didn't care that it was Ash Wednesday although my personal observance of it yesterday meant a lot to me and I intend with all my heart to be faithful to my promises through the forty days.

What I hope is happening is that in light of my Christian feminist studies, I am filling these old male conceived modes of worship with new meaning. Jan Aldredge says:

> New wine must be put in new wine skins. "We have drunk the new wine of Christ Sophia, and we cannot

be contained in old structures and old symbols. Old language will not suffice. Old rituals do not satisfy. Our vision can be stifled no longer. We cannot wait for official authorization or approval.[5]

Her statement is an echo of the words of the Old Testament prophet, Habakkuk.

> Then the LORD answered me and said: Write the vision; make it plain on tablets, so that a runner may read it. For there is still a vision for the appointed time; it speaks of the end, and does not lie. If it seems to tarry, wait for it; it will surely come, it will not delay. (Hb 2:2-3)

New visions become new realities. We are bursting out of old language and old rituals. My prayer is that feminine language for God will become that new vision. In 1 Corinthians 1:24, the writer says that Christ is the power of God and the wisdom of God. Wisdom is a feminine name for the Holy One.

2/11/05

Christ-Sophia. Nowhere I go does anyone talk feminine theology. Everyone is trying to put forth ideas that will save the church and save the world, but none of them are feminist ideas...When I see starving children I regret that I am no longer doing anything to help them. And then I think that You are calling me to preach and proclaim that Your nature is male and female. I believe that is the way the church and the world will be saved. But who am I to do it?

I wouldn't be doing it. You would. Use me, Lord, to accomplish whatever you can. Make me brave and articulate. Keep me always near You.

---

5   Jan Aldredge Clanton, *Praying with Christ Sophia,* (**Eugene, OR.** Wipf & Stock Publishers, 2007) 35.

2/15/05

There is a picture of Mary Magdalene on the cover of Susan Haskins book about her.[6] She looks at me and makes me think of You. Wonderful Woman of God. I know You don't look like that, that You have no human form, but seeing a woman's face convey Your incarnation is very unsettling. I don't know why.

Maybe it is because I don't want another woman to see into me as deeply as she appears to be seeing.

Maybe it is because she is very serious and will not let me get off easily in being who I genuinely am.

There is also a slight smile on her lips as if she knows I don't always like who I am—especially when it comes to speaking my thoughts and opinions.

2/23/05

...each day I launch into the search for you full of expectations, knowing instinctively that my quest pleases you immensely[7]

3/5/05

In getting ready to lead a workshop on the liturgical year at the spring gathering of Presbyterian Women of the Presbytery, I am reading a collection of quotes from Henry Nouwen's book, *Eternal Seasons*. He wrote,

> If you want to talk about hope, you have to talk about despair. If you want to talk about joy, you have to talk about darkness. If you want to speak about salvation, or redemption or freedom, it's very important that you're willing to speak about what you are redeemed from.

---

6   Susan Haskins, *Mary Magdalen: Truth and Myth* (CT, Konecky and Konecky, 1993).

7   William Cleary, *Prayers to She Who Is* (New York, Crossroad, 1997) 2.

The spiritual life is a constant choice to let your negative experiences become an opportunity for conversion or renewal.[8]

I am not sure what this means except in terms of feminist theology's need to tell the history of women's experience in order to see what freedom would be like. Maybe it says something against a faith that is too Pollyanna-ish.

3/17/05

Please help the world! I just read the flyer for the One Great Hour of Sharing offering about fishermen in India who have been fishing near the shore in homemade boats. Now they have to go out farther to get any fish and they need sturdier boats. So owners of big boats, rent out their boats and take half of the fishermen's catch as rental.

At circle we talked about the hundreds of women in Mexico who have been murdered in Cuidad Juarez.

Please help the world! I used to help You help the world, but what am I doing now? I love doing the things You have given me to do. When I write it that way it sounds like I am doing what I should be doing. I can't do as much as I used to—that was my job wasn't it. Just take me and use me however and wherever You can.

When I wrote this prayer I was getting close to finishing *Learning a New Language,* and was spending all my time on it. When I had thought I was finished with it, Norm offered to read it out loud to me so that I could hear how it flowed (or not). I had already submitted it to a couple of publishers. It still needed work so I was rewriting parts of it that Norm and I discovered needed more work. It was so good to have him share in the writing of the book.

3/25/05

You were present with/in such power last night at the Tenebrae service. I cried and cried. ...Thank You that I had only four verses (Mt 27:51-54)

---

8   Michael Ford, ed., *Eternal Seasons, A Liturgical Journey with Henry J. M. Nouwen,* (Notre Dame, Indiana, Sorin Books, 2004) 17.

to read in the dark and that I memorized them and didn't need to use a flashlight. That may have been one of the factors that so connected my heart and soul to You.

It was also a great blessing and relief to feel Your Jesus self so real after all the stuff I have been reading in recent months that discounts Jesus' power and Jesus' being God.

O Lord Jesus, I know You are God. I know You are who I have felt You to be my whole life. I praise Your Holy Name forever and ever and ever! Help me praise Your Holy Name forever and ever and ever!

My face felt so hot and I am sure I was flushed. I wonder if that happens because You fill my heart.

3/30/05

Thank You for guiding me to Jan L. Richardson's book, In Wisdom's Path.[9] She writes so beautifully and so much of what she writes really speaks to me. One thing she wrote was about how her throat tightens up when she is keeping silent about something she should speak. Maybe that is why I have this stuff in my throat and have to cough so often and why I dream about there being stuff in my throat. Help me speak.

4/17/05

Who am I? If someone had told me any time in my life that I would be asking that question when I am sixty-nine, I would have not believed them or I would have wondered why.

5/1/05

Thank You that my friend and I are participating in the Mary Magdalene retreat. Yesterday was so good! Such good, knowledgeable, enthusiastic speakers. But I just felt like a big, dumb old clump! And I don't know why. Everyone was nice and I already knew ninety percent of what they said. When I did make one comment, the speaker said it wasn't true—about

---

9   Jan L. Richardson, *In Wisdom's Path, Discovering the Sacred in Every Season* (Cleveland, Ohio, The Pilgrim Press, 2000).

the position of women in Roman society—and I answered back about the church accommodating itself to patriarchy.

I wonder if it was the new age stuff that made me feel that way. I hear it and think it is something I should have, but they don't relate to You as a person. I wouldn't trade Your Presence with me for any amount of chakras or spirits they express.

5/2/05

As I watched more news of bombings and deaths in Iraq last night, I could see and feel that events like that occur because You are "missing." I have thought things like this before but it came to me with such clarity at the retreat as Margaret Starbird talked about the feminine being removed from You and about the royal wedding that would make You and earth and all things in the universe whole again. It connects right to She Who Is and Learning a New Language.

I felt better about myself yesterday. At the end of the day the woman who had been leading our "celebrations" revealed that she is a Pagan. She hadn't done anything that was offensive, but I couldn't understand what she was saying. I didn't get the meaning of her words. Her words of gratitude were addressed to nothing I could grasp. You, Jesus-Sophia, were not there for me. I know now that however much I respect their religions I need You, God-Sophia incarnate.

5/5/05

While working on the manuscript I found these messages in Sirach which seemed to be addressed to me at this time approaching publication of our book—a time when I am nervous and afraid of putting my words and work—our words and work—out there:

> do not be ashamed of yourself. . . (Sir 4:20b)
> do not refrain from speaking at the proper moment, and do not hide your wisdom. . . (Sir 4:23)

It seems I am always in need of encouragement. May I remember these words and come back to them every time I need to.

5/29/05

Voyager One is years and years away from the earth and will be traveling many more years and it still won't be at the "edge." You are the Life, the Energy of all that is out there. Even "great" is a puny word to describe You.

6/3/05

Please keep reminding me that You wanted this book written and how You answered my prayers for thoughts and words. This may be the hardest time in the whole process. I am doubting if it will ever be done. I am doubting if anyone will read it. I am doubting if it is worth reading. I am doubting if it is accurate. I am doubting…I am doubting…I am doubting. Help me remember and concentrate on its origins—You and why You wanted me to write it.

6/13/05

Thank You for Carol P. Christ and for her writing this book.[10] I have been speed-reading it but still getting confirmation of things I already know and ideas I have written in Learning a New Language. This is a friend's book. I will buy my own copy and read it again especially for my personal faith journey. It may even be of help in organizing a book on my prayer journals.

6/22/05

Finished reading the manuscript yesterday. I imagine all kinds of possibilities when the book is out there: one that nobody reads it; another that some people read it and there is a flurry of activity that dies out; another that it will lead to teaching and preaching opportunities. It is already so amazing to me that I have done this. Whatever else happens with it is in Your hands just like the writing of it was. Take me and use me.

---

10   Carol Christ, *She Who Changes, Re-Imagining The Divine in the World* (NY, Palgrave McMillan, 2003).

7/14/05

For days I have been trying to think of a sermon topic for Celebration of Life Church. Last night as I was trying to fall asleep I asked You for it. And, if I am not mistaken, You gave it to me almost immediately: She Who Is. I preached on "Naming Toward God" last time I preached there. I think this will follow up. I don't want to preach like other preachers. I want to preach like someone who knows You as both male and female. Thank You and praise be to You for hearing my prayer and answering so clearly and quickly. I hadn't asked before and was feeling like the well is empty.

After worship Norm told me it was a good sermon. I thought it was too.

8/2/05

I did it! I submitted "our" book to iUniverse.com yesterday. It was easy but when it came to clicking on the final submit button I paused for a few seconds. It turned into a prayer that You, dear Sophia God, see it on its way and accompany it. And when it is "out there" finally, that You will be able to use it in many, many ways with many, many people! May it make a difference in the world, to the world.

I want to be called on to talk about it and share it. Let that not be arrogance or pride. I do believe that giving women equal status with men by recognizing You as feminine would change the world and relieve suffering, bringing more shalom to all peoples. May Learning a New Language be part of that change.

8/18/05

Dear Creator God, what beautiful, awe-inspiring places we saw yesterday between Williams and Kingman. The space, the colors, the shapes. Outside our window is the Colorado River. Here in Laughlin it looks like it was made for people to play in and on. But just a ways north it flows, sometimes rages, through the Grand Canyon, having carved that awesome place. Farther south it provides water for veggies for our nation. And all along the way and at distances it provides water for the daily use of humans. What a gift of abundance it is from the hands of You who are a most generous God!

8/21/05

The proofs of our book came on August 16! It amazes me and scares me! I know we co-created it and that it will bring glory to Your Holy Name and it will be of help to people and to the world. Now I need to work hard to get it out there. Help me do that and please speak to the hearts of those who read it.

9/1/05

After Hurricane Katrina:

Oh, Parent of the Poor, Guardian of the Desolate, abide with all the people in New Orleans, the sufferers and the rescuers, the repair people. Everyone. Comfort the bereaved and calm the children. Guide all who have public decisions to make. May they make them wisely.

Chapter Thirteen

9/3/05

Dear Divine Sufferer, how Your heart must be bleeding and Your tears used up as You abide with the people of New Orleans. Forgive us as a nation and as individuals that we allow and even contribute to the existence of such poverty anywhere in the world. We fall so short of who You dreamed we would be when You created us. Forgive us Americans and use this catastrophe as a way to help us see the truth of suffering everywhere. Make us better people because of this great loss.

At the same time Your heart must swell with joy and pride at all the generous and heroic deeds that are being done—like the family who took two evacuee families into their home.

May today be the dawning of hope for the victims of the hurricanes.

9/4/05

When Norm came out of his room I was sitting in the Lazy Boy reading. He said, "You must be sick. You are not at the computer or the dining room table." I told him I was at loose ends. That I didn't know what to do with myself. He said, "I feel a book coming on."

I do need something that big to do. I believe You have put it in my heart to write another book, but I don't know what it is. Your Presence is so real in my heart as I write this I know You are affirming my feelings, my need.

O Enabling Friend, help me know what it is You want me to write about. I think about writing something on my journals and something more on feminist theology. I keep thinking that I need to write a proposal letter to a "real" publisher, but maybe not. So far it has worked out fine to do it through iUniverse.

9/7/05

You are working such wonders with the evacuees from Katrina. So many people are helping in such amazing ways. Norm needs to watch it all on TV and he sighs such deep sighs. I can't watch it for very long at a time because I cry. CNN is showing pictures of all the missing children in New Orleans. Help their parents find them and keep them out of the clutches of pedophiles and other evil people.

9/13/05

Cleanse from my heart the ashes of old angers and the still glowing embers of not so old ones. And make my heart such that new angers and hurts will die quickly leaving no residue to clog my heart.

9/17/05

iUniverse is sending me five copies of the book.

9/29/05

When our granddaughter, Bailey, was two years old, Norm and I went with her and her mom and dad and her other grandfather to Tuscany and Germany. Dave and Nancy, and Don had been there before but it was our first trip to Europe. It was a special time for many reasons and one of them was that they took us to the places they had enjoyed most in the past.

It was Bailey's first ever long trip. She was amazing! She spent most of the trip strapped in a car seat or strapped in a stroller. In spite of her confinement she had only one breakdown the whole two weeks. Needless to say, she did run and jump and dance whenever she got a chance. In Volterra, Italy, Don took her for gelato and to a place to play while the rest of us visited the Guarnacci Museum which was founded in 1761. It contains beautiful, elaborately carved burial urns of ancient Etruscans. In the back of the museum is a garden.

Thank You for Volterra! I felt Your Spirit as soon as we walked in the gate and in the museum garden. The picture of Christ and St. Veronica in the little chapel down the street is etched indelibly in my mind. Thank You and praise be to You for the way it touched and continues to touch my soul.

Dave, Bailey, Nancy and me on the steps of the duomo in Florence, Itlay.

Bailey eating gelato in Florence.

10/9/05

In Berlin, we were hosted by David's aunt and uncle who had a little house in a lush garden not far from where the Berlin wall had stood.

O God of peace and love and beauty, You are worthy to receive all honor and glory and praise and adoration and love and blessing. Thank You for the peace and serenity I felt in Manfred and Gudren's garden. And then we walked and walked and walked a path that followed where the Berlin Wall had been. I don't understand how You can forgive human beings for the hurt and pain they cause. Praise be to You for Your grace and mercy.

10/14/05

Yesterday I saw our book in published form for the first time. It is beautiful! Thank You for it! Thank You for Your unfailing faithfulness and patience and wisdom in guiding me through it!

Now may I be as faithful and wise abut marketing it. I know You will bless all of that. Help me work hard and smart to get it out there.

Help me be able to understand and have confidence in what I have written when I speak to anyone. Help me use my time to Your glory and for the good of Your people. It seems I have two choices—I can drift along from day to day enjoying my life or I can do challenging service. Now that I have written those words I think it may be a reflection of the summer, my reaction to the heat, and the lull waiting for the book to be published.

There will be plenty of opportunity to serve as church gets started again. I do want to start another book, but I need You to show me the topic and to say, "Go!" My journals are on my mind, but so is Hattie Williams and further elaboration on topics in Learning a New Language. Help me hear You speak.

10/15/05

In Siena, Italy there is a vast brick basilica which contains the head and one little finger of St. Catherine of Siena. When we drove into Siena the only place we could find to park was near the entrance to the city that is nearest to this basilica. We certainly weren't interested in seeing the head of a long dead saint, but the building was beautiful and we went in to see what was there besides the relics.

I had heard of St. Catherine but didn't know much about her. After looking at the huge, fantastic paintings of her and her miracles, I went into the book store, as I am wont to do wherever we go. There I found a three hundred and ninety page book called *The Dialogue.* It was written by St. Catherine in 1377 so I bought it as a souvenir, little knowing that it would become one of my favorite devotional books. St. Catherine's spirit speaks to my spirit.

> In the Prologue to the Dialogue, Catherine of Siena wrote about souls (herself and me). …And loving, she seeks to pursue truth and clothe herself in it. But there is no way she can so savor and be enlightened by this truth as in continual humble prayer, grounded in the knowledge of herself and of God. For by such prayer the soul is united with God, following in the footsteps of Christ crucified, and through desire and affection and the union of love He makes of her another himself. [1]

I want to pursue truth and be clothed in it. I want to be like You. Fill me with your Spirit, Sophia.

11/10/05

The Dialogue takes the form of conversations between God and Catherine. She was a mystic who was born in 1347 and died in 1380. She is one of only two women who have been granted the title of doctor by the Roman Catholic Church. Not only was she a mystic, but she served the poor in her city and acted as a mediator in the battle between the cities of Rome and Florence over where Pope Gregory XI and his successor , Urban VI, should reside.

I want to know God "in a special manner" as God said to Catherine. These friends of God know Him "Beyond the knowledge of ordinary love, these taste of it and feel it in their very souls."[2]

---

1   *Catherine of Siena, The Dialogue,* trans. Suzanne Noffke, (NY, Paulist Press, 1980) 25.

2   Ibid., 116.

11/11/05

Writing about the distractions that come to a person who is meditating, Catherine wrote:

> How does one come to know lively faith? By persevering in virtue. You must never turn back for anything at all. You must not break away from holy prayer for any reason except obedience or charity. For often during the time scheduled for prayer the devil comes with all sorts of struggles and annoyances—even more than when you are not at prayer. He does this to make you weary of holy prayer. Often he will say, 'This sort of prayer is worthless to you. You should not think about or pay attention to anything except vocal prayer.' He makes it seem this way so that you will become weary and confused, and abandon the exercise of prayer. But prayer is a weapon with which you can defend yourself against every enemy. If you hold it with love's hand and the arm of free choice, this weapon, with the light of most holy faith, will be your defense.[3]

For Catherine there are only two reasons for interrupting your scheduled time of quiet meditation. One is that if God calls you away to do something else. The other is if someone arrives at your door or you get a call from someone who is in desperate need of your help.

11/26/05

In her writing Catherine sometimes writes as though it is God speaking and sometimes it is herself speaking. When she is writing about herself she uses the third person. In this passage God is speaking to her.

> When she has experienced my consolation and my visitation within her in one way, and then that way ceases, she goes back along the road by which she had come, hoping to find the same thing again. But I do

---

3   Ibid., 122.

not always give in the same way, lest it seem as if I had nothing else to give. No, I give in many ways, as it pleases my goodness and according to the soul's need. But in her foolishness she looks for my gift only in that one way, trying as it were to impose rules on the Holy Spirit.[4]

I love my prayer time journal writing. It is like food for my body and air for my lungs. But from time to time I have wondered if I should be trying something else or something more. Is this what Catherine heard You saying to her? Guide me, Holy Spirit. Help me follow.

She is humbled, for in constant prayer (that is, in holy and true desire) she has come to know herself, and in herself she has come to know my affectionate charity.[5]

12/5/05

Coloring mandalas in my Sunday School Adult class was a great success! The class really got into it and shared how peaceful it was. One man said it felt good to be playful. Another man asked if everyone could show theirs and tell about it. It is amazing how inspired and surprised people are when they finish a mandala and find the meaning in it that came from the Holy Spirit moving in them. It was wonderful! Praise be to You for Your great goodness! For Your constant Presence with us all.

Mandalas are as old as the caveman and as universal as all civilizations. The word mandala comes from the Sanskrit word meaning circle. Sacred images based upon or containing circles can be found in cultures as diverse as the Aztecs, Navajos, Australian Tjuringas, Celts, Christians, Buddhists, and Hindus. In the West the rose windows in cathedrals are an example of mandalas. They can also be observed in nature in such things as snowflakes, whirlpools, year rings of trees, our eyes, atoms, and even in fruits such as pears, bananas and apples.

---

4   Ibid., 129.
5   Ibid., 136.

Inside the circle of a mandala are geometric and symmetrical shapes that invite you to color them. Coloring a mandala is both creative and reflective. The best mandalas I have made I have done with colored pencils. That is the creative part. Some people are so creative that they draw their own, but I use patterns from books on mandalas or by going online to find them. In the process of creating a mandala a person is stilled and able to listen to the Spirit. That is the reflective part. Indeed, my experience has been that the Spirit even chooses the colors and the message of the finished art is quite often a surprise to the one who colored it.

1/12/06

Holy, holy, holy is the Lord of Hosts; the whole earth is full of his glory." (Is 6:3) The triple repetition of 'holy' expresses the superlative degree; but rather than leave the enthroned One simply sitting as the awe-inspiring subject of worship, the text radiates this holiness as glory upon the world.[6]

Thank You for Beth [Elizabeth A. Johnson] and the way You have used her to teach me about who You are! She speaks forth Your transcendence and Your immanence so beautifully and so faithfully. I know You are so real in my life in large part because of her! Bless her in all she does.

Thank You that I took the time last night to read Friends of God and Prophets. It was great to be able to read so much of it at one sitting. Two ideas that spoke to my current emotional condition were:

…your lives can be danced to the rhythm of the love of God better than dancers keep time with their bodies and their feet.[7] …struggling to remain faithful amid the many temptations that illness brings. As many situations as there are in human life, that is how many

---

6   Elizabeth A. Johnson, *Friends of God and Prophets, A Feminist Theological Reading of the Communion of Saints* (NY, Continuum, 2005) 52.

7   Ibid., 81.

opportunities there are for showing courage and love of God.[8]

1/20/06

Thank You for Mom and Daddy. I had begun to think of them as dead. Dr. Johnson writes about life eternal in her book, Friends of God and Prophets. What she writes is so beautiful and makes me realize that they do still exist in some way that is full of Your love and beauty. Praise be to You forever and ever. Amen.

1/24/06

I am reading Devil's Highway about the Mexican immigrants who got lost in the desert. In the paper this morning is an article about Humane Borders producing maps for the crossers. Protect the crossers and the courageous people at Humane Borders.

I watch so many beautiful Mexican children and loving Mexican parents here. I am writing about this piece at what we call my "McStudy" almost four years after I wrote this prayer. It is my habit to come to this particular McDonalds every morning to write, hence the name. This past Friday night and Saturday, Norm and I were part of a group from our church who went to Ajo, Arizona to learn more about the work of Humane Borders in providing life-saving water to immigrants. A ranger from Organ Pipe National Monument where the water stations are located told us about the danger to the border patrol agents and the ecological damage to the desert by the thousands of people crossing the border.

After we carried water and did some repairs at the two water stations we went to a place near the border fence where we had a brief service of worship and prayer for the immigrants, for the border patrol, for our governments and for ourselves. In essence we prayed for peace and justice along this border.

During a presentation on Humane Borders we were shown the maps which produced such a controversy across the country in 2006. These

---

8   Ibid., 83.

maps were described falsely in the media as maps showing Mexicans the best places to cross the border undetected. In truth, the maps were prepared with the help of the University of Arizona to show, not paths to get here, but rather how many days it takes to walk across the Sonoran Desert in Arizona and how dry it is here. At the bottom of each map, printed in large bold Spanish letters were the words:

DON'T DO IT!

IT'S HARD!

THERE'S NOT ENOUGH WATER!

These maps were handed out to people and posted at various places on the Mexican side of the border. Business people and church folks, who know the dangers of crossing the desert, were happy to receive the maps because they see the hope and the suffering on the faces of thousands of people who pass through their towns seeking a better life for their families.

2/3/06

I will have a book signing tomorrow at the Big Event. I am doubting, worried that not many people will want our book. It is in Your hands, Sophia. Help me not stew and not be discouraged if not many sell. Guide me to get the word out about Learning a New Language.

Cokesbury sold sixteen books. I signed eleven of them.

2/14/06

Annie Dillard quotes Teilhard de Chardin as saying You (God) are "profound and punctiform."⁹ I want to know what that means.

3/1/06

I could cry tears of gratitude at the sure knowledge that even though my attention to You is meager Your attention to me never fails.

---

9   Annie Dillard, *For the Time Being* (NY, Vintage, 1999) 71.

4/4/06

Thank You for always creating new understandings in me. Three times over the past week or so I have seen jealousy and what I describe as contrariness in me, not just passing over me, but dwelling in me, deep, deep inside me. I am so sorry for it and pray that You will grow me out of both.

4/7/06

My sinuses and everything else were healthy was the report from the doctor. I cried. My throat had been sore for a long time and it felt like there was a lump there. I was thankful that I was healthy, but I wanted an explanation for the lump.

I said maybe it is because I don't have a voice. Norm said, "You do too have a voice." What I meant and what may be true is that I have a voice and I don't use it the way You want me to or as much and as bravely as You want me to.

Help me, please. Help me know what to do about it. Help me live with it. Or overcome it. Maybe it is unspoken words. Or uncried tears. Maybe it is unreleased sobs. Maybe I am way too over-dramatic!

4/14/06

You know how I need help with what might be called my "wilderness." I am not sure what makes my wilderness, but I am sure I have one. I don't know if last fall's bad times are part of it or if this is different. A wilderness is where there are many things, threats one might have to deal with.

Over the years what have been my defenses?

Not talking.

Laughing or giggling when I am not sure my words will be accepted.

Avoiding direct confrontation.

Giving in to what others want.

Assuming I am wrong and the other person is right.

Pouting or sulking about the whole thing, about all of these.

I don't think my pouting and sulking have affected my relationship with You, but how could it not? I insult You as my Creator and Friend when I think I am inferior. When I pout in another's presence I am being unfair to them and thus unfair to You.

4/24/06

O sweet, strong, wise Sophia, Your love and Your blessings surround me like the air! Like the sunshine! Forgive me that even so surrounded by Your grace and love I still have times when I am angry or upset or lack love for myself. If only I could become Your friend through and through. If only all my thoughts and actions could be full of You just as You surround me. I want to be Your image. I want to feel it for myself. I want others to see it. Always for Your glory and for the sake of peace and love in the world.

4/30/06

Dear Mighty and Powerful Spirit and always near Loving Presence, You are so amazing, so divine. Praise be to You for yesterday's workshop at the women's retreat. The word that keeps coming to me is a burst. It was as though You used me (and I felt that so strongly because at first I felt lost) to put water on a seed and it burst open. Or like moonshine on the cereus that causes the buds to burst into flowers, or like a match to kindling.

Those women were so open to hearing about You, our dear Mother God. And at the end they all wanted other women to have a chance to hear about these ideas.

Thank You and praise be to You is not enough to say! Hear the song of my heart! See the tears on my cheeks! Forgive me for the times I have wondered what I was going to do next. The writing of Learning a New Language was "our" work and You will not let it die on the vine. Take me and use me.

The awesome power of the words of the Lord's Prayer filled my heart again, recently, in a shimmering moment at this women's retreat when we prayed the prayer after Communion. I had been using the metaphor, Mother, for God for several years in my personal prayer time, but never in the Lord's Prayer. This day when I said, with this group of women, "Our Father. . ." the words seemed to glow and expand. My having called this Divine person "Mother" caused the word "Father" to take on a new and lively meaning in my heart. It convinced me beyond a shadow of doubt that using feminine metaphors for God is a good and legitimate way to look deeper into the nature of God and to be drawn nearer to the Divine Being who is a mystery beyond all mysteries.

5/8/06

Dear Harmony of the universe, Song of my soul, Rhythm of my life, praise be to You for who You are and for how You act in the whole world and in my own little life.

5/25/06

Yesterday it dawned on me who I am!
I am first of all a woman of deep faith.
I am a woman who believes in and practices prayer.
I am a woman who has received the gift, the great and wonderful gift of feeling Your Presence.
I am a smart woman.
I am a compassionate woman.
I am a good wife.
I have been a good mother, not perfect, not always doing what was strong, but always a good loving mother.
I was an effective Hunger Action Enabler, accomplishing much for the churches in Chicago Presbytery and helping, working toward alleviating hunger in the U.S. and the whole world.
I was a well-loved and influential organizer for Bread for the World.
I was a lover of that organization—its goals and its life style and its work.

6/1/06

Every morning I will praise You and thank You that I have slept well! O Lord whatever it was that was causing my insomnia is gone, has been gone for the past nine nights. I haven't taken any drugs in that long. Last night was the best. I don't know what happened. You heard the pleadings of my heart and answered them. You are worthy to receive all honor and glory and praise and thanksgiving and blessing and adoration and love. May I thank You with my life. With who I am and what I can do.

6/2/06

Dear God of Wonder, Gift of Life, Lord of Wondrous Patience, You are my life and my breath and my strength. You are my reason for being. In all Your mystery and glory You care about me and about all whom I know and love and even those I don't know and don't love. Praise be to You from all corners of the universe forever and ever!

6/12/06

Has it ever been possible for a human being to continually sustain the feeling of Your Presence? Even a cloistered person? I think not. It would be too much. It would be like coming too near a fire. Praise be to You that I know You and feel Your warmth in my heart for even brief periods of time. As long as my attention span holds and there are no interruptions.

7/22/06

I read about a man who asked another man who prayed in silence what was going on. The pray-er replied: "I look at God and God looks at me." In my "best" prayers that is what You and I do. I look at You and You look at me. Or maybe You look first. At any rate, thank You and praise be to You for this most precious gift of time aware of Your Presence!

8/18/06

Dina Rees, a powerful spiritual guide, wrote what she calls a lullaby. It is a hymn to God.

> Beloved,
> Great is my yearning for You.

You have opened my heart so,
Through everything
I can see and feel,
Through You
Let me become one
With You.
Let me be quite Yours.
Nothing shall belong to me
Until I am eternally one with You,
Beloved.
My yearning is so great,
Free me from all bonds
And let my heart sob,
Let me be surrendered to You Forever, eternally,
Let me be with You,
 One with You.
You, my Beloved
Hear my yearning.
Take my heart,
Hold it in Your Hands.
Take my all.
Let the perfume
Of all roses
Rise up to You
And let the perfume
Of my heart
Rise up to You.
Let it be
United with You
For all time, Amen.[10]

"Let the perfume of my heart rise up to You." That phrase not only told of my love for You, but reminded me that sometimes what rises for my heart is not perfume. Rather it is stink. Forgive me and make me clean.

---

10 Regina Sara Ryan, *The Woman Awake, Feminine Wisdom for Spiritual Life* (Prescott, Arizona, Hohm Press, 1998) 119. Private translation from the German by Polly Doge, from: Rees, Dina, *Nimm Mein Herz: Gebete von Dina Rees,* Freiburg:Verlag Johannes Galli, 1990, 92-93.

8/21/06

5:30 a.m. I have been awake all night. Took Tylenol at 8 p.m. and natural sleeping pills at 11 p.m. after reading in Woman Awake. At 2 a.m. I got up and drank a glass of wine and played spider solitaire until 3. Got up at 4 and worked on history of women's ordination for the retreat. I thought I might as well do while I am awake what I will be too tired to do when it is day time.

I had stopped taking Ambien because I was groggy the next morning and I was afraid of becoming addicted to it.

8/22/06

In *Woman Awake*, Ryan writes about Hildegard of Bingen. She writes that Hildegard became so ill that she often had profound pain and was even partially paralyzed. At that time she "received an inner wakening which opened the world for her...As she reports in her writings, the enlightenment was so profound that it confined her to bed for several days. Only when she had forced herself to get up and begin to put into form what she had been "given" did her energy and health return."[11]

What she was given was "an illumination of scriptures, an understanding of theological concepts beyond anything she had formally studied, an insight into the liturgy together with a deepened knowledge of nature, of healing, of music, and many other gifts besides."[12]

I would not expect anything of that wide a scope to happen to me, but what I can learn is what Regina describes as Hildegard's "'legacy' to women of our time which is to afford us another glimpse of the immense possibility and abundance which each woman possesses to transform her ordinary, day-to-day reality into a life of art, creativity and beauty regardless of whether that art is ever seen or appreciated outside the confines of her own home."[13]

> Woman, simply in being herself, is creative, full of seeds, imagination, intuition. When, like Hildegard,

---

11 Ibid., 308.
12 Ibid., 308.
13 Ibid., 310.

she is willing to lay herself open to the teaching of the Divine Gardener and to exercise the patience, courage and persistence which is called for in the cultivation of those seeds, she finds no end to the harvest that is reaped in and through her.[14]

8/29/06

How I love You, Sophia! How I love You and seek You. I have been reading in Woman Awake about the need each woman has for a teacher, for a guru. I believe I have many teachers in the books I read, especially Elizabeth A. Johnson.

I can't understand the devotion Regina Sara Ryan and some of the other women she writes about have for their male gurus. Maybe that kind of devotion is out of my reach, maybe beyond my spirit. But I really don't want it. Even if I was free to go to an ashram and have a guru, I wouldn't. The one talks to and about her guru as though he is You. Hmmmmm. Maybe that is the point of their devotion that they see You in their teacher.

9/9/06

Maybe what I feel is the sorrow of women from all times and places. Maybe my tears are for the suffering and abuse of women from all times and all places. That sounds way too dramatic but maybe I can't talk about half of God missing without sorrow and despair. Even in the midst of the good, good life I have.

Maybe the lump in my throat is for all the women of all times and places who have not been allowed to speak or have been afraid to speak. Maybe I can't talk about them without hurting. Maybe my stomachache is for all the women of all times and places who have led lives filled with conflict about which they could do nothing.

Maybe I have gone too far. Help me not be crazy.

---

14 Ibid., 304.

9/11/06

Dear God, She Who Is, She Who Suffers with us, comfort all those who today still mourn or mourn again the deaths of the people killed on 9/11 five years ago. It looks to me like we didn't learn much from that awful event. I think we took the entirely wrong road to deal with it and that has just led to more hatred and killing and dying. Forgive us all and help us do better.

You see the whole picture so You see what manner of good has come from it. I ask that there be some.

10/10/06

My mother preceded my father in death by nine years. When he passed away my sisters and I knew that if we didn't make a plan for getting together on a regular basis we would see each other only rarely. So for several years we have had annually what we call reunions, taking turns to host them in our homes. In 2006 they came to Arizona and we spent one day in Sedona. Not only did we enjoy the beauty of the red rock formations and the canyons, but we also shopped in the fine art galleries and the delightful boutiques that fill Sedona. A brief, light shower passed over while we were in the shops. Soon we heard people gasping and saying, "Look! Look!" We went out to look and there to the east were two complete rainbows! They were the high point of that reunion.

And then You gave us the rainbows! Oh, my goodness! People left their shopping to go outside in the cold rain to look at them and point out better vantage points to others who came out. Even clerks came out of the stores to look.

I understand why the ancients said You put it there as a sign of You covenant with us! It is pure beauty, pure beauty. As I looked at it I felt the part of You that is in me connecting with those rainbows that are also part of You. You are too great for words!

Sisters and waitress at the Superstition Saloon, Tortilla Flat, Arizona

Husbands and waitress at the reunion.

10/28/06

The keynote speech I gave at the fall gathering of the Presbyterian Women in Grand Canyon Presbytery was not good.

Dear Lord, my God and my Friend, did I do a good job this morning? Did I please You? I told the "story" of my prayer journey, but there were many things I meant to say and didn't. Several women thanked me and told me how good it was. One lady said it was compelling. Another said I always inspire her. I was so tired (not much sleep last night) and drugged from Ambien and codene. Did I please You?

That is what I want more than anything else. To please You and to live in Your flow, in harmony with You.

Help me leave that keynote speech behind me. I am usually able to leave a speech or a sermon in Your hands and not think back on it too much. Please don't let my talking about my prayer journey so much take anything away from what I experience when I turn to You in prayer.

The mandalas workshops I led (thirty-four women in two workshops) were so good! I did a good job and the women were wonderful! One lady said she was a skeptic when we started but afterwards she described coloring a mandala as a wordless prayer! Others found such symbolism in the mandala and the colors they chose. When I asked them if they came with these thoughts in mind they said no. One woman said that the mandala tells you what to think and how to color it. All of the mandalas were beautiful! I know every one of those women was blessed by You!

I need a rest, don't I? I'm not thinking now about the rest I still need to get over this virus, but a rest from being a leader and speaker...I need time to write and study.

About my keynote speech yesterday. Red Auerbach (famed coach of the Boston Celtics) once said, "What counts is not what you say, but what they hear." I pray that what the women heard yesterday was not what I said but what You wanted them to hear.

11/11/06

Our son gave us a gift of a vacation to Maui. While we were there we took a day trip to Pearl Harbor. As usual the National Park Service has done an excellent job of setting up the interpretive aspects of the site.

After touring the center we boarded a launch for the short sail to the remains of the USS Arizona. As we neared the dock the captain of the launch asked that we be quiet as we walked around on the monument which is built over the sunken remains of the battleship. He really didn't need to tell us.

There is an air of sacredness about the place. Parts of the battleship rise from the water and the beautiful flag that flies over it flies from the flag mast of the ship. Part of the memorial lists the names of the men who were killed there, but you don't even need to read the names to feel the presence of their spirits. A person wants to be silent in that place which is the final resting place of 1,102 men who went down with the ship when the Japanese bombed Pearl Harbor on December 7, 1941

Today is Veterans' Day. When will there be a victims' day? A victims' memorial—Holocaust Museum. The guide on the Battleship Missouri told us about the firepower of the ship when she was refitted for the Gulf War. He pointed out the Tomahawk Missiles and another system AUM (armed unmanned) that were so accurate they could travel down streets and alleys and come in your front door. Is that true? I don't think so. That's a spin trying to avoid accusations of "collateral damage."

The video of the actual movies taken during the bombing of Pearl Harbor were very well done. No flag waving, chest thumping super America deal.

A little dove just walked over my foot. (I was sitting on the balcony of our hotel when I wrote this prayer.)

12/4/06

You are so perfectly present when I call upon You! You are so perfectly present even when I don't call upon You! Night before last when I was meditating in my room before I went to bed I felt Your presence more strongly and for a longer period of time than I ever have! Praise be to You for such a great gift! I thought about the really great believers who have done miracles and received the stigmata and I thought it is no wonder they did and do work wonders. They were so full of You that You burst out through them in loving healing power!

May I be open to the full measure of Your Spirit that You want to give me. I want to be filled with You, to be Your woman as much as is possible for me, for who I am and what You want me to do.

Chapter Fourteen

12/12/06

For a number of years I have cried sometimes when I pray. For the past few weeks as I have started meditating before I go to bed (in an effort to get over the insomnia) I have cried almost every night. Sometimes more than other times. I had also noticed that sometimes when my stomach hurts so much crying seems to lessen it. You talked with Catherine of Siena about tears and I want to understand what you said to her and what that means for me.

Then God, gentle first Truth, spoke:

O dearest daughter whom I so love, you have asked me for the will to know the reason for tears and their fruits, and I have not scorned your desire. Open your mind's eye wide, and I will show you, through the spiritual stages I have described for you, those imperfect tears whose source is fear.

First of all, there are the tears of damnation, the tears of this world's evil ones.

Second, are the tears of fear, of those who weep for fear because then have risen up from the sin out of fear of punishment.

Third are those who have risen up from sin and are beginning taste me. These weep tenderly and begin to serve me. But because their love is imperfect , so is their weeping.

The fourth stage is that of souls who have attained perfection in loving their neighbors and love me without any self-interest. These weep and their weeping is perfect.

The fifth stage (which is joined to the fourth) is that of sweet tears shed with great tenderness.

And I want you to know that a soul can experience all of these different stages as she rises from fear and imperfect love to attain perfect love and the state of union.

I want you to know that all tears come from the heart. Nor is there any other bodily member that can satisfy the heart as the eyes can. If the heart is sad the eyes show it.[1]

A couple of nights ago when I was praying with tears I began to feel in a very faint way the presence of Catherine. I wanted her to be with me. I wanted her to like me and I wanted to like her. That kind of feeling was new to me and seemed strange. But I do believe in the Communion of Saints.

12/19/06

I have always needed you but it seems I need You more and more partly because I am getting older but also because I am learning more and more about who I am and who I want to be. You alone know where I am going and what I can do yet. I would never have thought that I would like the idea of slowing down but I do. Not quitting, but slowing down. Mom said before her cancer, that she was spending more time sitting in the porch swing. Slowing down must be a natural thing to do.

12/30/06

These were topics of my prayer this day just as I wrote them down.

---

1   Catherine of Siena, *The Dialogue*, 161.

US elections: Two more women were elected to the Senate. Klobuchar MN and McCaskill MO now 16 out of 100. 71 women in the House net increase of 4, 16% (435) 46 more women to state legislatures, 1,732. The United States now has 23% of elected officials throughout all levels of government who are women. The world average is 16%.

Letter to the Editor re Mike Foley: (He was involved in a sex scandal involving pages in the House of Representatives): Perhaps the highest office even above president should be Mother. Not to form committees to investigate, but to say right out that he did wrong!

Illegal immigration: The building of a wall on the border with Mexico. Berlin Wall. Israel's wall to keep Palestinians out. Robert Frost's poem "Mending Wall". "Something there is that doesn't like a wall."

1/13/07

O wonder-full, mysterious, awesome God, I heard on NPR yesterday about "dark matter." The scientist could only say that they know it exists; that some of it is hot and some is cold, that the hot expands and is widening the universe while the cold opposes it to keep things together. How do they figure out such things?! You know all about it. In fact maybe you are it. Or better it is part of You.

Thank You that you moved Norm and me to go hear Father John Dear last night. He is truly a prophet and a preacher. I will write an article for the UPC newsletter about his work and his message. It was so powerful. He is on fire with the message that You are NOT a god of war! That You desire peace for all people and all creation! He is forty-seven and has been arrested seventy-five times. Once was with Daniel Berrigan when they beat on a jet fighter with hammers—symbols of beating swords into plowshares.

He said we have the spirituality of warfare down to a fine art. War can't stop terrorism. War is terrorism. He lifted up the Scripture passages in which Jesus denounces violence. Jesus was never violent and he got killed "it is part of the job description that does not go over well."

1/18/07

Dear Heart of my heart, Life of my life, Spirit of my spirit, You make me who I am in my best moments. You fill me with any goodness that is ever in me. You fill my heart to fullness when I pray and I believe the tears that fall as I meditate before I go to bed are also Your doing.

Why, I don't understand. Well, yes I do. You fill me so full that something has to happen to my body as well as my spirit. I read some things on the web last night about tears and mostly it is orthodox priests who talk about it.

2/6/07

I had a big cry before I fell asleep. I wrote a prayer, meditated for about twenty minutes and then crawled into bed. My brain wouldn't stop until I admitted I need to cry and got out of bed and did it!

I cried hard and those sobs for Jim turned into sobs and prayers for the whole world of suffering mothers and children. You filled me powerfully.

> *I cry for my son. Deep heart wrenching sobs*
> *because he has no money,*
> *because he has a job that keeps him living in his eighteen-*
> *wheeler truck*
> *not earning any money for three and a half days.*
> *He sounds on the phone as if he would cry too*
> *if it wouldn't ruin his tough guy persona.*
> *Maybe he cries to himself.*
> *I cry deep heart wrenching sobs*
> *for other suffering mothers and their sons and daughters.*
> *Mothers who are too poor to take care of their children.*
> *Mothers who have lost or are losing their children.*
> *Mothers who watch their children cry because they are*
> *hungry.*
> *Mothers whose children are too different and are not accepted*
> *by others.*
> *I cry deep heart wrenching sobs*
> *and Mother God fills my heart to bursting with*
> *Her strong and sure Presence.*
> *She knows what it all means (my crying). I don't know.*
> *How She must cry and sob and grieve.*

The Divine Mother of the World would not, could not cry less, suffer less for Her children than the human mothers She has created.

You saw me today! What is wrong with me! I believe that sometimes my tears are a gift of Your Spirit. And maybe these are too. Somehow cleansing me of something. Help me understand what I need to understand.

Jim in his eighteen-wheeler, 2007.

3/11/07

You are Energy and Love. You connect us with the cloud of witnesses, with people who have gone before us. I am reading Ettie Hillesum's diaries[2] and letters and feel a connection with her even though she, a Jew in Holland who was killed at Auschwitz, was so different from me. In those two years of her writing she grew in her knowledge of You, of herself and of others around her. She keeps telling how much she wants to write down her ideas and that someday she will. She is inspired by Your wonderful creations in nature. She tries to love people but not be dependent on them to an extreme.

---

2   Ettie Hillesum, *Ettie Hillesum, An Interrupted Life The Diaries, 1941-1943 and Letters from Westerbork* (NY, Henry Holt, 1996.

Our situations could hardly be more different and yet her spirit touches mine. Thank You and praise be to You for witness of the people who have gone before us and are with us still.

3/12/07

Thank You that I read about Etty Hillesum. She has enriched my spiritual life! I will think about things she wrote at greater length tomorrow and in the days to come. She died in Auschwitz in November 1943. She is one of the great cloud of witnesses. Thinking about her in that way is helping me think of my loved ones who are also part of the great cloud of witnesses.

4/1/07

I feel badly that I haven't been meditating for several nights before I go to bed. I have been tired and just crawled into bed and fallen asleep. I think that when I meditate first I bring a whole lot of people and situations into my mind which then circle around and around in my thoughts. Please guide me in this as You guide me in other matters. Help me be in Your flow. Help me be in Your flow in all things.

Take me and use me. That is a phrase from my teen-age prayers. And it is still the deepest prayer of my heart—that I will be of use to You. However, today, these latter days, I don't so much see our relationship as one where You pick me up and use me as a tool, but rather as You being in me and letting me, asking me, luring me to work with You. That You move in my gifts.

4/11/07

Thank You for the way I have been sleeping! Like I did nights before the insomnia started. This started happening when I started writing about the journals, about my spiritual life. I do believe there is a connection between writing and sleeping for me.

I am not sure where the writing is going but I think that is a matter of trusting in You, so help my mind and my heart be open to Your leading, to Your thoughts and ideas and words.

Forgive me for imagining vain things like I just did—two or three books by the time I am finished, an agent who would be a soul sister and books published by a major publisher, selling lots of copies.

Forgive me and help me write what You want me to write. Help write me what will bring glory to Your Holy Name and what will help other people.

4/13/07

I don't need to "figure You out." You will reveal as much of Yourself as I can handle to me. All I have to do is love You. That loving is the key that opens my heart and my soul to You. Praise be to You. My heart sings. My soul praises Your Holy Name. …Even in the midst of a spiritual high like this time is, my mind wanders. That is my being human. But I love You, Sophia God, Sophia Jesus, Sophia Spirit. I want to know You and abide with You and you with me. I want that more than anything else.

Writing this book about my prayer journals is important. It must be important because You have put it in my heart and my will for such a long time. It must be important because for all these years You have called me to fellowship with You and You have moved in my heart so I would respond. Least of all, it is important because since I have started it I have been able to sleep at night. Not quite like I used to but still I am not up and wondering around the house at all hours.

I believe there is a purpose for this book. I believe You will write it with me just like You did Learning a New Language. I love You, Sophia, and pray with my whole heart and mind and soul and body that you will never let me fall away from You. That I will never want to fall away from You or that my love for You will ever be dulled. May it only grow and grow.

4/14/07

There isn't much left when the breath leaves the body. As my friend caressed and patted the body of her mother with such love and tenderness it was really the memory of her mother alive that prompted her. The same when I kissed my Mom's forehead when her body was in the casket.

Are they now part of the life and breath and energy of the cosmos in a different way than when they inhabited a body. I would like to think, I want to believe that I will see Mom and Daddy again as Mom and Daddy. I want to! But maybe that is not the way it is. Quite likely the way it is is way better than I can think or imagine. That would be like You—to provide for us in a way beyond our imagining.

4/17/07

You are so generous and so exuberant and so luxuriant. These are some of the words I found when I was coloring a mandala in Coloring Mandalas, Circles of the Sacred Feminine[3] *last night. Fincher described You as fecund. I could not color the mandala without looking that word up. What an abundance of good words are synonyms for fecund and my heart tells me they can all be used to describe You: productive, fertile, fructiferous, fruitful, generating, proliferant, rich, propagating, inventive.*

5/7/07

For weeks I have been writing the book on my prayer journals. Now it is time in the process to read what I have written. But I really don't want to. Actually, I am afraid to. What if I don't like it! What if there is nothing there! I should be ashamed of myself because I have felt that You are my Author Within. And that You are present in the whole project. Dear Sophia, help me with this. Help me read with Your eyes, with Your wisdom and show me what to change. Always for Your glory.

Such was the beginning of this book, *From Heaven to My Heart, God's Journey With Me.* The method of author, writer Tom Bird is to write your thoughts in a large drawing pad without editing your writing at all. In doing that you are free from the constraints of lines and margins and rules. It is a great way to write. My drawing pad contained thirty-two pages, approximately 21,000 words of prayers copied from my journals. I even compiled a kind of table of contents.

---

3   Susan F. Fincher, *Coloring Madalas, Circles of the Sacred Feminine* (Boston, Shambhala, 2006).

5/18/07

Dear Sophia, You are so steady and so sure, so strong and so dependable! I can always count on You to be present with me. What is unsure is me. I go from strong to weak, from happy to sad, from confident to inferior in the blink of an eye. Forgive me and help me be focused on You more and more of the time. When I am focused on You I am strongest and I am sure more of a witness to You.

5/31/07

The journal book consists of essays—about eighty-five of them now which really need more work. My plan is to finish typing them into the computer today. Then I think it will work out for me to rework them one at a time. Please guide me. Show me a style that won't sound egotistic.

And most of all hold me close to You! I don't want to lose my closeness to You in prayer time. I want it to deepen.

6/21/07

O God of Mystery and…I should say, "O Mysterious God, Unknown God whom I seek to know, fill me with Your Spirit as I seek to feel Your Presence and to be present with You. The mandalas I have been coloring in Circle of the Feminine have depicted Hindu goddesses. Who are they? How are they related to You? Can any worship that is good and produces good be true worship?

7/31/07

O dear Sophia, praise be to You for all the goodness You have created. People who are seriously ill, trapped in illness are heavy on my heart this morning. Also people who need medicine and can't afford it. …May our next president be able to lead us to health care, good and affordable for everyone.

Be with the candidates and all the citizens that they may tell the truth and we may be discerning.

8/9/07

The struggle to understand who God is shows itself repeatedly in my prayers. This poem written by Benjamin Myers about Karl Barth is a great comfort to me in this quest. Great minds of all generations have been absorbed in this seeking. They join us who have "brains small, confused and dim" in the final words of this poem: who as we fall on our faces in failure to know God fully we fall safely into Her hands.

You are God. You are specifically God. You are the Presence in my heart. I don't know why I am thinking about this this morning but if You are everything then are You anything? I know I can see You and feel You in all good things but are You those good things? I know You are in me but does that mean I am You? No.

> Barth's brain was charged with the grandeur of thought,
> It swirled out, like soap suds in the sink,
> It smeared reams of paper like the ooze of ink
> spilt. Must we all then follow him?
> Generations adored, abhorred, or fought his thrall
> Moltman went beyond him,
> Panneberg disproved him,
> Torrence hung awe-rapt on every word: and all
> Of us (brains small, confused and dim)cobble systems
> fat or thin.
>
> Yet for all this, God does not fling us off;
> He crouches at our system's edge, peers hungrily through holes;
> Sneak-watching for the moment when we sigh and say
> "Oh, bugger! All these thoughts I can't command"
> Then breathless as a madman or a child, God lunges
> And trembling floorward fall our thoughts, while
> we fall into ah! Safe hands.[4]

I found this on the web and am so moved by it! Think and ponder as much as we will and the bottom line always is—even with thinkers like

---

4   Benjamin Myers is an Australian scholar, who teaches systematic theology at Charles Sturt University's School of Theology in Sydney. This poem is on his blog, Faith and Theology, which is a forum for conversation about theology, books and culture.

Barth—that we don't know who God is. Except that we are in Her safe hands.

From the safety of Your hands may I keep seeking You and/or responding to You seeking me.

8/23/07

O Great God of heaven and of earth, great and mysterious are Your ways! You created the mountains and the plains, the rivers and the seas, the skies and the stars. You made them to move in harmony with each other. And You rule over all. You created creatures of all kinds and taught them how to live. You created human beings and gave us Your way of steadfast love, righteousness and faithfulness to live by. Everything is so beautiful and so perfect when we live the way You created us to live. But we forsake You too often! Forgive us and keep showing us Your way.

Christiane Amanpour's series on CNN, "God's Warriors," is so disturbing! She shows the militant groups in each of the three major religions. They all behave in warlike ways -- all in Your name. How can they do that?!

It is all so ugly! Their thoughts and activities are in total contrast to who You are and what You stand for. Your beloved human creatures. How you must grieve!

May all those of us who know better live better. May we work to spread the word of Your steadfast love, Your righteousness and Your faithfulness.

9/8/07

O Holy Christ our shepherd,
we bleat before you.
O Holy Ghost our inspiration,
we dance before you.
O Holy one, even our foolishness brings you praise.[5]

I turned to this prayer book (it is new) because I couldn't think of words to write to praise You this morning. I felt You in my heart but I didn't know what to write. Then when I found this I was dismayed by his saying we "bleat" before You.

---

5   Jon M. Sweeney, *The St. Francis Prayer Book, A Guide to Deepen Your Spiritual Life,* (Brewster, MA, Paraclete Press, 2004). 105.

I remember the bleating of those sheep at the Howard County Fair. It was not a pleasant sound to me. But if I was the shepherd I am sure it would be. It was simple and forceful and expectant. Those sounds come naturally from those creatures. They are how You created sheep to sound. May I make the sounds You have created me to make. May I bring glory to Your Holy Name by being who You created me to be.

9/13/07

The first thing I did this morning was read Thursday from the St. Frances prayer book. These words were words spoken to me.

> God has sent workers to the vineyard to cultivate it, to root out briars and thorns. "These men and women have cut back the overgrown branches and pulled up the brambles and shallow-rooted offshoots so that the vines might produce sweet fruit."[6]

I believe with my whole heart that this is what the church needs! Calling You by feminine names can help weed out dead branches and make room for new growth. May I please be a part of cleaning the vineyard.

The whole collect on page ninety-three is one that I need to learn and to pray over and over again as I try to be a worker in Your vineyard.

> Grant your servants, O God, to be set on fire with your Spirit, strengthened by your power, illuminated by your splendor, filled with your grace, and to go forward with your aid. Give me, O Lord, a right faith, perfect love and true humility. Grant, O Lord, that there may be in me simple affection, brave patience, persevering obedience, perpetual peace, a pure mind, a right and clean heart, a good will, a holy conscience, spiritual comprehension, spiritual strength, a life unspotted and upright and after having finished my course, may I be happily enabled to enter your kingdom.[7]

---

6   Ibid., 92.
7   Ibid., 93.

10/11/07

Words cannot express my thanks and my adoration so I ask that the way I live each day will be a show of what words cannot express.

Thank You for the clear and to me powerful insight which You gave me yesterday by way of answers to the professor's question: why are feminine symbols so important in the religion of oppressed and marginalized people? What, I believe You gave me to understand and to say was that it is men, fathers, who crash in with swords and helmets riding their horses over the people (we had just seen a video on the Virgin of Guadalupe so I was thinking of conquistadors). It is women who hide their children when husbands flee, who bind up the wounds. Who at the risk of their own lives stand up to conquerors and say you will not kill any more of my children. It was an insight that gave me understanding of much that I have been reading, writing and saying for some time. It is a helpful synopsis. Thank You for it.

11/27/07

Last night I was too achy to sleep so I got up and read a little in a book titled, Women in Praise of the Sacred. A woman named Kassiane touched my soul with something like a light of recognition. She lived in the early 800s and was like Hildegard of Bingen in being gifted in writing hymns. She was born in Constantinople. I will learn more about her. A quote of hers that touched me so deeply was:

I hate silence when it is time to speak.[8]

I have been hating the silence that Norm and I maintained Monday in class when we could have thanked the professor and the students. And I hate the silence I kept yesterday at circle when I could have spoken up and said more about how PW is going. Both were prime opportunities and we/I missed them. Forgive us Lord and help us/me speak more freely. Give us/ me confidence.

---

8   Jane Kirchfield, ed. *Women in Praise of the Sacred* (NY, HarperCollins, 1994), 53.

12/2/07

O Holy Sophia
make me holy too.
My heart's desire is to be like You.
To be so filled with You that Your glory
shines in me.
To be so filled with You that I am always in
Your flow.
My heart and my soul sing praises to You!
My heart and my soul sing thanks to You!

12/5/07

"One foot in the grave and one foot on a banana peel." My Dad used to give that as an answer to the question "How are you?" In my memory he was saying it when he was not really very old. He had a great sense of humor and knew or made up many humorous phrases, so I think this was a joke he thought funny.

At my age now, seventy-three, I don't think my life is that threatened, not that I might slip into my grave at any time now, but I do think about it. I think about it in a way that causes me to grieve that so much of my life is behind me. One night I was sleepless from thinking about the shortness of time I have left so I got up to read in one of my favorite books on prayer. I found this passage.

> There seems to be no limits to the possible growth of the human psyche in its fellowship with God. One probability is that life in the hereafter is a continuation of the same growth process begun within the world of space and time.[9]

I like the sound of this! I like the idea! I don't know what he bases it on but he is a man in touch with You and I trust him.

The way You have grown me my whole life has been wonderful and amazing. Because You love me that much and that patiently it would make

9   Morton Kelsey, *The Other Side of Silence, A Guide to Christian Meditation* (NY, Paulist Press, 1976) 129.

sense that You would not just be done with me when my body wears out. You have a lot of time and effort invested in me and it would make sense that You will continue to love me and grow me forever and ever.

Now how much more can I grow in these years to come and how can I maximize that growth. Kelsey says over and over again that his goal of meditation is not to merge with You but to relate to You and as a result relate to the world.

12/29/07

I write about wanting a new vocabulary of ways to praise You. Joseph Campbell says, ...a vocabulary not of words but of acts and adventures when he talks about life as a poem and a person participating in the poem. "A vocabulary of acts" that is what I want!

1/27/08

I stayed home from worship this morning in the interest of getting over a sinus infection. I decided to spend the time reading Elizabeth A. Johnson's Quest for the Living God. I had already started it. It is so rich!

Last night I was reading Elizabeth Gilbert's book, Eat, Love and Pray (thank You for her! And that I found her!) She went to an ashram in India after spending four months in Italy eating. She wrote that everyone needs a guru (means darkness to light). I thought, like yeah! I'm really going to do that and then realized that I sometimes wonder if I need a spiritual director.

> You come to your Guru, then, not only to receive lessons, as from any leader, but to actually receive the Guru's state of grace. ...And this is why you came to a Guru: with the hope that the merits of your master will reveal to you your own hidden greatness. ...The theory is that if you yearn sincerely enough for a Guru, you will find one. The universe will shift, destiny's molecules

will get themselves organized and your path will soon intersect with the path of the master you need. [10]

What a moment it was when I read that! Dr. Johnson is my Guru! She has been for almost ten years. Before Beth it was Hattie! Those two women caused my universe to shift, the molecules to organize—You used that process to bring them to me and they were that process in my life. Beth continues to be. Praise be to You forever and ever.

1/28/08

My prayer this day was inspired by what Elizabeth Gilbert wrote:

> …instead of admitting to the existence of negative thoughts, understanding where they come from and why they arrived, and then—with great fortitude and forgiveness dismissing them.[11]

That is what I was able to do yesterday. It took a conscious effort. She also wrote:

> …the rules of transcendence mean that you will not advance even one inch closer to divinity as long as you cling to even one last seductive thread of blame. As smoking is to the lungs, as is resentment to the soul; even one puff is bad for you. I mean, what kind of prayer is this to imbibe—'Give us this day our daily grudge?' You might just as well hang it up and kiss God goodbye if you really need to keep blaming someone else of your own life's limitations.[12]

---

10   Elizabeth Gilbert, *Eat, Pray, Love, One Woman's Search for Everything Across Italy, India and Indonesia* (NY, Penguin Books, 2006) 123-124.

11   Ibid., 178.

12   Ibid., 186.

3/22/08

Having knee replacement surgery is a snap. The pain and the suffering from the weeks of therapy that follow are anything but a snap. Some people find it easier than others. I stayed pretty much home bound for a month after my knee surgery. I needed so much pain medicine that my surgeon said, half-jokingly, that if he gave me any more of it he would have to send me to drug rehab.

I think it is hard to move from being an "invalid" in your sheltered home, the center of everyone's attention back into the world where so much is going on and people are paying attention to each other. And now I need to take on responsibilities again. Even though it hurts it is almost easier to be sick.

3/26/08

A prayer I found while working on Gifts of Women Sunday Service. It could be mine. I have not been able to find anything about the writer, Jennifer Duke, except that at the time she wrote it she was in Atlanta, Georgia.

Lord, I Sing Your Praises.
Oh, Lord, I praise your holy name
for your endless mercy upon me.
Empowered by your vision
I boldly speak your promises.
You have given me the voice of authority.
You enable me to dream dreams.

Oh, Lord, I will stand next to you
for the rest of my days,
refreshed and new.
I will sing praises unto you until
my work is done.

4/13/08

A friend got to talking about why the church is diminishing in membership. In the course of that conversation he said he decided on his theology when he was in communicants' class. How sad that is! That may well be why the church is not growing—people's theology does not grow.

6/12/08

Sometimes when I can't sleep I cry and then fall asleep. I had not heard about the gift of tears very often so I copied from the web twenty pages written by Pope Shamada about holy tears. I want to know if my crying (when it is not from self-pity) could be a spiritual gift from You, compassionate God.

My questions about tears go back as far as 1993 when I included a definition of tears in one of my prayers. It was that the gift of tears is a mark of compassion and extreme openness to the divine. I found it in a book by Brenda Meehan titled, *Holy Women of Russia.*

When my prayers are deep—whether prayers of joy or intercession—I frequently cry. For the past few weeks I have been asking if there is a spiritual gift of prayer and if I have it. Then I add, "That's weird."

6/15/08

Dear Sophia, abide with women where every day life is a misery here in this country and in all the countries of the world. Women who are murdered like Du'a Kahlil Arval[13] and women who are being killed in spirit and in mind.

Be with all the children who are suffering unimaginable horrors in the sex trade and in famine stricken countries and in places where there is war in their nation and violence in their homes.

Be with people who are suffering from the effects of the war in Iraq and Afghanistan.

God of peace and love and joy, how you must suffer over all these things and more, like the destruction of this fantastic planet. As I wrote that I

---

13   Du'a Khalil Aswad was a seventeen year old Iraqi girl who was because she fell in love with a man who was not of her faith. She was stoned to death by the men of her family on April 7, 2007.

thought that process theology deals with those cosmological environmental problems and that feminist theology deals with personal problems but that is absolutely not true! Feminist theology deals with it all in a way that could solve it all. The "missing" part of You is who people need to find. The idea that You are only like a man is the idea that men dominate everything. It creates the idea of dominion of some humans over other humans and of humans over all of creation. Mother God use me to preach this. Use me to speak bravely about it. Help me plan the retreat bravely. Find places for me to speak and lead so that You, Sophia, may be found.

6/18/08

A friend recommended the novel (placed with religious fiction at Barnes and Noble), The Shack. It is a strange but thought-provoking, soul-touching theology book. Thank You for William P. Young. Thank You that I am reading his book. Help me understand truth that is in it.

His depiction of You as a Trinity of Papa (a large' black woman), Jesus (a carpenter of Middle Eastern descent), Sarayu (the Holy Spirit, who is mainly wings or cloud or mist of beautiful changing colors.) It reminds me so much of Dr. Johnson's idea of the Trinity as three friends. Praise be to You. May it mean to my growth in You what You want it to mean.

He writes about God being a verb.

He has Mark, the main character in the story, ask Sarayu why he doesn't know that she is always with him. Her answer is "For you to know or not…has nothing at all to do with whether I am actually here or not. I am always with you, sometimes I want you to be aware in a special way— more intentional."[14] That expresses the way I know You are with me—at special times like this prayer time and other moments of created beauty or of relationships. It also expresses my firm belief that You are always in my heart and I can touch You there any time I want or any time You want.

I spent too much time looking on the web to find out who William P. Young is and why I should try to understand what he wrote.

"Believe from your own experience of me."--God

One way to believe it is to see the shack as the place I live when I am depressed/foggy/angry/resentful. But it can and does become the amazingly beautiful cabin when I open myself to You. It is what I have been feeling for

---

14   William P. Young, *The Shack* (Los Angeles, CA windblown Media, 2007) 155.

several weeks: that I can be on the underside where it is gray and gloomy or I can be on the up side where You are (no, You are on the underside with me.) The up side is where living is a joy.

6/21/08

Dear mysterious, complicated God, You are unimaginable and yet You give us clues and hints about who You are. The result is so many religions and so many philosophies, and so many theories and so many ways of picturing You. Praise be to You that You want us to know You!

6/22/08

I spent this half hour reading the chapter on the Trinity in Elizabeth Johnson's book, Quest for the Living God. She uses the word "perichoresis." In the novel, the Shack, You were perichoresis. Help me think about these things. May I think your thoughts after you!

> Perichoresis is a Greek term coined by eastern Christian theology to describe the inner life of God. . . .the Greek term describes a revolving around or a cyclic movement like the revolution of a wheel. When applied to the life of the Trinity, this metaphor indicates that each of the "persons" dynamically moves around the others, interacts with the others, interweaves with the others in a circling of divine life. While remaining distinct, the three co-inhere in each other in a communion of love.[15]

Those who have read *The Shack* will recall with delight how the three persons of the Trinity enjoyed each other and how each had a part to play in the transformation of Mack.

---

15 Elizabeth A. Johnson, *Quest for the Living God, Mapping Frontiers in the Theology of God* (NY, Continuum, 2007) 214.

Chapter Fifteen

6/27/08

The main purpose of my writing the book, *Learning a New Language*, was to use it as a basis for conversations with groups of women about using inclusive language for God. In my search on the web for groups who needed speakers or workshop leaders, I found the Evangelical and Ecumenical Women's Caucus. The EEWC is an international organization of inclusive, Christian feminist women and men who believe that the Bible supports the equality of the sexes. When I emailed the woman in charge of a conference they were having in Indianapolis, Indiana she invited me to apply to be a workshop leader. I was accepted and traveled to Indy not knowing what I would find there.

Dear Sophia, I belong here! I belong here! I haven't even met anyone but the two registrars yet. But I have been reading the material and I belong here at the Evangelical and Ecumenical Women's Council conference! Since its beginning in 1973 the EEWC has proclaimed that the Bible supports the equality of the sexes.

6:20 p.m. What a day! I have been hyper all day. Mother God, I feel Your loving, laughing presence with me as strongly as I felt Mom's loving, laughing presence with me when she gave us girls unexpected gifts!

I didn't slow down to feel You until I had gotten back to my room with a sandwich from Au Bon Pain and a Starbucks frappaccino. I called Norm before I began to settle down. When I thought about You as I ate I felt You laughing because You watched all day as I lived into this wonderful amazing gift You have given me!

I had no idea it would be so electric!

I wrote this prayer before an evening session.

Now if You can just settle me down for twenty minutes.

On the flight here I read Call of My Heart, the Journey to Ecuador and Beyond, by Nancy Conley Burke. She went to Ecuador to explore what it would be like to be a shaman. She and her group experienced such strange things—some wonderful to me, some totally distasteful. Most of the time I was totally absorbed in her stories but not moved to want to do what she did even if I could go to Ecuador.

She had such warm, loving, real contact with You as Packamama, the Great Mother. As I read I wondered if I could experience You like that without going to some exotic place like the rainforest of Ecuador. Today I did! In Indianapolis, Indiana! How strange and wonderful You are!

6/28/08

Dear Sophia God, Jesus Sophia, Spirit Sophia, You are using this conference which is called "A Place at the Table" to bring me into a sense of being at the table in a new way. Praise and honor and glory be to You forever and ever.

The text for the conference is: "Come eat of my bread and drink of the wine I have mixed. Lay aside immaturity, and live, and walk in the way of insight. (Prov. 9:5-6)

Later in the day.

It has been a great morning, but I am shaking like a leaf! My workshop is at 3:30 and I am nervous. I don't know if it is the four prednisone pills I took at eight or fear of failure. There are so many scholarly women here. Maybe none of them will come to my workshop.

Much calmer after a twenty minute nap.

Virginia R Mollencott (author of thirteen books who advocates for Lesbian, Gay, Bisexual, Transgendered rights and Christian feminism) said this morning that Your love flows into a pure soul like light into a glass vase. O, dear Sophia, I want to be a pure soul. I want Your love to fill me and shine like light in this workshop and always. May it be so.

7:10 p.m. You did it! You always do! You spoke through me in ways I had not thought of and can't even remember. You and the people are always the key ingredient. Thank You, Sophia, for bringing me here.

7/2/08

One who rises early to seek her will have no difficulty,
for she will be found sitting at the gate.
[15]To fix one's thought on her is perfect understanding,
and one who is vigilant on her account will soon be free from care,
[16]because she goes about seeking those worthy of her,
and she graciously appears to them in their paths,
and meets them in every thought. (Wisd. of Sol. 6:14-16)

Something is changing in me. It has been always, many things, but this feels like something big. I may be feeling relief from the drugs after my knee surgery five months ago. It really feels good.

But this feels like a major change in my being. I really do think I am slowing down from a headlong rush to do all things and control all things as far as time is concerned. And letting go of some negativity.

It seems like You have been working on this in me for a long time and that You laid Your hand upon me to seek it in a special way when You stood by my shoulder and laughed in delight at my surprise at how good the EEWC conference was.

You are a wonder and a marvel and a surprise.

8/21/08

Dear Sophia, don't ever let me fall or turn away from You! I am reading, Praying with Our Eyes Open, Engendering Feminist Liturgical Prayer, *by Marjorie Proctor-Smith. She is pretty harsh about the words we currently use in prayer. She is hard on You. Help me think through what she is saying. Meet me in every thought so that I will know a little more who You are and how prayer works.*

Prayer is our relationship—how You are alive in my heart all the time and how I feel You when I look into my heart. But I still ask You for things. You give me so much, even more than I ask, but not all the things I ask.

8/27/08

O Giver of Life, Taker and Regenerator of Life, Renewing and Eternal Earth, Energy and Unfolding, You are most certainly beyond our understanding, beyond our describing. These are names for You that Carol Christ names— activities of the Goddess.

I believe You are these verbs but I just can't call You Goddess. I believe You are God acting in all those ways and more. And that some are gendered and some are not.

I do know You as Sophia, so feminine is definitely, in fact mostly, how I feel You. Praise be to You for guiding me along this path to You. Walk with me, take me nearer and nearer to You. Fill me with Your Spirit.

8/28/08

I had been in Corvallis, Oregon for a week playing with my granddaughter, Bailey, while she was on a break from Montessori School.

Last night Bailey and David were talking about Tuesday when he is going to stay home with her. She was so excited that it would be just the two of them. Then she stopped and said, "Where will Grandma be?" It made her sad when David told her I would be gone.

Swirl around her always. Whatever she is doing. Wherever she is.

Six year old Bailey at the beach in Oregon, 2010.

Bailey and Jim, June 2010.

Norm and me, 2008.

9/21/08

Yesterday at the library I ran across two books by a man named Gregg Braden. The prayer book, Secrets of the Lost Mode of Prayer, the Hidden Power of Beauty, Blessing, Wisdom and Hurt, appealed to me. When I got home I started reading the other book, The Isaiah Effect, and it just seemed strange because he believes in Nostradamas and Edgar Cayce and such.

He threw me off right in the beginning when he wrote that the biblical prophets were reporting on future events just like the seers he tells about in the book.

I didn't check out the other book because I decided I would buy a copy, but now I am not so sure. I want to write more but I need to get ready for church.

9/25/08

Abide with Congress and the President and Paulson and Bernancke as they work out how to handle the financial crisis in the best way possible. The way that will help the most people and our nation and not reward those who were greedy and dishonest. A good, workable plan is not just for our sake but for the sake of all the countries of the world.

9/28/08

I am happy with my life and the research and writing I am doing but something seems to be missing. I don't paint or sew or crochet any more. Maybe I need to be doing something creative like that. Maybe the writing and the studying is enough and I need to do it more.

10/4/08

While cleaning yesterday I found an old National Geographic that had an article about the search for the God particle at the Large Hadron Collider. Scientists are trying to "crack the code of the physical world, to figure out what the universe is made of, in other words to get to the very bottom of things." The press labeled it the God particle but the scientists call it the Higgs field or Higgs boson, Higgs particle or simply the Higgs.

The Higgs mechanism was postulated by British physicist Peter Higgs in the 1960s. This is absolutely fascinating to me. If only I could understand it.

I am on a search for You. To know who You are and how I relate to You. I don't expect to know You fully and truly until my earthly life is over. Will these scientists and this big "machine" find out all about You? I don't think so but they will find more about our universe. Which is maybe You.

11/10/08

Earlier I told about writing the prayers I wanted included in this book on a large drawing pad.

I can't believe that I had written a whole manuscript (40,000 plus words) and then forget I had done it! How does a woman spend that much time and energy and produce something like that and forget she has done it. Maybe I did a year and a half ago and the knee surgery wiped out my memory of it.

Now the questions are: Is it something people will read? Is it finished? Who will publish it? What I have read so far I have enjoyed. Is it finished? Do I want to ask my friends in the study group to read and critique it for me?

You must have helped me write it or it wouldn't even exist. Help me find a publisher.

11/15/08

And help me, please help me find the passage in the Koran that says "A man does not believe until he loves for his brother what he loves for himself." I quoted it in Lesson six of the articles for Horizons Magazine and I haven't a clue where I got it. The editor needs to know. Help me find also the story about the immigrant who found the sick child in the desert and went to the border patrol for help.

11/16/08

I spent the afternoon at the library looking for that passage. Last night I googled the Golden Rule. And there it was—along with many other forms of it from practically all the religions of the world! What a great and wonderful God You are!

11/17/08

I found this in Sufism: Love and Wisdom. It is one of the most beautiful descriptions of You that I have ever read.

> According to a famous holy utterance, God says, 'I was a hidden treasure and I loved to be known, so I created.' Here the purpose of creation is explicitly tied to God's desire to be known; He wished to manifest His inner perfections, and there is one way of becoming known, that is, knowing Himself outwardly, as distinct from knowing Himself inwardly.[1]

---

1   Jean-Louis Michon and Roger Gaetani , *Sufism: Love and Wisdom (Bloomington, IN, World Wisdom, 2006), 227-228. I left out references to an important Sufi*

This for me, is such a beautiful, transforming view of You.

11/24/08

At 1:30 a.m. I got up to eat Graham crackers and read Einstein in Love. In 1916 he wrote, "I feel that the real joke that the eternal inventor of enigmas has presented us with has absolutely not been understood as yet."² That name for You most certainly describes the path my search for You is taking me, not that I have been on for years! I love it! You are indeed the inventor of eternal enigmas.

12/10/08

Thank You that I am reading the seven hundred page book, Einstein, by Walter Isaacson. I don't understand the math and the physics but I marvel at the way he discovered things and how often he referred to You, "the dear Lord." Both Overbye in his book and Isaacson in this one say that Einstein was not a religious man but reading about him and his work is like reading theology.

It makes me more amazed at what You have done and are doing in this whole universe and in individual people. The part I struggle with is how to pray to You in the light of quantum physics.

I know without a doubt that You are present in me! I know that You are my life and my breath and my strength. You are my reason for being. You give me what are great ideas and great thoughts just as You did Einstein and Mozart.

How does it fit if You are all there is and we are parts of You that parts of You discover You? Create in You? If we are You shouldn't things here on earth and everywhere be perfect and complete?

I feel the feminist concept that You are like a pregnant woman who makes room in her womb for us Your human creatures and for nonhuman creatures. That You nurture us and care for us and want us to be who You created us to be.

---

scholar, Ibn 'Arabi, in the interest of making clearer what touched me so deeply.

2   Dennis Overbye, *Einstein in Love, A Scientific Romance* (NY, Viking, 2000), 306.

1/15/09

Dream: I was in a ramshackle old farmhouse with two or three old women. By old I mean old timey-old women. It was out by Hanover Church and cemetery because I told them about Grandma and Grandpa Heeren living so nearby, but they didn't remember them at all.

When I woke up I calculated it and they would have been little children if they had even been born yet when Grandma and Grandpa lived there. They had been a little leery of me until I told them that.

Then the lady whose house it was wanted me to go through her wardrobe to pick out what I wanted to wear. Her clothes were all frowsy (as she and the other women were) and hanging on a plumbing pipe along a wall in the room.

Before we left we sat at the table and the one lady tape recorded a song for me. She was not a very good singer but it was pleasant. I think we got into a really old car at the end of the dream.

Where did these ladies come from? One gave me clothing, one gave me music, maybe the third gave me wheels. One was kind of bossy. One was encouraging. One was almost invisible. I can't help but draw some likeness to You in three persons. If You have a message or some new understanding for me please give me Your wisdom to understand.

1/20/09

What a day this is! The first African American President of the United States! I cry just thinking about it! Obama's election night party—no when we knew he was going to win was when this propensity to cry started. I am sure this is the greatest event of my lifetime.

O Lord our God and Precious Mother, keep him safe from all harm! Thank You for him and for all his great gifts.

1/23/09

I question prayer to ask not whether it works but rather how it works. I will never learn the answer fully but keep drawing me nearer to You in my searching.

1/26/09

When we went to church I took Jay McDonald's book, Of God and Pelicans, A Theology of Reverence for Life, to read in the prayer room if no one came. Here is what I found:

> ...God can be experienced as a personal presence: as a Mother, Lover, or Friend. But God can also be experienced as an imageless reality, a feeling discovered in silent, wordless prayer. Amid such prayer we can feel the sheer given-ness of an embracing love that includes us within its scope, that wells up within us if we are open, and that extends outward to include the whole creation. This is a love we do not earn or create, yet nevertheless it lies at the center of our existence and that of everything else. To intuit the suchness of God in this way is to understand that the adventure of the universe as One is closely united with our own deepest self, that God is the very Heart of our hearts.[3]

That phrase was soft background music for my soul during the whole worship service. It sang to me of God's relationship to me, to everyone else in the sanctuary and to all of us in the body of Christ.

1/28/09

I gave copies of the manuscript to the readers yesterday. May they speak honestly about what they read. And fill me with Your thoughts and words as I write. May this book, From Heaven to My Heart, God's Journey with Me, be a tool in Your hands to touch the hearts of others as You have touched mine.

---

3   Jay B. McDaniel, *Of God and Pelicans, a Theology of Reverence for Life* (Louisville, KY, Westminster/John Knox Press, 1989) 101.

2/6/09

It is a little disconcerting to be immersed in the prayers from my past and view prayer as I see it now. More accurately, it is disconcerting to see myself as I felt long ago in the reality of who I am now. I thank You and praise You for that growth and that it will show through in the book....Last night I started to read Marjorie Suchoki's book, In God's Presence. She is going to be at University Presbyterian Church this weekend. Her book is hard to understand, but it seems like it will give me some wisdom about prayer. She asks some of the same questions I do.

2/7/09

I read more of Suchoki at the park today. Her words are hard to understand, but they ring true. Help me think about them and understand what You are saying in them.

She speaks right to my thoughts about prayer—when Nancy got diabetes and I prayed would You heal her if You could and could You? Intercessory prayer is really where I need help. Prayer as life with You, relationship with You is full and rich for me. Praise be to You always and forever!

2/13/09

I don't sit here for very long any more. I justify that by thinking that my writing the prayer book is prayer and it is. Also by thinking that the times during the day when I feel Your Presence are prayer and they are. However, my experience is that I need and want this specific, sitting-still time with You. Thank You for teaching me to have it the last thing at night too. Anytime I am open to You, full of You is a good time, the best time.

2/17/09

I was listening to NPR. It was a story about a Returning Warriors program the Navy has for sailors and spouses. How it must grieve You heart to have all soldiers and their families go through these horrors!

...Three hours at McStudy working on the prayer book. It was truly prayer time—constantly and even after I left to go to the store. Praise be to You forever and ever.

2/18/09

We saw the movie "Australia" yesterday. At the beginning Drover said, "Your story is all you own. Make it an exciting or interesting one." In the middle, Drover's brother-in-law said, "If you don't have love in your heart, you don't have a story." Nulla, the young aboriginal boy, said at the end, "Telling stories keeps people belonging."

These are true and wise sayings. They fit the church as well as this movie.

2/28/09

Irresistible Beauty, I find You in the buttes and the mountains that make this valley. I find You in the desert plants and birds. I find You in the sunsets. When we are in the Midwest I find You in the trees, thick and green. I find You in my backyard and out the window of the study. You are as near to me as my own heartbeat.

3/4/09

The prayer I read this morning from Prayers to Sophia *is truly a statement of my life's purpose.*

> Wise and faithful Guide,
> you lovingly abide in my depths
> and graciously guide my every step.
> You lead me to ever stronger growth
> and draw me more fully toward inner freedom.
> I thank you today for the awesome ways
> in which you constantly enter my life
> as I pledge my heart to you again.
>
> This day I renew my life's purpose

of being faithful to our relationship.
I give you my openness,
trusting that you will lead me on paths
that are meant to help me grow.
I re-commit my intention
To listen to you in all of life.

I promise you my daily discipleship
so that I may be an instrument of your love.
Most of all, I give you the loyalty of my heart.
May I do all in the circle of your wisdom
and learn from your dance of compassion
in every corner of this universe.

Source of Inner Luminosity,
thank you for being a loving radiance.
May the lantern of your perpetual goodness
always shine in me and through me.[4]

This prayer is so true for me I think You want me to use it to close our book, From Heaven to My Heart. *It is a perfect summary of what I have prayed and will continue to pray because it expresses where I still want to go. Who I want to be.*

4/5/09

"How far do you want to go?" That is Sophia's question to me. I keep saying to Her, "I want to be Your person." She is and has been for awhile saying to me, "How far do you want to go?"

Then She brought me to St. Teresa of Avila. Her thoughts and prayers and spiritual experience seem so like to mine—up to a point and now Sophia is asking me if I am really serious about wanting to be Her person.

---

4   Rupp, *Prayers to Sophia, A Companion to "The Star in My Heart"*, 34.

4/20/09

A pile of tinder waiting for a spark. That is the best way I can describe the women at the retreat. They were ready to take fire and they did. It was so amazing! So wonderful! So incredible!

It had happened once before at a retreat for Presbyterian women and it happened again at a retreat for Episcopalian Christian educators who were all women. The topic was using feminine language for God. The language and reasons for using it were new to most of the women and they were ready and waiting for it even though they couldn't have expressed their need before they heard of the possibilities. The first session of the retreat started out as though it was an ordinary—good, but nothing new—talk by a speaker. As the session progressed with each woman choosing a biblical woman to describe herself, things began to change.

These women who were mostly strangers to each other grew close as they heard each other's stories. Some of the stories were joy filled, some were sad. Oppression, abuse and neglect surfaced as the women talked.

As the leader, I used feminine pronouns for God whenever God came into a sentence. That is vey jarring to people who haven't heard it before. Some of those women were shaken by it, but this is when I began to see the tinder catch fire. Before the evening was over many of them were using feminine pronouns as well and their excitement was becoming evident.

Worship that evening was couched in traditionally male words, but by the time of the next morning's worship the man who was leading worship had rewritten the liturgy addressing God as She. It truly was like a fire burning in our hearts, in our midst.

4/30/09

I had a dream. Another woman and I planned an elaborate worship service. When it came time for it I was asleep in a chair in the sanctuary. My clothes looked like I had slept in them and so did my robe which was hanging over the pew in front of me.

A trumpet blew which was the signal for my part to begin. As I was hurriedly putting on my robe a young nerdy man took over. When I got to the big oversize pulpit I couldn't get behind it on one side because it was very close to the edge of the platform. The other side was also a narrow space. But I made it.

However, there was a group of large posters and pictures that had been leaning against the wall behind the pulpit but they had fallen forward and were leaning against the pulpit where I was supposed to stand. They were so heavy I couldn't move them to lean them back against the wall. That was the end of the dream.

Since Monday night's worship I have been thinking about the desperate need for someone to make Sophia known through nondenominational conferences. I thought it could be me, but I don't know how, but I could throw myself into it and with Your blessing do it.

Now I think this dream is telling me first of all that I am not ready. And secondly that I can't move the obstacles.

5/4/09

Dear Sophia, I feel so sorry about how I pouted after Sunday School yesterday. It was an ego trip. I am sorry. Please forgive me and keep me from doing it again. There were only five people to study Sophia. Last Sunday there were twelve. Thank You for helping me realize that the five who were there were very moved by You. What You gave me to say to them was important. Bless them on their journey with You, Mother, Lover.

5/15/09

I am such a mystery to me but You know me through and through.

6/3/09

Here is one of the most beautiful expressions of Your grandeur and majesty I have ever read. Even more or just as beautiful as any Psalm. It was written by a woman named Dhouda who lived in 841. Let this be my praise to You, sweet Sophia.

Surely, if sky and meadows were unfurled through the air like a scroll of parchment and if all the gulfs of the sea were transformed, tinged like inks of many colors, and if all earthly inhabitants born in the world from the beginning until now were writers (by some increase of human genius, an impossibility contrary to nature!), they would not be able to seize upon the grandeur, the breadth, the loftiness, and be able to tell the depth, of the sublimity, and divinity and wisdom, and goodness, and mercy of him who is called God.

Furthermore, trust that God is above and beneath, within and without, for he is higher, lower, deeper within and farther without. He is above, because he presides over us and rules us; he is sublime and as the Psalmist says, 'his glory is over all the heavens.' He is beneath us because he supports us all. ...In him we remain always. He is deeper within, because he fills us all and satisfies us with good things....He is farther without, because with his unassailable ramparts he surrounds and defends and protects us all.[5]

6/5/09

Praise and thanks be to You for President Obama! You have given him such wisdom and such understanding. He has been in Egypt and Saudi Arabia this week and is now in Germany. He speaks so wisely about a new beginning. That is exactly what the world needs from the U.S. New understandings and new ways of acting of treating others.

Keep him safe wherever he goes.

---

5   Rita Nakashima Brock, Rebecca Ann Parker, *Saving Paradise, How Christianity Traded Love of This World for Crucifixion and Empire* (Boston, Beacon Press, 2008), 251.

6/14/09

Thank God for school vacations! I went to Oregon to babysit Bailey during her week's Montessori school vacation. On the weekend her Mom and Dad and I did one of our favorite things—we went to the beach.

The enormity of You! That was what I felt at the beach today. The enormity of the ocean is a metaphor for You! It is impossible to comprehend the width or the length or the dept or the power of it. It is impossible to comprehend the width or the breadth or the depth or the power of You, great God of all that ever has been, is or will ever be!

I feel Your Presence and Your realness in my little study or in this little room, but out there You are too big for me!...Even those forests of tall trees somehow close You in with me. Even the desert in all its vastness prompts me to know You. But the ocean!

6/30/09

Dear Lord our God Sophia and Precious Mother, Christ Sophia, Spirit Sophia, forgive me and keep me close to You. Forgive me for many things but at this very moment, forgive me for wanting to write beautiful prayers because I want them in "our" prayer book. I am sorry.

In the introduction to the book I wrote about my fear that I would lose the gift of prayer if I talked about it. It's not the talking about it that is the problem. It is the need to show off, to be thought well of that will spoil my prayer life.

Forgive me for harboring these thoughts. I do want to write beautiful prayers to You, but "to You" is the key phrase.

7/28/09

O Great Wisdom, loving Lord, You are my life and my breath and my strength. You are my reason for being. I want to—but I am afraid to--write that I want to be a mystic. I am afraid because You might expect more of me, demand more of me. And yet, I want with my whole heart to be closer and closer to You! It is my deepest desire to be as close to You as is humanly possible in this life. I want to be fully the person You want me to be. By Your love and Your grace.

8/1/09

When we were in Powell's book store (which covers a whole city block) in Portland, Oregon, I bought Dorothee Soelle's book, The Silent Cry and Mysticism, Mysticism and Resistance. I started reading it last night and it looks like it will teach me a lot about being a mystic. I am going to read it as part of this quiet time with You. May it draw me ever nearer to You. I love You!

The three stages of grace described by Walter Hilton who died in 1395 describe my prayer life.

> People reach the first stage by faith alone and the second by faith in God and the imagination of the humanity of Jesus. In the third stage the soul beholds the divinity that is united with the humanity of Christ.[6]

8/2/09

> It is not suspicion that turns people away from the church; it is hunger that drives them to seek help wherever their dignity and their right to have a life are being respected.[7]

8/5/09

> Creation is the book that God wrote.[8]

---

6   Dorothee Soelle, *The Silent Cry, Mysticism and Resistance* (Minneapolis, Fortress Press, 1001), 18.
7   Ibid., 48.
8   Ibid., 100.

8/7/09

All mystics know that the incomprehensibility of God grows rather than diminishes when God's love comes close to us.[9]

8/10/09

Dear God, ruler of the universe and Life of all that is in it, praise be to You forever and ever! Dorothee Soelle writes about prayer being purposeless. I am not sure what that means. I think it is that a person does not come to You with a motive, with something to ask for. Rather she comes to You only to share Your love for her and her love for You.

My purpose in coming to You is always to praise and adore You. But my other purposes are to feel the power of Your presence and to ask to be in Your flow in all I do.

8/18/09

Soelle writes so much about resistance. As I read that I think I am resisting nothing. Reading pages 204-205 this morning it came to me that I am! I'm not working or resisting on behalf of the immigrants (which makes me sad) but I am resisting in all the things I do to help people see You as whole, as complete in feminine and masculine. What a relief! Praise be to You! May my whole life praise You!

---

9   Ibid., 130.

Chapter Sixteen

8/21/09

About Dag Hammarskjold Soelle writes:

> As for many mystical thinkers, the question remained also for him whether this is about a personal God or life's energy and power. 'I don't know Who—or what—put this question, I don't know when it was put. I don't even remember answering. But at some moment I did answer Yes to Someone or something.'[1]

I know you are Someone. Can you be both Someone and life's energy and power?

8/24/09

> Prayer is its own end and not a means to obtain a particular goal. The question 'What did it achieve?' must fall silent in face of the reality of prayer.[2]

---

1   The Silent Cry, 227.
2   Ibid., 294.

8/25/09

Dear Sweet, Strong, Sure Sophia, You never cease to amaze me! I just finished copying into the manuscript the prayers from the pink prayer journal. And there in Soelle's book, The Silent Cry, is the last chapter of the journal book! It is absolutely amazing how it comes to an end with her wisdom—and I just bought her book in June at Powell's in Portland.

It is not the end of my prayer journey but it is the end of this book! She wraps it all up.

8/29/09

The Buddha is quoted as having said, "To insist upon a spiritual practice that saved you in the past is to carry the raft on your back after you have crossed the river."

With this quote are you telling me that writing in a journal needs to change for me somehow? I would be afraid to give it up because I might lose touch with You. I don't want to give it up. It anchors me in You. What would I do instead?

9/2/09

Dear Friend Sophia, my desk calendar for says for today: "Merciful God, help me learn to accept my age with grace and dignity. May Your spirit renew my hope and help me discover new directions this day."

9/3/09

We cease trying to make ourselves the dictators and
God the Listener, and become joyful listeners to Him,
the Master who does all things well.[3]

These words certainly describe the changes in my prayer life: "this inner level has a life of its own, invigorated not by us but by a divine source."[4]

---

3   Testament of Devotion, 14.
4   Ibid.,17

This explains how Your ideas come to me out of the clear blue sky. What a gift You have given to me! I am dull this morning but You, the Light within me are lively. Praise be to you always and forever!

9/15/09

Nor is the God-blinded soul given blissful oblivion but, rather, excruciatingly sensitive eyesight toward the world of men.[5]

It is strange how sometimes the evil present in the world feels so real to me. The evil and the suffering it causes. Maybe not so strange in light of what I just quoted. My question is why do people act the way they do—ways that are ugly and harmful? And all this hatred and ugliness towards President Obama. Keep him and his family safe, O Lord. Keep them safe.

9/16/09

While I was writing yesterday, I came upon this passage by Joyce Rupp. It goes hand in hand with what I copied yesterday from Kelsey.

The ache in me goes deep when faces of starving children and bodies of people in war-torn countries stare at me from the newspapers or the evening news. I weep for the people of the world who are in pain. And I weep for the elements of the universe because we are all webbed together in this cosmic dance.[6]

Then I saw on the web news page a story about a twelve-year-old girl in Yemen who labored for three days and then died in childbirth. Some people would say that it is cultural for young girls, children to be married young. Cultural or not it is pedophilia and it is wrong. It must grieve Your heart! Forgive those who do it and all of us who are indifferent to it.

---

5   Ibid., 40
6   *The Star in My Heart,* 19

10/4/09

A friend prayed this prayer when we had a short worship service at the United States and Mexico border fence.

> Heart of Jesus, full of love and mercy, I want to ask You, for my migrant brothers and sisters, have pity on them and protect them as they suffer mistreatment and humiliation on the journey, when they are labeled as dangerous, when they are marginalized for being foreigners.
>
> Make them to be respected and valued for the dignity that Your blessing has provided. Touch with Your goodness the many that see them pass. Care for their families until they return to their homes, not with broken hearts, but rather with hopes fulfilled. Let it be so.

Dear Sweet Sophia, let it be so. It is Your heart's desire that not only these immigrants but all people everywhere be treated with respect and dignity. It is, we, privileged, most privileged, of Your people who will not let it be. Forgive us and make us better.

10/10/09

Yesterday morning President Obama was awarded the Nobel Peace Prize! Thank You and praise be to You. Forgive all the people who are complaining about it and saying he hasn't done anything to earn it. He is changing so much what the world expects from the United States--from self-centered to wanting to be part of a one world community. Others who favor him are critical as well—not his receiving the prize, but of how he "hasn't done much." What do they expect! Protect him from all evil.

10/12/09

Dear Lord of love and justice, You would rule this world with love and justice and equality for all! It would be a world where all people had everything they need to be healthy and happy and give love and glory to You! Why are people so greedy and so selfish? Even people who call themselves Christians.

I just read an article that Jim emailed to me to print out about the bonuses the CEO and CFO of his company are receiving: $10 million in stock to four company leaders! At the same time they are cutting out holiday parties for their employees and annual salary raises based on merit and mandating approval for overtime.

So many people are losing their jobs, have lost their jobs. Help our leaders get this all straightened out. Not that they can take away greed, but that they can put a stop to some of it. May Congress approve the President's plan to regulate financial institutions.

And may a really good health care plan be passed by Congress.

Praise be to You for Barak Obama! His winning the Nobel Prize is, for me, an affirmation of his righteousness. Protect him from all who wish him harm.

Protect the immigrants who are crossing the desert today. Protect the agents who are there.

10/20/09

Thank you that I got through typing the first part of the manuscript into the computer. Actually I was only formatting. I want to make plans for my adult Sunday school class which starts Sunday, but it feels empty not to work on the book. Sometimes I have such doubts about how good and useful it will be. That maybe it has just been busy work for me—no, no busy work because I have been drawn nearer to You through writing it and will still be drawn nearer to You.

11/3/09

It is so strange that as I sit here at the dining room table so I can watch the moon go down, that after all these hundreds of years of humans knowing better, I still think in terms of the moon moving! My whole life it has been known that it is the earth that moves. This morning, for some reason, I am acutely aware of that. And it is a metaphor for the old, old language about You that lingers in my mind even when I know better, more lively language for You.

Thank you for giving me the new language. Help me find people who want to learn it.

11/9/09

It seems I have less desire or need to write these morning prayers. Is it because I feel You more often and for longer periods of time at other times of the day? Or is it because I have been spending so many hours with my prayers from the past?

Writing my prayers has the great advantage of holding my attention instead of my heading off to do other things. As much as this is my choice, may I choose the best. As much as it is Your love luring me to You, may I follow where You lead.

12/14/09

Thank You that I was able to read Sor Juana Ines de la Cruz's book, The Answer. She was an amazing woman. I didn't feel the sisterhood with her that I have with Catherine of Siena and Theresa of Avila. I think she is too much of an intellectual for me. She would intimidate me. But there are parts of The Answer that spoke to my heart. One of them is that "God is the center and the circumference." It sounds like process theology and it fits with Teilhard de Chardin: punctiform and profound and with Einstein's: God is the inventor of eternal enigmas.

You are the Alpha and the Omega! You are the creator of all things and You are in all things. Praise be to You forever and ever and ever world without end.

12/16/09

This is what I like and what I want—being so full of Your Presence that I cry! And yet I want to rush on to the things I have to do. Please forgive me and never, never, ever give up on me! Where would I go? What would I do if I dwelt in Your Presence this way for longer and longer periods? I am better at it, but I want more!

1/7/2010

Thank You and praise be to You for the way my heart becomes alive to You! The way it awakens!

This prayer, written before I began writing this chapter this morning, describes exactly how prayer is for me now today. God is no longer someone out there from whom I beg for favors. Not one who is there to grant my every prayer God dwells in my heart.

At the beginning of this book I expressed my fears that by talking about my prayer life I might lose it. But on the contrary it has grown and deepened.

1/9/10

I believe You are in other people. I have been thinking about how that affects me as I have been writing this book on my prayer journals. My well-being is added to by the prayers of others for me and in the loving looks I get from complete strangers. I have wondered for some time if those looks come to me because people see You in me. That may be part of it but I think more and more that I see You in them looking at me.

What mysteries and adventures You hold out to me. May I ever be faithful in being open to them, open to You.

Thank You and praise be to You for the prayer filled time I had at McStudy yesterday. That is another mystery—how that place is so special to my spirit. I even felt Your Presence when I was eating a Happy Meal! (I did that to get the toy for my granddaughter.)

You are so amazing, so divine. When we were flying home from Nancy's we saw the snow-covered Cascades and then the Sierras. The sun was setting and there were some clouds. It was so beautiful! And I could feel You in the beauty but I could not comprehend You in the wider universe out there.

I know I can never know You in Your fullness, but I want to know You as much as I am able, as much as You want me to. Help me be ever faithful to You.

1/21/10

When I reach through the hole at my center the gift eludes my grasp. Whatever it may be I can possess it only as that mystery which beckons from the greatest distance and draws my heart deeper into the quest.[7]

---

7   Meinrad Craighead, *The Mother's songs, Images of God the Mother* (NY, Paulist Press, 1986), 55.

Epilogue

God has come from that far off place, where I felt him at first, to my heart. The journey has been a struggle with my seeing God not as a separate entity in some celestial sphere, but God as always, everywhere present in all things, including me. The great gift of where I am now is that the experience of God in my heart happens more often at unplanned times and in unusual places. My longing for more of God in my life is being met by this God who journeyed from heaven to my heart.

As I feared when I started sharing my prayer life in this book, my prayer practice has changed. But rather than being a fearful thing it is a beautiful thing, a blessing. I still sit down every morning to write a letter to God. However, now I spend more time in wordless prayer than I do in writing.

So much more can be said and has been said about prayer. I hope you will turn to some of the books I have named to learn more. But most of all my prayer is that you will faithfully seek God who lives in your heart.

A Short List of Short Reviews of Special Books

These short reviews are of a few of the books I have mentioned in *From Heaven to My Heart*. These are books that I read and reread as I continue on my prayer journey.

The Story of Ruth, Twelve Moments in Every Woman's Life. Joan Chittister has been a leading voice on spirituality for over twenty-five years. She is always good! In this book Chittister has reclaimed the story of Ruth as a powerful model for contemporary women who are seeking a fully spiritual life. The breathtaking artwork of John August Swanson illustrates twelve moments in every woman's life. Each chapter speaks to a woman's search for wholeness. Her books, *A Passion for Life, Fragments of the Face of God,* and *There is a Season,* are also deeply moving and beautifully illustrated. All three of these books were topics for a book discussion group of women that I belong to and I tell you with complete confidence that a group of women using these books will never lack for conversation and soul sharing.

Prayers to She Who Is. William Cleary. It should come as no surprise that this would be on my favorites' list since Elizabeth A. Johnson, the author of *She Who Is,* is one of the most important teachers of prayer that I have had. Poet William Cleary turns Dr. Johnson's third person classic theology into second person prayers that everyone can say. Cleary gives one page quotes from Johnson's work and then adds personal prayers expressing what she has written. These prayers not only touch my heart deeply, but they help me speak to God who is female as surely as she is male.

The Prayers of Susana Wesley. W. L. Doughty ed. This book is small in size, fifty-nine pages, but is huge in inspiration. The short biography of Susanna tells us that she was born in 1669, married Samuel Wesley and was the mother of John and Charles Wesley, the founders of Methodism. She was the mother of eighteen or nineteen children whom she home-schooled. She made time to pray by pulling her apron over her head which was a signal to her children not to bother her. Her prayers cover such topics as when you have too much to do, calamities, confession and giving glory to God.

Meditations with Julian of Norwich. Brendan Doyle. Whenever you need new insights into the nature of God to enliven your prayer life, Julian of Norwich is the woman to read. This book contains some of the prayers of this fourteenth century nun who experienced sixteen mystical visions. One of the amazing things about this book of prayers is that a woman who lived so long ago in such a different situation can speak so movingly to twenty-first century people.

On Becoming a Musical, Mystical Bear, Spirituality American Style. Matthew Fox. Like Joan Chittister, Matthew Fox is always good. Mystical Bear is the first book of his that I read decades ago and it is still an inspiration to me when my prayer life lags. Fox was censured by the Vatican in 1989 and then dismissed by the Dominican order in 1993. He is now an Episcopal priest. From the beginning of his writing he has espoused what is called Creation Spirituality which maintains that we are born in "original blessing" rather than original sin. Any book of his that you pick up and read will inspire you and lead you to read more of his writings

A Testament of Devotion. Thomas R. Kelly. These five compelling essays in this classic of devotional literature urge us to center our lives on God's presence, to find quiet and stillness within modern life, and to discover the deeply satisfying and lasting peace of the inner spiritual journey. Even though it was copyrighted in 1941 it still speaks to our desire for conversation with God.

The Other Side of Silence: a Guide to Christian Meditation*.* Morton Kelsey. This book is truly a how-to book on Christian meditation. In it Kelsey writes about the climate for meditation, preparations for the inward journey, and uses of images in meditation. It is an excellent guidebook for the kind of prayer life which we seek.

Guerillas of Grace. Ted Loder. It is amazing how these private personal prayers that touch your heart so deeply also create feelings of unease and the need to set out in new directions in your inner soul and in the world at large. The prayers offer inspiration and motivation in a poetic style that is unique to Ted Loder. In the margins of this book I have written comments such as, "Yes! Yes!" and, "Yes, Lord, Yes!"

Of God and Pelicans: a Theology of Reverence for Life. Jay B McDaniel. My copy of this book is full of underlining and notes in the margins. The four chapters reveal new thoughts about understanding God's relationship to all living things, the foundations and guidelines for an environmental ethic, the understanding of Christian spirituality, and feminism in a nonhierarchical world.

With Christ in the School of Prayer. Andrew Murray. This was one of the first books I read on prayer and it had a great influence on my spiritual journey. His books that I own are a mess! They are old and yellowed, marked up and dog-eared. If you truly want to go to school on prayer, Andrew Murray is one of the best teachers.

Amazing Grace: A Vocabulary of Faith. Kathleen Norris. As the subtitle says this is a vocabulary of the Christian faith. From Norris's struggle with her faith come definitions of words common in Christian theology that often intimidate people: judgment, prayer, faith, dogma, salvation, sinner. Her definitions come from her life situations and are understandable and delightful.

Catherine of Siena, the Dialogue. Suzanne Noffke, trans. I return to this book again and again for understanding about God's love for me and about how that love leads me to love other people. It is another case of a woman who lived in such different times in such a different way from me, yet has so much to say to me about God.

Prayers. Michel Quoist. Agnes M. Forsyth and Anne Marie de Commaille, trans. Norm gave me this book in 1982, but the prayers on everyday topics still speak to the longings of my heart.

CPSIA information can be obtained at www.ICGtesting.com
Printed in the USA
LVOW101619261111

256560LV00002B/171/P

9 781450 259934